D1521810

British Catholic Merchants in the Commercial Age

Studies in the Eighteenth Century
ISSN: 2398–9904

This major series from Boydell & Brewer, published in association with the British Society for Eighteenth-Century Studies, aims to bring into fruitful dialogue the different disciplines involved in all aspects of the study of the long eighteenth century (c.1660–1820). It publishes innovative volumes, singly or co-authored, on any topic in history, science, music, literature and the visual arts in any area of the world in the long eighteenth century and particularly encourages proposals that explore links among the disciplines, and which aim to develop new cross-disciplinary fields of enquiry.

Series editors: Ros Ballaster, University of Oxford, UK; Matthew Grenby, Newcastle University, UK; Robert D. Hume, Penn State University, USA; Mark Knights, University of Warwick, UK; Renaud Morieux, University of Cambridge, UK

Previously published

Material Enlightenment: Women Writers and the Science of Mind, 1770–1830, Joanna Wharton, 2018

Celebrity Culture and the Myth of Oceania in Britain, 1770–1823, Ruth Scobie, 2019

British Sociability in the Long Eighteenth Century: Challenging the Anglo-French Connection, edited by Valérie Capdeville and Alain Kerhervé, 2019

Things that Didn't Happen: Writing, Politics and the Counterhistorical, 1678–1743, John McTague, 2019

Converting Britannia: Evangelicals and British Public Life, 1770–1840, Gareth Atkins, 2019

British Catholic Merchants in the Commercial Age

1670–1714

Giada Pizzoni

THE BOYDELL PRESS

Published in association with

BSECS
British Society for
Eighteenth-Century Studies

First published 2020
The Boydell Press, Woodbridge

ISBN 978 1 78327 438 3

The Boydell Press is an imprint of Boydell & Brewer Ltd
PO Box 9, Woodbridge, Suffolk IP12 3DF, UK
and of Boydell & Brewer Inc.
668 Mt Hope Avenue, Rochester, NY 14620–2731, USA
website: www.boydellandbrewer.com

A CIP catalogue record for this book is available
from the British Library

The publisher has no responsibility for the continued existence or accuracy of URLs for
external or third-party internet websites referred to in this book, and does not guarantee that any content on such websites is, or will remain, accurate or appropriate

This publication is printed on acid-free paper

To my father

Contents

Maps

How a bonfire sparked my interest in Catholic history

On the Fifth of November 2011, I attended the Bonfire Night celebration in Lewes, Sussex. It was an impressive display of fireworks,
complete with effigies of the Pope and Guy Fawkes, blazing tar-barrels,
and crosses symbolising the local Marian martyrs. I was not aware that the
town had been renowned for these celebrations since the late seventeenth
century. In fact, I did not even know what the celebration was for or what
it symbolised. I was told by a fellow spectator that it was an old tradition of which the local bonfire-running societies were very proud. And
although he could not remember the exact meaning or origin of the event,
he was confident I would enjoy the legacy it had left. A few days later, out
of curiosity, I looked for some material on its background and found the
renowned book by James Sharpe, *Remember, Remember*. I was aware that
Sharpe was giving his own twist to modern folklore, nevertheless it raised
my interest in Catholic historiography.[1]

The Fifth of November celebrations hark back to the foiling of the
Gunpowder Plot of 1605, a Catholic scheme to blow up Parliament along
with King James I and other members of the royal family. The aim was to
reinstate a 'tyrannical' Catholicism, and one of the protagonists was the
Yorkshireman Guy Fawkes. The event traditionally represents the sense
of anti-Catholicism, Catholic tyranny, and absolutism from the time. But
throughout the centuries the meaning has shifted with the annual celebration reinventing itself. In Lewes, festival-goers don't just burn effigies
of Catholics and popes, but of devils, and politicians including Thatcher
and Tony Blair – indeed of anyone deemed unpopular enough in any given
year. Nowadays, children no longer request 'a penny for the guy' and in
most cases don't even know the story of Guy Fawkes and his plot; instead,
the Fifth of November has found a place as a winter festival, along with
Halloween, which has overshadowed the Christian holy days of All Saints

---

[1]   James Sharpe, *Remember, Remember the Fifth of November: Guy Fawkes and the
Gunpowder Plot* (London: Profile Books, 2005).

and All Souls. It still has popular allure and is one of the very few British traditional festivals still celebrated today.

While reading Sharpe's book, I became fascinated with this uniquely British – or perhaps English – celebration, which seemed crucial to the process of building a nation. The story of the British nation had so far been told in providential terms, constructed against tales of papal oppression and atrocities. God had demonstrated providence to the English, with the short reign of the Catholic Mary Tudor, the extensive rule of Elizabeth I, and the defeat of the Spanish Armada. The position of Catholicism became problematic with the Tudor dynasty. Regarding persecution, however, implementing laws proved to be a mission in itself; Catholics were part of society, and there was solidarity among gentlemen, among neighbours, and within the community. Catholicism survived because it became a religion headed by the gentry. Despite existing in uncertainty and danger, the faith was kept alive and its community was protected. Paradoxically, some Catholics even prospered, filling important offices during the reign of Elizabeth I. The experience of Catholics in Britain at this time was very different from contemporary narratives. Tensions and conflict with the community were still strong, but their public display became less common, and throughout the decades became mixed with folklore. Today its meaning may have shifted, but what fascinates me is that the Bonfire celebration remains an integral part of communities. Bonfire Night was my first understanding of how the British nation was constructed and how it defined itself. Festivities are a cultural product and the celebrations of the Fifth of November represent the crucial role played by anti-Catholic feelings and fear. It prompted me to reflect on the position of Catholics in the country, and after that night in Lewes, the history of the community intrigued me even more.

As Sharpe, I also want to start with this commonly sung rhyme:

> Remember, remember, the Fifth of November,
> Gunpowder, Treason and Plot.
> I see no reason why Gunpowder Treason
> Should ever be forgot.[2]

I agree that anti-Catholicism and treason should never be forgotten, if anything for reflecting on the marginalisation of a religious community and making a mockery of extremism. But, I wonder if, like me on that night in Lewes, even Catholics in the seventeenth century took part in the celebrations.

---

[2]   Ibid., 1.

At the end of 2011, while looking for answers, I began with a survey of the archival records of Sussex, one of the counties which attested a strong Catholic presence. I started in Lewes and Chichester in the hope that more localised material might help shed light on the various Catholic families who gained prominence in England in the early modern centuries. The material allowed me to map the Catholic presence and, after integrating it with the literature, offered a valuable insight into individuals' occupations, where they lived, and the extent of their properties. I gained an understanding of the degree to which these families were well established, and how long they had owned estates. From estate records and rental agreements, it was possible to investigate their properties and their values and also discover with whom they entered into contracts. Catholic parish registers allowed me to access their social interactions (if they lived among co-religionists), if they intermarried, and to view a survey of the frequency with which Catholics attended mass or received communion. Finally, in London, at the Westminster Diocesan Archive, the reports of the apostolic vicars made it possible to identify the economic networks of this community, its activities, and its social relations. These studies have offered insight into the gentry's families and their lives.[3] Indeed, I saw that among the gentry, interaction at all levels with Protestants was indeed possible, as families were linked by common values and blood relations and so easily disregarded religious affiliation.[4] Certainly, it is true that upper-class Catholic families were defined through bonds of amity and marriage, and these offered patronage to their communities. Support from Rome was lacking, and the gentry had become the backbone of a self-supporting structure. However, I still wondered if this established pattern of integration could also be seen among other social classes.

---

[3]   The archival research started in the East Sussex Record Office in Lewes and the West Sussex Record Office in Chichester. Regarding the literature, the two most valuable texts consulted there were: N. Caplan, 'The Sussex Catholics, c. 1660–1800', in *Sussex Archaeological Collections*, vol. 116 (Lewes: S. A .C., 1978), 19–30, and Mary K. Kinoulty, *A Social Study of Roman Catholicism in West Sussex in the Eighteenth Century* (Chichester: W. S. R. O., 1982), 28–31. Usually Catholics lived only a few miles from the gentry's household, though a few people were located in rural areas or far from the noble families. The most prominent Catholic families in the south of the country were the Carylls in West Grinstead, the Montagues in Easebourne, the Norfolks in Arundel, and other families along the Sussex–Hampshire border.

[4]   P. Marshall and G. Scott, *Catholic Gentry in English Society: The Throckmortons of Coughton from Reformation to Emancipation* (Burlington: Ashgate, 2009); Colin Haydon, 'Eighteenth-Century English Anti-Catholicism: Contexts, Continuity and Diminution' in *Protestant–Catholic Conflict from the Reformation to the Twenty-First Century: The Dynamics of Religious Difference*, ed. J. Wolffe (Basingstoke: Palgrave, 2013), 46–70.

Despite being fascinating, this material did not offer convincing answers to my question. So in January 2012, I began studying the account books of Bishop Richard Challoner at the Westminster Diocesan Archive.[5] Challoner was Vicar Apostolic for the London Catholic Mission between 1758 and 1781, and his ledger books show a deep commitment to the financial life of the government's maritime companies. From here, I thought these sources might hint at an untold story. From Challoner's documents, we can see how the financial operations of the Catholics were carefully coordinated. They suggest how the community subscribed to government maritime companies – particularly the South Sea Company, funded the national debt, and ultimately financed charitable work across England. My questions now were turned to who directed these vast investments and I began to investigate Challoner's relationship with the Catholic Dukes of Norfolk.

It soon became clear to me that the Norfolks were one of the most prominent families in the south of England. Their possessions were seemingly untouched throughout the centuries, and the political roles of family members as Earls Marshall raised questions about their status. If Catholics were being ostracised, how could the political and social influence of the Norfolks be explained? This question moved my research focus from London and East Sussex to Arundel, which had been a stronghold of the Norfolk family since the Middle Ages. Arundel offered a real understanding of the importance of a patron. The family's residence, Arundel Castle, towered over the town, and historically, through the figure of the Duke, religious and political authority merged. Rich families became the lynchpin of Catholicism as they provided financial and spiritual support, as well as offering employment in their households. Like their peers, the Norfolks hosted and sheltered priests in their private chapel in an act which ensured the survival of the faith in the area. Historians have also recognised this political role: the Dukes had been close to the House of Stuart and the Hanoverian dynasty and were amongst the petitioners for Catholic toleration in 1778.[6]

The story of the Norfolks in turn led me to the Aylward merchant family. The tenth Duke of Norfolk was the grandson of John Aylward, a London merchant and banker of Irish origin; yet who is recorded in the *Irish Genealogist* as a merchant of St Malo.[7] Certainly, his family was from

---

[5]   Here I studied the account book (WDA, B 1536 *Challoner's Ledger*) of the Bishop and his correspondence with Rome and the district. Two record books offer a list of the most prominent Catholic families in the country.

[6]   John Bossy, *The English Catholic Community*, 77–107; Aveling, *The Handle and the Axe*, 253–283; Glickman, *The English Catholic Community*, 252–257.

[7]   Julian Walton, *The Irish Genealogist*, 5 (1974): 216.

Waterford, Ireland, and in 1672 it is known that he moved to Malaga in Spain, where he stayed until 1687. It is not clear where John himself was born, but what is certain is that he was part of the London Anglo-Irish community of the time and that it was in Spain that he met his wife, the Englishwoman Helena Porter. Daughter of Matthew Porter (also a merchant of Irish origin), Helena was the widow of French trader Jacques de la Herse Trublet (probably of St Malo). She married Aylward on 27 April 1687, and the couple went on to have three daughters including Marie-Alsen, who married Henry Charles Howard of Greystoke in February 1708 and gave birth to a son, Charles, who would eventually become Duke in 1777. John and Helena Aylward moved to St Malo in 1687, where they stayed until 1698. They then returned to London, the city where John died on 24 April 1705, leaving his wife to administer his legacy.[8] From studying the Aylwards, it soon became evident that here was the potential to tell a very different story on Catholics and trade in the early modern world, leading me to this project to further explore a new history.

Acknowledgements

When thinking about how many people I have met since starting this project, and how many I should thank, I do not even know where to start. I must acknowledge, first and foremost, my stay in the UK and say that this book would not have been possible without the help and support of my family, especially during the times in which I lost sight of the aim of my work. It is dedicated to them: my mother, Gisa, my sister, Clarissa, and my aunt Fiorella. It is also dedicated to the memory of my father, Claudio, and our dear friend, Françoise Lenoble, who both always believed in this project and unconditionally supported me from the first day I started my research.

A great many friends have made these eight long years of research enjoyable and a particular thanks goes to Colleen Roberts, Sara Sirci, Karin Brandmayer, Lise Hinke-Guldberg, and Mike Mesquita, whose advice and criticism helped me improve my work and my well-being. I will be forever grateful for their time and efforts. Regarding guidance, I cannot fail to mention my wonderful friends Hannah Smith, Rebecca Lonergan, and Kay Martin; the long writing days have been joyful with them. A great thank you goes also to the archivists and staff of Arundel Castle Archives and of the Westminster Diocesan Archive. Their insight and knowledge has helped me discover groundbreaking material and this book would have never been written without their knowledge and auspices. I would also like to thank His Grace the Duke of Norfolk for his kind permission to reproduce the Aylward Papers. The Catholic Record Society has a special place in this project as well, funding my research expenses when no one else was willing.

Finally, I owe the completion of this work to my supervisor Emma Hart and my mentor Mark Knights. They taught me how to write History and I deeply appreciated their patience, pedantry, and kindness. Richard Whatmore and Trevor Burnard have a special place in my academic life too, for giving me the opportunity to study and work in reputable institutions, and for their constant encouragement.

This work brings closure to a very challenging chapter in my life and I will be forever grateful to all the people that I met throughout this journey, in particular my St Andrews, Warwick, and Leamington friends whose kindness, camaraderie, and input have helped me endure difficult days when the purpose of this work was being questioned.

Abbreviations

Archives

AY	The Aylward Papers, Arundel Castle Archives
CO	The National Archives, Kew, London
WDA	Westminster Diocesan Archive

Coins and Measures

Arroba	25 pounds (one pound would cost between 1 and 6 silver pesos)
Fanega	Castilian measure which varied. It could be 4.4 *arrobas* or 110 *libras* (a *libra* was a Castilian pound)
Mds	*Maravedis:* one piece of eight was formed by 34 *mds*
Rs	*Reals de vellon plate* or piece of eight, the Spanish silver coin

Legislative Terms

Indulto	tax on commerce
Pragmatica	ordnance

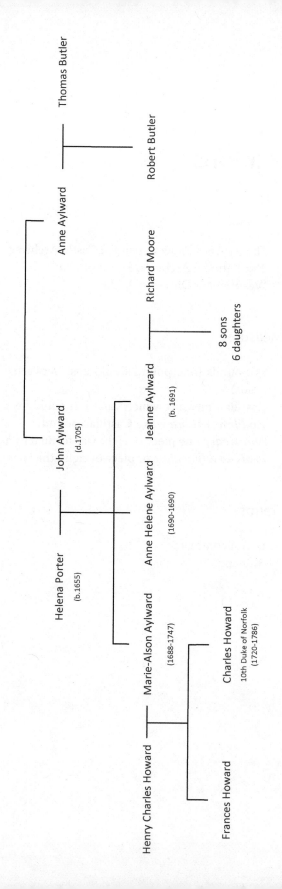

Introduction

This project was initially inspired by Weber's provocative opinion that Catholicism has never been associated with the 'spirit of capitalism'.[1] Although much debated – and many would say outdated – the theory left me thinking about the position of Catholics in Britain. This was just after I had completed my Masters dissertation on seventeenth-century Dutch Catholicism and the practices of tolerance (and intolerance) in the Netherlands. After concluding that the country at this time had adopted a pragmatic attitude of acceptance towards Catholics, I wondered if the same pattern could be applied to communities in Britain. Perhaps it was being from a very Catholic country that sparked my curiosity, and I wanted to understand how it would have been to live as a Catholic in a country where the religion was not so influential. But also what in particular it meant to be a Catholic in a Protestant country in the early modern world, when tolerance was a contested concept. I started to navigate the literature with Weber's thesis in mind.[2] What I found was a belief that Catholics did not embrace risk, were less ambitious in business and more concerned with their place in the 'other world' than in pursuing success in this life. On the other hand, there was a widespread belief and acceptance that Protestants, in particular Puritans, were being called to fulfil their roles within society and that success in this life meant proof of being part of the elect and of God's benevolence. Indeed, Weber argued that Protestant minorities successfully engaged in a variety of economic activities at this time, even when operating in predominantly Catholic countries, as is evident in the example of the Huguenots in France. The same, however, could not be said for those Catholics living in Protestant countries such as England. Weber contended that religion profoundly shaped culture and ethical behaviour, a rather bleak depiction of Catholicism and one that certainly did not match later studies on the community and its endurance. Certainly, the influence of

[1]   Giancarlo Poggi, *Calvinism and the Capitalist Spirit: Max Weber's Protestant Ethic* (London: Macmillan Press, 1983), 40–78.
[2]   Max Weber, *The Protestant Ethic and the Spirit of Capitalism* (London: Routledge, 1992), 3–50; Poggi, *Calvinism and the Capitalist Spirit*, 40–78.

religion on culture cannot be underestimated, and much has been written to refute this controversial theory, with recent literature showing instead how much the spirit of enterprise has been a feature of other religions such as Judaism. Indeed, Snyder and Trivellato are among many to affirm how, like Protestants, even Jews pursued economic success while leading a profoundly religious life.[3] So, could this same formula be applied to Catholics? And importantly, were British Catholics, like the Dutch, somehow tolerated, if anything, through pragmatism?[4]

Existing studies of England's Catholic communities and religious authorities in the late seventeenth century focus almost solely on the social and political context, to the neglect of substantial economic or financial analysis.[5] As a result, despite the extensive literature, I was left wondering how this community of Catholics actually survived. Most of all, how did they act within a Protestant society; how did they relate to the new economy; and is it correct to talk of a faith on the social and economic margins? In recent decades, Catholic history has tackled the theme of integration, assessing inter-faith relations among the upper classes. But there is no clear answer as to how the mercantile community sustained itself with such success at this time in history.

A New Catholic History?

The Aylwards' trade had international, almost global, reach from the West Indies to Ottoman Greece, and their business papers offer a wealth of information on the British expatriate communities in European ports. When studying their fascinating letters, I became convinced that the Aylwards and their associates could have been the key representatives of Catholic involvement in the newly born British Empire during the early modern centuries. Their business accounts call into question the extent to which

---

[3]   Francesca Trivellato, *The Familiarity of Strangers: The Sephardic Diaspora, Livorno and Cross-Cultural Trade in the Early Modern Period* (London: Yale University Press, 2009); Holly Snyder, "'Under the Shadow of Your Wings': Religiosity in the Mental World of an Eighteenth Century Jewish Merchant', *Early American Studies: An Interdisciplinary Journal,* 8 (2010): 581–622.

[4]   B. J. Kaplan, B. Moore, H. Van Nierop, and J.Pollmann, eds, *Catholic Communities in Protestant States: Britain and the Netherlands, c. 1570–1720* (Manchester: Manchester University Press, 2009). In this edited collection, various authors analyse the level of toleration towards Catholic minorities in both countries. They depict a narrative that moves away from usual assumption of marginalisation.

[5]   The works of John Bossy and Gabriel Glickman on the English Catholic community have been seminal for my research.

the Catholic community was economically marginalised and highlight the dynamic nature of merchants and financial enterprises within imperial economies. A comprehensive study of Catholic economic activity has until now been missing, and there is need for a clearer understanding of the nature of the commercial world and its players at this time. The Catholic merchants analysed here were certainly a major part of the British mercantile community. They prospered in the trading world for more than three decades, from the early 1670s until the early eighteenth century, and faced significant risks in everything from the vagaries of the weather to privateering, to political turmoil. In 1688, they endured the Glorious Revolution and juggled their businesses through both the Nine Years War (1688–1697) and the War of the Spanish Succession (1702–1714). Their correspondence shows exchanges of information about politics, commodities, and prices, and also about their families and communities. These British Catholics were traders well integrated in the Mediterranean–Atlantic commercial world. But how are they representative of the wider Catholic community?

In recent historiography, the analysis of Catholics and their part in trade mostly focuses on Irish expatriates.[6] Over a century of English colonialism profoundly shook the fabric of Irish society, and the first wave of reforms, in the early seventeenth century, triggered the Irish diaspora. The most crucial moment was the Flight of the Earls in 1607 when, after the Nine Years War (1594–1603) against Elizabeth I, the earls left a political vacuum in the north of the country, which the English government tried to fill. Irish Catholics fled to the continent and joined the Catholic communities of expatriates in Spain, France, and the Spanish Netherlands. A second wave of Irish immigrants arrived on the Flemish coast and in Bruges after the Cromwellian Wars in the early 1650s. For English Catholics, they had since the sixteenth century endured loss of land through confiscation. This forced them to move away from the manorial estate and offered the opportunity of

---

[6]   *Irish and Scottish Mercantile Networks in Europe and Overseas in the Seventeenth and Eighteenth Centuries*, ed. David Dickson et al. (Gent: Academia Press, 2006); Jan Parmentier, 'A Touch of Ireland'; Nash, 'Irish Atlantic Trade in the Seventeenth and Eighteenth Centuries', 329–56: from 1685 until 1731, Irish–French trade was quite lucrative as Ireland was excluded from English colonial trade and therefore needed to find new outlets; Thomas Truxes, *Irish–American Trade, 1660–1783* (Cambridge: Cambridge University Press, 1988) 84; Cullen, *Economy, Trade and Irish Merchants at Home and Abroad*; L. M. Cullen, 'Galway Merchants in the Outside World, 1650–1800', in Galway, *Town and Crown, 1484–1984*, ed. Diarmuid O'Cearbhaill (Dublin: Gill and Macmillan, 1984), 63–89: From 1689 until 1713, the Irish–French partnership suffered from embargoes enacted during the wars. Gabriel Glickman, 'Catholic Interests and the Politics of English Overseas Expansion 1660–1689', *Journal of British Studies*, 55 (2016): 680–708.

more imaginative economic strategies.[7] The continent was in many ways an optimal destination, with flourishing trading centres and hubs of privateering and contraband. The Irish in particular have always had a special relationship there, particularly in Spain, with tales of a common origin and the same religious beliefs. This trading relationship had begun as early as the medieval age with exchanges between the south Irish ports of Waterford, Limerick, Dublin, and Galway; and the Iberian harbours in Bilbao, Cadiz, San Sebastian, and Lisbon. Cadiz held the most numerous Irish expatriate community and was fast becoming a prominent Atlantic port. But the Irish in Spain, although welcomed for their religion, were viewed with suspicion due to their allegiance to the English crown and commercial partnerships with English merchants.[8] Indeed, Schuller has introduced the concept that Catholic ties often proved to be a useful economic tool in such circumstances;[9] in line with Croft's study on the Irish, Scottish, and English merchants who operated in the same harbours in the late sixteenth century. In fact, both studies primarily focus on Spain, where Protestants and Catholics from the British Isles worked together to secure continuous trading relations with their homeland even in times of war, while also reaping the profits of the Spanish transatlantic trade. In fact, although they were seen to be linked with Britain, in Spain the Irish and English Catholic merchants were able to avoid those restrictions placed on Protestants. This theory has been buttressed by Recio Morales, in 'Identity and Loyalty', where he suggests that Catholic merchants had an ambiguous position: being able to form part of the Spanish transatlantic trading circles, while at the same time participating in the British–Atlantic deals with the American colonies under British control.[10] Del Carmen Lario and Herzog have also researched Catholic merchants and their privileges in Spain, investigating how often royal decrees granted them the rights of natives, prior to their settlement

---

[7] Glickman, 'Catholic Interests and the Politics of English Overseas Expansion 1660–1689'.

[8] *Irish and Scottish Mercantile Networks in Europe and Overseas in the Seventeenth and Eighteenth Centuries*, ed. David Dickson et al. (Gent: Academia Press, 2006).

[9] Karin Schuller, 'Irish–Iberian Trade from the Mid-Sixteenth to the Mid -Seventeenth Centuries', in *Irish and Scottish Mercantile Networks in Europe and Overseas in the Seventeenth and Eighteenth Centuries*, ed. David Dickson et al. (Gent: Academia Press, 2006), 175–196.

[10] Oscar Recio Morales, 'Identity and Loyalty: Irish Traders in Seventeenth Century Iberia' in *Irish and Scottish Mercantile Networks in Europe and Overseas in the Seventeenth and Eighteenth Centuries*, ed. David Dickson et al. (Gent: Academia Press, 2006), 197–210.

in the country.[11] This right of naturalisation offered excellent opportunities as it implied free access to trade or any related activity. As in the south of Europe, Catholics mainly found homes in Cadiz. In the north they moved to France and the Flemish territories, and in the former settled in the port cities of St Malo, La Rochelle, Nantes, and Dunkirk,[12] as well as the port of Ostend, where there was a strong Catholic presence. Indeed, Ostend served as a gateway between England and Europe, a crossroad of Dutch, English, and French markets and a place for smugglers and privateers linked to Dunkirk.[13] Through those ports large groups of merchants had opportunities to tap into the Channel privateering business using both lawful and illicit means to access the transatlantic riches. During the second half of the seventeenth century, all of these ports had become part of an international trading block which saw the rise of West Indian commerce. Jamaica, in particular, thanks to its position and natural resources, soon became the epicentre of contraband and privateering, mainly between the English and the Spanish – to the extent of transforming its fate from Cromwell's 'consolation prize', in 1655, to England's colonial 'gem'.[14] Indeed, it was in Jamaica as well as Barbados, Monserrat, and North America that Galway families and English Catholics such as the Gages joined the race, forming Catholic oligarchies that commanded colonial trade and plantations. Ultimately, all over the Atlantic and the Mediterranean, ties of kinship and religion

[11]   Maria Del Carmen Lario de Onate, 'The Irish Traders of Eighteenth Century Cadiz' in *Irish and Scottish Mercantile Networks in Europe and Overseas in the Seventeenth and Eighteenth Centuries*, ed. David Dickson et al. (Gent: Academia Press, 2006), 211–30; Tamar Herzog, *Defining Nations, Immigrants and Citizens in Early Modern Spain and Spanish America* (New Haven: Yale University Press, 2003), 83.

[12]   Xabier Lamikiz, *Trade and Trust in the Eighteenth Century Atlantic World: Spanish Merchants and their Overseas Networks* (Woodbridge: Boydell Press, 2010), 133–4; L. M. Cullen, *Economy, Trade and Irish Merchants at Home and Abroad, 1600–1988* (Dublin: Four Courts Press, 2012): Agreeing with Cullen, Lamikiz further argues that these merchants and businessmen intermarried with each other.

[13]   Jan Parmentier, 'The Sweets of Commerce: The Hennessys of Ostend and their Network in the Eighteenth Century' in *Irish and Scottish Mercantile Networks in Europe and Overseas in the Seventeenth and Eighteenth Centuries*, ed. David Dickson et al. (Gent: Academia Press, 2006), 67–92. Jan Parmentier, 'A Touch of Ireland: Migrants and Migration in and to Ostend, Bruges and Dunkirk in the Seventeenth and Eighteenth Centuries', *The International Journal of Maritime History*, 27, 4 (2015): 662–679.

[14]   Ronald Findlay and Kevin O' Rourke, 'World Trade, 1650–1780: The Age of Mercantilism', in *Power and Plenty: Trade, War, and the World Economy in the Second Millennium*, ed. Ronald Findlay et al. (Princeton: Princeton University Press, 2007), 227–310. A. McFarlane, *The British in the Americas, 1480–1815* (London: Longman, 1992).

assured a constant relationship between the two continents which, in terms of trade, survived until as late as the nineteenth century.[15]

Indeed, it is through the historiography that I have been able to reconstruct the networks of the Aylwards and formulate a wider theory that can encompass the whole of the Catholic mercantile community. Scholars have extensively analysed the Catholic communities in Atlantic and Mediterranean ports, and mercantile dynasties are attested as operating in these waters from the late 1600s well into the nineteenth century. For over four decades the Aylward Papers attest to exactly those men and women, who among many others, for centuries played a prominent role in international trade. Suggesting them as representative of a well-established diaspora with extensive networks enriches recent beliefs that Catholic merchants successfully operated in commerce. Indeed, in Spain, the most prominent families identified by scholars (such as Lynch, Walsh, Porter, Blake, and Fitzgerald) worked constantly with the Aylwards on deals that spanned from the West Indies to the Caribbean. The longevity of their business is further buttressed by the records showing the same names already operating in the same ports in the late sixteenth century – particularly the Butlers or the Blakes, whose relatives in Cadiz and London were still active in the 1730s. Those families feature consistently in the Aylward Papers as business partners and family, notably the Butlers and the Porters, alongside whom they worked in Spain, France, and England in times of peace as well as war. It is also worth noting that it was with the help of Catholic partners including the Arthurs, the Blakes, the Brown(e)s, and the Lynchs that the Aylwards mastered their contraband activities through the Channel and in Port Royal and were able to operate in the colonial world as well as the continent. In fact, many of these colonial planting families were active in Atlantic trade as well as in continental exchanges. The continent, indeed, was always of primary interest as it made Atlantic trade viable, and the British focused particularly on Spain and France – far more so than on Holland, which had traditionally been an English partner. Between the British Isles, France, Spain, and Portugal, trade of provisions and ordnance had flourished, and the north European centres contributed to sustaining these exchanges, often by moving Spanish, French, and English goods when the countries were at war. Indeed, as previously mentioned, Ostend, St Malo, and Dunkirk became renowned exchange centres where merchant dynasties including

---

[15] Parmentier, 'A Touch of Ireland'; D. Dickson, 'Catholics and Trade in Eighteenth Century Ireland: An Old Debate Revisited' in *Endurance and Emergence: Catholics in Ireland in the Eighteenth Century*, ed. T. P. Power and Kevin Whelan (Dublin: Irish Academic Press, 1990).

the Carews, Fitzgeralds, Porters, Goolds, Comerfords, Brownes, and the Cloots helped coordinate smuggling across the Channel, furthering deals that ultimately were inter-imperial. From the Channel, those families had strong links with London, where Irish and English Catholic families (the Gages, Kirwans, Lynchs, Bodkins, and Walshes) played prominent roles, and where the notable Arthurs, Fitzgeralds, and Cantillons mastered connections that went up to the court and out to continental financial markets. The geographical scope of Catholic business interests was wide and had an almost global reach of long-lasting networks which met the Aylwards' interests. The literature has not completely disregarded the Aylwards, identifying them as part of this vast diaspora whose interest spanned the continent and colonial America. Indeed, in Bergin's work they emerged as London–Irish merchants, moving within the London mercantile community, where national and religious differences were blurred. It was in London that Zahedieh saw them as import–export merchants operating from the late seventeenth to eighteenth centuries and with trading interests in Jamaica – one to which John Aylward was introduced by the Halls, nephews of the Protestant Thomas Brailsford.[16] Ultimately, in my work the Aylwards are part of the Catholic diaspora but as integrated traders furthering not only individual but national interests. The Aylward Papers ultimately enable a further understanding of the Catholic communities which were operating in the Atlantic and the Mediterranean at this time.

Catholics in Trade

The Aylwards acted as would any other merchants dealing in international exchanges, but their story offers a new perspective on how the commercial world functioned at this time. In the marketplace, just like other widely studied families, the Aylwards saw their Catholic network as a strength but instead of only moving between national borders they also successfully moved beyond their own religious circles. As merchants of the late seventeenth century, they were involved in West Indian trade, one of the most lucrative at the time. Although they had once relied on family and Catholic partners, they soon realised that wider networks would be far more profitable and used this to great advantage. As Haggerty clearly stated, any ambitious dealer knows that moving outside close-knit circles and using the benefits of new acquaintances to provide information is a major key to

---

16   Zahedieh, 'The Merchants of Port Royal'; John Bergin, 'Irish Catholics and their Networks in Eighteenth-Century London', *Eighteenth-Century Life*, 39, 1, (2015): 66–102.

success. The Aylwards maximised on the idea and succeeded when dealing with non-Catholics. This study does not aim to deny any religious dimension to their business, as at times fellow Catholic contacts were used to further their economic careers, but argues instead that religion was seen as a private matter. Perhaps due to the nature of the correspondence, there is very little disclosure on private life and beliefs in the records. Catholics have been identified through past scholarship, with their rare remarks on observing 'the Oration', supporting King James II, and most crucially through the explicit Protestant request of the 'Romanist's Pass', which fostered collaboration and a sense of belonging.[17] In fact, in the 1670s and 1680s, religion allowed British Catholic merchants to base themselves in Spain where they could offer their Protestant partners in England a share of the riches of the Spanish Empire. The agreement perfectly suited the English mercantilist principles of supplying the home country with bullion and raw materials and ultimately increasing its wealth by promoting exports.

Commercial relations with the continent, particularly with Spain, had been vital for England since the late middle ages. The strategies and interfaith collaboration that this book will discuss have been examined by Croft for the Spanish community in the late sixteenth century when Irish, Scots, and English traders worked in partnership to further the interests of the British Isles. In order to close the deals, especially when there was an English ban on trade, Catholics had offered aliases and covers, bribes, and forgery, as well as access to French and Flemish ports where English vessels could change identity in order to make their way to Spain. Mirroring this study, this book expands the lens of inquiry to include other continental centres to investigate how British merchants pursued their interest in furthering their exchanges despite the disruptions, and about their underlying faith as they showed pragmatism and solidarity. Patriotism and religion at this time ultimately proved less strong than the motive of profit, with merchants caring more for their livelihoods than foreign policy.[18] A century later, at the time explored in this book, Spanish relations were still crucial for the British Isles and history shows that as commerce thrived so did relations between Catholics and Protestants. Ultimately, work among merchants fostered a sense of community and, I believe, national belonging. This study is set at a time in which British national identity was shaped and renegotiated. Indeed, as the analysis of papers from the 1670s to the 1680s led to

---

[17]   AY 18, Business Correspondence. Letters to John Aylward from Thomas Brailsford and Richard Horde at London, Oct. 1688 to Sept. 1689.

[18]   Pauline Croft, 'Trading with the Enemy, 1585–1604', *The Historical Journal*, 32, 2 (1989): 281–302.

the theory that Catholics were operating as any other merchant involved in transatlantic dealings in moving beyond the community, further research into activity during the 1690s and 1700s has shown potential to widen the story, suggesting the crucial importance of the Catholic community on a national level.

Catholics in the Nation

The year 1688 was a turning point in British history. The flight of the Catholic monarch James II set in motion changes that would influence British politics and religion for decades to come, and change the nation's relationship with the continent. Across the British Isles, following the excommunication of Queen Elizabeth in 1570, Catholics had already been labelled as the enemy within. From 1688 they took on the potential to also become political enemies as Jacobites. Jacobitism emerged as a force in the 1690s and soon began an ideology of opposition to the government. The British Isles witnessed several Jacobite plots, beginning in 1708 when a fleet supported by the French tried to invade Scotland as an act of protest against the Union. Jacobitism was seen as treasonous activity but it was also inconsistent, incoherent, and influenced by the ebb and flow of national politics rather than being clearly identifiable with either the Whig or the Tory party. Particularly after the rebellions of 1715, Jacobitism became mainly a sort of nostalgia, a fantasy solution to the nation's ills and a force which expressed dissatisfaction with the policies of William III. In social terms, Jacobitism was not strong among all Catholics, and had little connection with social class. The landed elite were traditionally associated with the Stuarts but some gentry were ambivalent, maintaining their contacts in case the Stuarts should be restored, but at the same time advocating for a monarch with limited powers and respect for the majority Protestant faith. The staunchest supporters of James were perhaps the ones who had followed him in France but, ultimately, the position of the French King was not clear. After the death of James II in 1701, he had proclaimed James III as King of England, yet active support in terms of money and men was never extensive.[19]

Perhaps, rather than Jacobitism, it is possible to talk about Jacobitisms. In terms of geographical distribution, the idea remained popular in Scotland, particularly in the Highlands where again the religious element was strong, but also because the Scots were dissatisfied with the policies of

---

[19]   J. Smyth, *The Making of the United Kingdom, 1660–1800: State, Religion and Identity in Britain and Ireland* (London: Longman, 2001).

William III, seeing in him a foreign monarch more interested in commerce and foreign affairs and ignorant of the country that he was meant to rule. Moreover, the Stuarts were Scottish and this heritage strengthened political allegiance. However, more than a commitment to the Stuart restoration, the Scottish Jacobites expressed dissatisfaction with post-revolutionary developments and with a union that had disregarded their betterment and failed to deliver on its promises. Among the three Kingdoms, the Irish Catholics were perhaps in the most difficult position. After 1691, the land and faith had been destabilised by the new Williamite regime and the position of Catholics was weakened but this did not necessarily lead to support for the Stuarts. Not many Jacobite rebellions happened in Ireland and, as argued in *Loyalty and Identity*, it was perhaps a removal from positions of power and politics that hindered any organisation of protest.[20] Regarding the English Catholics, Monod and Glickman agree that perhaps this community was torn between an allegiance to the Crown and support for the Stuarts and their religious beliefs. If many supported the Stuart cause, the association of Jacobitism and Catholicism was not clear cut. Perhaps the Jacobite cause was mainly felt by the landed elite, if anything for their higher stakes in politics. However, for the purpose of this work, particular attention has been devoted to the mercantile class which seemed the most disenfranchised. In England, some Catholic merchants supported the Stuarts. Monod, in 'Dangerous Merchandise', explains how Catholic traders exchanged merchandise and seditious information across the Channel in support of James III.[21] Families including the Butlers, the Goolds, and the Lynchs were among the most renowned owners of privateer vessels at the time having operated similar business in the Channel for some years,[22] and the Aylwards partnered with them. However it can be seen from their papers that the vast network of London merchants involved in Channel contraband were mainly Protestants with an interest in furthering exchanges disrupted by the war rather than supporting a deposed king. Evidence of the Aylwards' activity therefore seems to support Parrish's argument that not all Jacobites were Catholic.[23]

---

[20] *Loyalty and Identity: Jacobites at Home and Abroad*, ed. P. Monod, M. Pittock, and D. Szechi (Basingstoke: Palgrave Macmillan, 2010).

[21] Paul Monod, 'Dangerous Merchandise: Smuggling, Jacobitism, and Commercial Culture in Southeast England, 1690–1760', *The Journal of British Studies*, 30 (1991): 150–182.

[22] Bromley, 'The Jacobite Privateers in the Nine Years War', in *Corsairs and Navies, 1660–1760* (London: Hambledon Press, 1987), 139–166.

[23] David Parrish, *Jacobitism and Anti-Jacobitism in the British Atlantic World, 1688–1727* (Woodbridge: Boydell & Brewer, 2017), 38–65.

As suggested by Linda Colley, merchants were perhaps more interested in social order than civil unrest which would have affected trade. Stuart restoration could have meant commercial policies favourable to France which would have considerably weakened British interests; therefore, merchants as a class were not fervent Jacobites and perhaps –as Colley said– far more ambiguous.[24] However, during the Nine Years War these strategies changed and the Catholic network became crucial for smuggling French goods into England through Spain. Finally, during the War of the Spanish Succession, religious contacts allowed merchants to introduce French and Spanish commodities into English ports through Portugal. Needless to say, none of these exchanges were legitimate. Indeed, the merchants defied many policies issued during times of war and for two decades their businesses survived through smuggling and privateering. Records of their illegal practices offer insight into the mechanics of European trade and, most of all, show how Catholics were crucial in keeping the wheels of British commerce spinning across Europe and beyond.[25]

Concluding Thoughts

The story of these trading communities examined by the literature is one of success, of Catholic success, which dispels stereotypes not only about early modern religion but also of the seventeenth- and eighteenth-century British commercial world. They prove that religious contacts at this time were not only an asset to use on occasion in the market, but could also determine a successful career. The integration of these Catholic traders into the British mercantile community also implies Protestant collaboration. They worked with non-Catholic others weaving a narrative of acceptance and also a new story about early modern commerce, in which religious beliefs were no longer crucial in defining policies; one in which capital was becoming the most important factor in commerce. This period of transition for Catholics would also be a time of rehabilitation. James II introduced a programme of modernisation that embraced a disconnection between Church and State: religious dissent became a political issue and the religious argument

[24] Linda Colley, *Britons: Forging the Nation 1707–1837* (New Haven: Yale University Press, 1992); Gabriel Glickman, *The English Catholic Community, 1688– 1745: Politics, Culture and Ideology* (Woodbridge: Boydell Press, 2009); Paul Monod, *Jacobitism and the English People, 1688–1788* (Cambridge: Cambridge University Press, 1989).

[25] Fernand Braudel, *The Wheels of Commerce: Civilization and Capitalism, 15th–18th Century*, vol. II (London: Collins, 1982).

for intolerance was abandoned by the King himself.[26] His reign was short-lived, but changes were already in motion. With the Glorious Revolution of 1688,[27] alongside the political and economic transformation, Stuart society also witnessed the beginning of a more tolerant and more pragmatic society, although the extent of it must not be overstated. Religion was undoubtedly still important but had become more of a political tool of convenience. Indeed, the Catholic penal laws became less harsh at this time and, despite being revived, were not necessarily always pursued. This emerging attitude of tolerance certainly resulted from various contingencies, not least the new economic spirit as James II himself believed that persecution failed to achieve its aims and conscience could not be constrained. Furthermore, the penal laws could affect property and employment, and with them the economy. Instead, pluralism and more pragmatic policies protected the interests of the country and of its people and in turn, markets and trade were spun by money which had no religious denomination.

When this project started in 2011, I was aware that the theme of British Catholic history had been very different. Glickman's admirable work at the time focused on what separated English Catholic politics from mainstream British life: their Jacobitism. But alongside more recent scholars, he paid more attention to the economic role of Catholics, which provided rehabilitation of the community. Indeed, Catholics in Atlantic–Mediterranean ports worked alongside fellow Protestants, eventually furthering a sense of belonging. Starting with the most basic levels of social experience and working out to the Atlantic context, I will unveil the full extent of the Catholic contribution to the changing society of the era.

The Documents, Structure, and Aims

The Aylward family's papers, made up of 10 account books and over 130 bundles of commercial correspondence written in three different languages, have allowed me to explore the wider context of British Catholics'

[26]   S. Pincus, *1688: The First Modern Revolution* (New Haven: Yale University Press, 2009), 278–302. Mark Knights, '"Meer religion"and the "church-state" of Restoration England: The Impact and Ideology of James II's Declaration of Indulgence' in *A Nation Transformed: England after the Restoration*, ed. A. Houston and S. Pincus (Cambridge: Cambridge University Press, 2001), 41–70.

[27]   Ibid.; Nuala Zahedieh, 'Overseas Expansion and Trade in the Seventeenth Century' in *The Oxford History of the British Empire: the Origins of Empire*, vol. I, ed. Nicholas Canny et al. (Oxford: Oxford University Press, 2011), 398–421. Regarding the period of transition in the community I refer to Bossy, *The English Catholic Community*.

enthusiastic participation in an emerging fiscal-imperial economy. For almost forty years the letters were sent from Cadiz, St Malo, and London to partners in Europe and beyond. In 1687, after almost twenty years in Spain, the Aylward family moved to St Malo, where they stayed until 1698, the year they moved back to England. In Spain, as in France and in Britain, the correspondence reached associates across the Atlantic and the Mediterranean. This book begins in the 1670s when the first business accounts of merchants associated with the Aylwards were recorded in Cadiz, and concludes in 1714 with the last letters sent by their associates in London. The work is structured chronologically and shows how Catholicism was not only an asset to the market, but could also be the determinant of a career, and significantly contributed to sustaining British trade. In particular, the role of Catholics grew in importance when the British Isles became embroiled in almost thirty years of uninterrupted warfare from 1688 until 1714. This work does not deny domestic Catholicism or Protestant intolerance, in particular the resurgent anti-Catholicism after 1688, but suggests how the new dynamics of trade allowed this proactive minority to integrate and support British trade. Important themes underpin the book and relate to the wider debates in social and economic history of the early modern world, namely the place of Catholicism in early modern Britain, the role of religious minorities in early modern trade, and the role of the Catholic minority in the formation of the British nation. Recent scholars have extensively studied the economic and religious features of the early modern world and aspects of trade, trust, family, religion, and nationality have all been examined and deeply analysed.[28] The newly born British state was undoubtedly a Protestant one, but the emerging fiscal-imperial economy was also sustained by various religious groups who set up and moved within their international networks. Up to now, Catholics during the age of mercantilism have been studied and recorded mainly as a marginalised group, with scholars more concerned about politics than economics.[29] The

[28] Lamikiz, *Trade and Trust in the Eighteenth Century Atlantic World*; Nuala Zahedieh, *The Capital and the Colonies: London and the Atlantic Economy, 1660–1700* (Cambridge: Cambridge University Press, 2010); Perry Gauci, *The Politics of Trade: The Overseas Merchant in State and Society, 1660–1720* (Oxford: Oxford University Press, 2010); Sheryllynne Haggerty, *'Merely for money'? Business Culture in the British Atlantic, 1750–1815* (Liverpool: Liverpool University Press, 2012); Hancock, *Citizens of the World*; Trivellato, *The Familiarity of Strangers: The Sephardic Diaspora, Livorno and Cross-Cultural Trade in the Early Modern Period* (London: Yale University Press, 2009); Tijl Vanneste, *Global Trade and Commercial Networks: Eighteenth Century Diamond Merchants* (London: Pickering & Chatto, 2011).

[29] Glickman, *The English Catholic Community*; Marshall and Scott, *Catholic Gentry in English Society*; Bossy, *The English Catholic Community*; Alexander Lock,

aim of this work is to offer new insight which dispels and contradicts this generalisation of the Catholic community.

Following the first chapter on Catholicism and the politico-economic context, Chapter 2 opens with the mercantile strategies of the British Catholic community in Cadiz during the 1670s and 1680s. Through a focus on the Aylwards, I reconstruct a group of traders who established themselves in Anglo-Spanish trade, maximising English exports while importing Spanish and West Indian raw materials. Their pragmatic behaviour was that of any other merchant group of the time, as they tapped into established networks of expatriates and closed deals with trustworthy partners. This book then analyses in depth why British Catholics were important in Atlantic and Mediterranean commerce. Chapter 3 focuses on the British Catholic community in St Malo and its strategies in times of political turmoil. It looks more deeply at how their business survived the Glorious Revolution and throughout the Nine Years War when their Catholicism allowed the traders to procure French commodities in high demand in England and overseas. Chapter 4 builds upon the previous three chapters and further analyses the Catholic community in London during the War of the Spanish Succession in which European trade became even more difficult. This is illuminating as it was during these years that British Catholics made great use of both their citizenship – which allowed them to live in London – and their religious contacts – which allowed them to thrive through smuggling. It is striking how during times of war they maximised profits and showed outstanding commercial skills. These four chapters form the core of the book and show how the experience of the Catholic merchants challenges prevailing assumptions about how the religious community was marginalised, hinting at a completely new story in which social ostracism was replaced by economic and, eventually, political inclusion.

These merchants reverse the stereotype of an idle Catholicism, showing instead how Catholics acted and integrated within trading communities. The fifth chapter focuses on their ability to establish inter-imperial connections which became crucial for the survival of British trade as Catholic ties allowed British merchants a constant supply of in-demand goods by connecting with various trading circuits. I analyse how trading strategies of the British Catholics abided by the mercantilist rules of the balance of trade where north European manufactured goods were exchanged for Mediterranean and Atlantic raw materials. I will also investigate how international

---

Catholicism, Identity and Politics in the Age of Enlightenment: The Life and Career of Sir Thomas Gascoigne, 1745–1810 (Woodbridge: Boydell & Brewer, 2017).

war affected the market and commodity prices, what merchandise retained its value, and what was worth smuggling during these years. The aim of this section is to argue that Catholicism allowed British merchants to successfully sustain their individual exchanges. Chapter 6 expands further the concept of economic integration by analysing the role of female Catholics within the new economy. It looks at a group of historical women and their economic and financial deals, exploring how they embraced new and lucrative financial opportunities while openly defying social conventions and religious beliefs about gender roles. These female merchants fit into the literature of widows in trade who, as shown by recent scholarship, were generally so accustomed to their husbands' dealings that they were able to take financial responsibility for the family's business following their bereavement. Their involvement in trade challenges the prevailing role of Catholic women as wives, patrons, or nuns and their stories shed light on the role of women and business which has been so far been overlooked by Catholic historiography.[30] Moreover, they enrich the argument formulated throughout the previous chapters. In fact, the previous narrative illustrates male Catholics as entrepreneurs, moving beyond religious and national borders in their quest for profits. This chapter therefore complements the

---

[30]   For the literature on women and business I mainly consulted: Haggerty, *The British Atlantic Trading Community*; Richard Grassby, *Kinship and Capitalism: Marriage, Family, and Business in the English-Speaking World, 1580–1740* (Cambridge: Cambridge University Press, 2001). Women usually ran parallel and minor trades, such as shop-keeping or retailing. If they remarried, they could lose the capital and the independence gained. Usually, they resorted to guardians. Hannah Barker, *The Business of Women: Female Enterprise and Urban Development in Northern England, 1760–1830* (Oxford: Oxford University Press, 2007), 3–10. Pamela Sharpe, 'Gender in the Economy: Female Merchants and Family Businesses in the British Isles, 1600–1850', *Social History/Histoire Sociale*, 34 (2001). Regarding Catholic historiography, the primary works are: Jenna Lay, 'An English Nun's Authority: Early Modern Spiritual Controversy and the Manuscripts of Barbara Constable' in *Gender, Catholicism and Spirituality: Women and the Roman Catholic Church in Britain and Europe, 1200– 1900*, ed. L. Lux-Sterritt and Carmen M. Mangion (New York: Palgrave, 2011), 99–114; Claire Walker, '"When God Shall Restore them to their Kingdoms": Nuns, Exiled Stuarts and English Catholic Identity, 1688–1745' in *Religion and Women in Britain, c. 1660–1760*, ed. S. Apetrei and H. Smith (Burlington: Ashgate, 2014), 79–98; Caroline Bowden, 'The English Convents in Exile and Questions of National Identity, 1600–1688' in *British and Irish Emigrants and Exiles in Europe, 1603–1688*, ed. D. Worthington (Leiden: Brill, 2010), 297–314; J. Goodrich, 'Ensigne-Bearers of St Claire: Elizabeth Evelinge's Early Translations and the Restoration of English Franciscanism', 83– 101 and S. Brietz-Monta, 'Anne Dacre Howard, Countess of Arundel and Catholic Patronage' in *English Women: Religion and Textual Production, 1500–1625*, ed. M. White (Burlington: Ashgate, 2011) , 59–82.

overall argument, showing that British Catholics, male and female, worked in trade and seized upon new economic and financial opportunities offered by the new commercial age.

The book also explores how the Aylwards and their partners exploited new systems created by the Protestants and sustained themselves in the era before emancipation. Catholicism might have entailed sectarianism and civic liabilities, but what these traders show is that this religious community was no stranger to the entrepreneurial spirit. During the age of mercantilism, society was deeply changed and the Catholics simply adapted to fit in the new world. Commerce and Catholic community form part of one story; they merged because, despite the hostile environment, Catholics acted in business 'merely for money'. They built coherent trading zones and through a broad range of connections were able to move beyond the borders of the European Empires, both national and religious, as they established international networks. Another aim of this work is to prove that Catholics were part of the Atlantic–Mediterranean economy, which was not dominated solely by Protestant and Jewish businessmen. It is possible to talk about Catholics in business and argue that they did not set up the equivalent of a 'Protestant International';[31] rather, they integrated within the mercantile communities, dispelling the myth of marginalisation and suggesting how the Atlantic economy transformed an entire system of beliefs. The emerging British Empire needed entrepreneurs and support and in time of political turmoil, investments were crucial and the identity of big moneylenders was irrelevant to the government. So, would their religious denomination be of any importance? Indeed, an attitude of public suppression and private connivance developed towards Catholicism and the new fiscal-economic policies issued during the age of Mercantilism (1650–1780) offered Catholics the opportunity for inclusion. The records of merchants examined here only strengthen this theory of Catholics who worked and supported Protestant partners and their institutions from the late seventeenth century and throughout the eighteenth. They answered the economic and fiscal needs of the new British state. Furthermore, decades of economic integration coincided with a new political environment in which the Catholic threat had entirely faded away.

Although the book focuses on activity during four decades, it complements a literature on Catholics in trade that has studied the same mercantile

---

[31]   Bosher, 'Huguenot Merchants and the Protestant International in the Seventeenth Century', 99–100.

communities from the late sixteenth to the early nineteenth centuries.[32] By integrating previous studies, this book confidently proposes a new theory for Catholicism in the long eighteenth century. I believe that profound political and social change can be partly explained through the changing economy in Britain at this time. The second half of the seventeenth century saw the birth of imperialism and a revolution in fiscal-military policies –changes which presented fresh economic needs and triggered new social dynamics. This was a period of crucial transformations in which the emerging economy offered an opening to non-conformists. The drive for wealth and success set the religious affiliation of merchants and investors at relatively minor importance, and a few decades later British politics was forced to acknowledge a de facto situation that this economy had already ushered in. Indeed, after the Seven Years War (1756–1763), France and Spain acknowledged British superiority, whereas nationally, the Stuart-Jacobites had been officially defeated.[33] After facing its enemies, Hanoverian Britain needed support and the time was ripe for new concessions. Therefore, it may not be entirely coincidental that Catholic rehabilitation was granted at the end of the mercantilist era, ultimately culminating in the passage of the Catholic Relief Act in 1778.[34] Throughout the eighteenth century, Catholics in Britain on the whole fared well: not only were they entrepreneurs working alongside Protestants, but they also felt themselves to be as British as anyone else in the country. They saw opportunity in change, embraced risk, and through the new imperial designs bought their 'relief', their place within the nation.

---

[32] Bergin, 'Irish Catholics and their Networks in Eighteenth-Century London'; Thomas Truxes, *Irish American Trade, 1660–1783* (Cambridge: Cambridge University Press, 1988) 84; Craig Bailey, *Irish London: Middle-Class Migration in the Global Eighteenth Century* (Liverpool: Liverpool University Press, 2013); Pauline Croft, 'Trading with the Enemy, 1585–1604', *The Historical Journal*, 32, 2 (1989): 281–302.

[33] Colin Haydon, *Anti-Catholicism in Eighteenth Century England* (Manchester: Manchester University Press, 1993), 170–176, 227. Haydon argues that the Seven Years War was seen as a religious war, when Britain and Prussia fought Austria, France, and Spain in 'Eighteenth Century English Anti-Catholicism: Contexts, Continuity and Diminution' in *Protestant–Catholic Conflict from the Reformation to the Twenty-first Century*, ed. John Wolffe (Basingstoke: Palgrave Macmillan, 2013), 49; C. Johnson, *Developments in the Roman Catholic Church in Scotland, 1789–1829* (Edinburgh: John Donald, 1983).

[34] Pincus, 'Rethinking Mercantilism'; Haydon, *Anti-Catholicism in Eighteenth Century England*.

Chapter 1
Religion, Trade, and National Identity: A Review

Catholicism and Nationality

The Aylward Papers primarily invite discussion about the role of religion within the mercantile early modern world. The main aim of this research has been to challenge and dispel stereotypes about Catholicism and to contribute to the recent scholarship on dissenters in the Atlantic world.[1] However, the Aylwards' letters tell us much more about religious groups within Britain as a nation, rather than simply its world of commerce. Unlike other scholars, Glickman's recent work suggests the British nation was not exclusively Protestant and the example of the Aylwards supports this argument.[2] The Catholic merchants here thought of themselves as part of a distinct national group, at least within the mercantile community and strove to further the commercial interests of their country. As Hancock said, the Atlantic world promoted the idea of a British community and this book hopes to contribute to the debate on Britain and its invented nation.[3]

The relationship between Catholicism and British nationhood is problematic. In the last twenty years or so, historiography has questioned the position of dissenters within Britain, their contribution to the nation-building

---

[1] J. F. Bosher, 'Huguenot Merchants and the Protestant International in the Seventeenth Century', *The William and Mary Quarterly*, 52 (1995): 77–102. Holly Snyder, '"Under the Shadow of Your Wings": Religiosity in the Mental World of an Eighteenth Century Jewish Merchant', *Early American Studies: An Interdisciplinary Journal*, 8 (2010): 581–622. F. Trivellato, *The Familiarity of Strangers: The Sephardic Diaspora, Livorno and Cross-Cultural Trade in the Early Modern Period* (London, Yale University Press, 2009).

[2] Gabriel Glickman, *The English Catholic Community, 1688– 1745: Politics, Culture and Ideology* (Woodbridge: Boydell Press, 2009), 1–18.

[3] Linda Colley, *Britons: Forging the Nation, 1707–1837* (New Haven: Yale University Press, 1992), 326; David Hancock, *Citizens of the World: London Merchants and the Integration of the British Atlantic Community, 1735–1785* (Cambridge: Cambridge University Press, 1995).

process, and their perceived identities.[4] After 1689, the position of Protestant dissenters was completely different from that of Catholics; they were tolerated and could access a level of the political system, including Parliament itself. Great Britain was not a confessional state: it was pluralist, but ultimately it was Protestant. There seems to be agreement between scholars that Britain was built by religion and that the various Celtic, Gaelic, and Anglo-Saxon elements were pulled together by anti-Catholic feelings, the only sentiment that found wide consensus. In short, that Britain was an invented nation and Protestantism was its cement.[5]

It is difficult to disagree with this argument, particularly in light of the official legislation that, as Colley said, enshrined the division between Protestants and Catholics until 1829. Until then, British Catholics had not been allowed to vote or hold state offices. They were subject to punitive taxation, forbidden to possess weapons and discriminated against in terms of access to education, property rights, and freedom of worship. Within the minds of the nation they were 'un-British', the 'fifth column', or 'the enemy within'. Catholics were seen as culturally too close to the continent in their education, their manners, and their baroque chapels; and they were also too close to foreign powers like the French, the Spanish, the Pope, and the Stuarts. In the eyes of Britain, they were disloyal and their culture was foreign.[6]

Instead in Britain, national history was told in very providential terms, as an unfolding of events that would progressively free the country from popery and pull together its three nations. Every year Britons would remind themselves who they were by celebrating anti-Catholic events: one among many was the day of the 1st of August, which remembered the Protestant accession of the Hanover dynasty. This dynasty symbolised the end of the divine right of the monarchs, a – partly foreign – national dynasty, in power for their faith and not for their family. They represented the country; providence had sent them and above all they responded to the Parliament, the embodiment of national unity. Protestantism might have meant intolerance, but it also made the nation possible.[7] The creation of

---

[4]   The leading scholars on this topic are Linda Colley, David Armitage, and Jeremy Black, *Natural and Necessary Enemies* (London: Duckworth, 1986). Also interesting is the edited work of B. Bradshaw and J. Morrill, *The British Problem, c. 1534–1707: State Formation in the Atlantic Archipelago* (London: Macmillan Press, 1996) which focuses on British national identity, although not on religion.

[5]   Colley, *Britons*; Tony Claydon and Ian McBride, *Protestantism and National Identity: Britain and Ireland, c. 1650–1850* (Cambridge: Cambridge University Press, 1998).

[6]   Claydon and McBride, *Protestantism and National Identity*; Colin Haydon, 'Eighteenth-Century English Anti-Catholicism: Contexts, Continuity, and Diminution'.

[7]   Colley, *Forging the Nation*, 11–54.

the British nation was deeply rooted in religious identity and the feeling of being British was fostered by a sense of being different from Catholic Europe, whose religion equalled despotism and obscurantism.

The other side of this narrative is that Catholicism was made responsible for the darkest times of British history. The Civil War was caused by the Catholic Queen Henrietta Maria who, with her scheming priests, 'led astray' Charles I; in 1666 London was burnt to the ground by Catholics, the Catholic Mary Tudor spilled much Protestant blood, and in 1605 the Parliament was almost blown up by the Catholic Guy Fawkes. Catholics were subject to witch hunts where folklore mixed with politics to express the fears, anger, and insecurity of the country. Britons turned against what was perceived as foreign or suspect, and international politics played a role in particular during war with France or Spain, when anti-Catholic pamphlets became an important part of propaganda. This included sermons, preaching that ensured the messages reached the illiterate, denouncing popish brutality and their iniquities on the continent. Harsh criticism was directed towards these two countries where the nobility and clergy were viewed as utterly unproductive parasites, the masses were poor and there was no promotion of progress.[8] However, what scared Britons the most was Jacobitism. The Jacobites, by supporting the Stuarts, showed that a Catholic restoration was possible and this was a threat which would influence British politics for more than fifty years. The anti-Catholic panic reached its zenith in 1745 when Charles Edward Stuart threatened to invade the country. In turn Catholics were accused of an internal conspiracy to undermine the country with their clandestine activity. In the 1740s, after the final defeat of the Jacobites at Culloden, attitudes changed and in some areas of the country Catholics were openly tolerated. Anti-Catholicism was closely tied to external threats and wartime scares, so when the fear of attacks from Spain or France diminished, so too did the fear of Catholics at home.[9]

Besides the widespread anti-Catholicism, I believe that it is possible to find a middle ground. By studying the ideological origins of the British Empire, David Armitage reached an interesting conclusion. He found that

---

[8]   Colin Haydon, *Anti-Catholicism in Eighteenth Century England* (Manchester: Manchester University Press, 1993), 170– 176; Tony Claydon and Ian McBride, *Protestantism and National Identity, Britain and Ireland, c. 1650–1850* (Cambridge: Cambridge University Press, 1998); Sharpe, *Remember, Remember.*

[9]   T. P. Power and Kevin Whelan, *Endurance and Emergence: Catholics in Ireland in the Eighteenth Century* (Dublin: Irish Academic Press, 1990); Haydon, *Anti-Catholicism in Eighteenth Century England*, 91, 81,170; Claydon and McBride, *Protestantism and National Identity*, 36. Regarding Jacobitism, see Colley's chapter on the Protestant Identity.

although anti-Catholicism gave Britons a clear vision of themselves as the chosen people, this was a negative force and that it is difficult to conceive of a nation that defined itself in a non-affirmative way, shaping its own idea against something else.[10] In fact, France was a powerful nation and a force to be reckoned with. Britons out of fear, or perhaps envy, depicted their Catholic enemy as inept, impoverished, and superstitious. Instead, Britain saw itself as non-continental, more liberal, and less backward,[11] and anti-Catholicism promoted national cohesion. However, the nation had been defining itself in negative terms, as a non-Catholic nation, with a non-Catholic Church, as something other. Therefore, Armitage asks, which kind of Protestantism built the nation? He is not even sure that Britain was ever one Protestant nation. Certainly, Scotland and England disagreed on religious terms, and faith has more often divided than united them but on the whole Britain was an accepting society and many Protestantisms coexisted. Anti-Catholicism also raised other concerns in the country as it was strong only among certain groups, and in certain regions. With this question, Armitage reopened a fascinating debate that this book aims to enrich: that in the eighteenth century, Catholic merchants began to perceive themselves as British. The mercantile world was known for its pragmatic acceptance and the Atlantic world forced the British nations to come together and see minorities integrated. It is difficult to assess whether this unity was reluctant or not, but it is indisputable that there was collaboration and through this a sense of belonging developed. British Catholic merchants became, and felt, part of the nation.

The most influential theory for this book is the recent argument presented by Glickman.[12] He read the English Catholic community in a different light, finally moving away from traditional historiography and enriching the narrative of inclusion that has been opened up by Bossy in *The English Catholic Community*. Glickman talks about an enduring English Catholic minority, with families of high social status and medieval ancestry who were not estranged from the political life of the country even though Catholics were not included in the Toleration Act of 1689. Catholic communities began to be seen as another form of dissent and their image in early modern England is not entirely clear cut. The community's religious life was more dynamic and creative than we might think, and it now

[10]   David Armitage, *The Ideological Origins of the British Empire* (Cambridge: Cambridge University Press, 2004), 69–99.
[11]   Colley, *Forging the Nation*.
[12]   Glickman, *The English Catholic Community*, and A. Lock, *Catholicism, Identity and Politics in the Age of Enlightenment: The Life and Career of Sir Thomas Gascoigne, 1745–1810* (Woodbridge: Boydell & Brewer, 2017).

re-entered, if it had ever really left, British public affairs. Glickman rejects the idea of a class in decay or one foreign to their country. Catholics very much participated in the debates of the kingdom, even if at times of revolution and change their identity and nationality might be questioned. The last decades of the seventeenth century were particularly crucial for Catholics in England as Bossy talks of a period of transition, both in the economy and in society and politics.[13] In 1685, the accession of James II seemed almost a vindication for Catholics who again became protagonists of national affairs. But this enthusiasm was short-lived, and ended with the revolution of 1688. The revolution had both a political and emotional impact on the Catholic community, with many aristocrats fleeing to the continent or organising rebellion at home. The Jacobite threat was real, but it was not universal. Not all Catholics wanted a Stuart restoration, especially the merchants worried about a potential civil war that would have disrupted commerce. Also, many Catholics simply objected to a Dutch ruler and in this case would fight for their country rather than their religion. Loyalty to the Stuarts was not unquestioned and Glickman disagrees with Bossy's argument that Catholics' devout patriotism was held back by it.[14]

Indeed, Catholics were ready to take the oath of fidelity to George I. They participated in local politics and questioned allegiance to the Stuarts – especially when it meant French encroachment. They were not all supportive of the religious policies of James II or of the struggle to restore him to the throne and they did think about possible new allegiances. Being Catholic did not necessarily mean being a Jacobite.[15] Their main problem with the oath to George I was not that it declared loyalty to the Hanoverians but that it rejected Catholic doctrine as superstitious. Nevertheless, Catholics were willing to rethink their own identity; regardless of faith, they believed that Catholicism was compatible with the English Constitution and wanted to assert their obedience to the sovereign.[16] Glickman concludes that the British national identity could not be solely Protestant.

---

[13]   John Bossy, *The English Catholic Community 1570–1850* (London: Darton, Longman & Todd, 1975).

[14]   Glickman, *The English Catholic Community*, and Colley, *Forging the Nation*. Gabriel Glickman, 'A British Catholic Community? Ethnicity, Identity and Recusant Politics, 1660–1750' in *Early Modern English Catholicism: Identity, Memory and Counter-Reformation*, ed. J. E. Kelly and S. Royal (Leiden: Brill, 2017), 60–81.

[15]   Agreeing with Glickman, Alexander Lock also supports the same theory on national identity and support for the Hanover dynasty.

[16]   This crucial point is discussed by Glickman and it is very much in line with the conclusion of J. P. Sommerville in his chapter 'Papalist Political Thought and the Controversy over the Jacobean Oath of Allegiance' in *Catholics and the Protestant Nation, Religious Politics and Identity in Early Modern England*, ed. Ethan H.

This book situates itself at this point. It acknowledges its debt to the work of Glickman and Colley and moves the debate further. The Catholic merchants examined here were not Jacobites, nor did they necessarily participate in local politics. They were informed about political events, but simply as dictated by the necessities of their profession. Furthermore, they thought of themselves as British, worked for a common goal, and despite living in various countries always pursued British interests. In British commerce at this time, as across the nation, 'access was not denied to any romanist'.[17]

The Catholic Narrative

In the late seventeenth century, the English Catholic community experienced a period of transition.[18] According to Bossy, Catholics were modernising, influenced by the society they lived in, where less traditional and more secular values emerged. With this, their new social and economic dimension, their political position shifted, being subject to the ebbs and flows of international politics. Indeed, since the Stuart Restoration of the 1660s, English Catholicism experienced a revival. Although Charles II was not a Catholic himself, he was surrounded by 'ostentatious Catholics' including his mother, Henrietta Maria, and his wife, Catherine of Braganza. Although the Queen Mother was held in contempt by popular opinion because of her alleged responsibility for events during the Civil Wars, the Queen herself was not seen as a threat by the people. Catherine had no interest in politics, barely spoke English, and bore no children. Rather, policies towards Catholics were influenced more by the international scene, in response to Counter-Reformation movements on the continent, such as the scares of the Spanish Inquisition and the persecution of the Huguenots in France.[19]

Shagan, (Manchester: Manchester University Press, 2005), 162–184. Sommerville argues that during the reign of James I, Catholics were torn between allegiance to the King and their religious beliefs. They somehow tried to accommodate politics and religion, although their attitude found the opposition of the Pope and of various 'papalist' political thinkers. It is interesting how already in the early seventeenth century, lay Catholics felt the need to acknowledge themselves as English subjects.

[17] AY 18, Business Correspondence, Letters to John Aylward from Thomas Brailsford, Oct. 1688 to Sept 1689.

[18] Bossy, *The English Catholic Community.*

[19] Haydon, *Anti-Catholicism in Eighteenth Century England*: Haydon argues that enormous resonance in propagandist terms in England had the St Bartholomew Massacre of 1672 and the Edict of Nantes of 1685. 'The Evil Empire and the Enemy Within' in Sharpe, *Remember, Remember*, 1–37. I. Deane Jones, 'The Theory and

However, hostile attitudes began to develop in the early 1670s when rumours spread about James II's religious conversion in 1672, and his refusal to take the Anglican sacrament in 1673. In the same year the fears intensified when he married his second wife, the Catholic Mary Beatrice of Modena. In response, the English Parliament promulgated the Test Act (1673), which integrated the Corporation Act of 1663 and required office-holders to reject Catholic doctrine, instead taking the Anglican sacrament and communion.[20] A priest could no longer say the Mass, under threat of imprisonment, and conversion to the Catholic faith would have been seen as a crime. Similarly, failure to submit to the oaths of supremacy and allegiance as prescribed by the Act would have meant disinheritance and the inability to purchase land – this latest prohibition being re-issued in 1700.[21]

In the late 1670s, the proximity of Charles II to Catholics and the conversion of his brother fuelled anti-Catholic sentiment. Anti-Catholicism was a constant factor in English politics and society of the time and provided a convenient explanation for disastrous events including plague, war, and even the Great Fire of London in 1666. This already tense climate led in 1678 to the denunciation of the Popish Plot, which at first appeared to be almost a new Gunpowder Plot. The infamous Titus Oates unveiled an alleged Jesuit scheme to depose and perhaps kill the monarch and return the country to Catholicism.[22] Parliament ordered an investigation and, although the accusations proved unfounded, a surge of anti-Catholic hysteria ensued. As a consequence, the penal laws were enforced and a second Test Act was produced. In 1679 tensions mounted with the exclusion crisis when the Parliament debated excluding James from succession. Despite all this, Charles II on his deathbed expressed his wish to be received into the Catholic Church, and great hopes were raised among Catholics all over the country when James II was proclaimed King. Now with a Catholic monarch, fears of a Catholic revival were justified and only a few months into his reign, James II faced an attempt by the Duke of Monmouth, an illegitimate Protestant son of Charles II, to take the throne. After taming the revolt, James began a period of Catholic 'rehabilitation', making religious appointments in important offices.[23] His policies exacerbated the prejudices of English Protestant opinion and things became worse still

Practice of Despotism: 1603–1642' in *The English Revolution: An Introduction to English History, 1603–1714* (London: Heinemann, 1966). 14–38.

[20] Colley, *Forging the Nation*, 1992, 326.

[21] Haydon, 'Eighteenth Century English Anti-Catholicism', 55.

[22] Sharpe, *Remember, Remember.*

[23] Pincus, *1688: The First Modern Revolution.*

when in 1688 the Queen gave birth to a son and Catholic heir. Until then, the Protestant establishment had been reassured by James having only two Protestant daughters, Mary and Anne, but with the new Prince of Wales, the problem of succession became an urgent priority. The boy threatened the country and it was not long before William of Orange, grandson of Charles I, son-in-law of James II, and third in the line of succession, was invited to intervene. On 5 November 1688, William landed in England and James fled the country. Parliament recognised William and his wife Mary on the throne and this dual monarchy would go on to preserve English liberties and religion in the eyes of Protestants. James II died in France in 1701 but he never gave up his hope of regaining the throne and his attempts gave life to Jacobitism, a movement that would influence the country's religious policies for more than fifty years. His departure had serious consequences for Catholics at home. It destroyed their hopes of a restoration and brought about further anti-Catholic legislation, including the 1695 Act which prevented them from becoming barristers, and prohibited them from keeping arms, ammunitions, or an expensive horse. The Act revived the former penal legislation and Catholics were further forbidden from voting in Parliamentary elections. When William III died in 1702, James II's daughter Anne took the throne; under her reign the penal legislation continued, in particular as anti-Catholicism was essential to the negotiations of a British state that emerged in 1707. Finally, in 1714, after her death, the power passed to the Hanoverians, beginning what was possibly Britain's most profoundly non-Catholic dynasty.[24]

During the Hanoverians' reign, the threat of Jacobitism was at its height and the British government responded by re-enacting fierce legislation against the Catholic community. Catholics found supporting the cause would leave their estates forfeited to the Crown and their owners imprisoned. After the first rebellion in 1715, an act was approved to force Catholics to register their names and estates, in order to tax their properties. Indeed, the Jacobite movement was well supported and even financed by the Catholic gentry of the North, including Northumberland and Lancashire, seeking to regain their lost power. The Jacobite rebellion of 1715 appeared as a Catholic crusade and thereafter the retaliation was harsh, but not equal all over the country.[25] It mostly depended on the relationships between the communities, and on local politics. Among the mercantile

---

[24]   David Mathew, *Catholicism in England, 1535–1935: Portrait of a Minority; Its Culture and Tradition* (London: Catholic Book Club Edition, 1938). J. C. H. Aveling, *The Handle and the Axe: The Catholic Recusants in England from Reformation to Emancipation* (London: Blond and Briggs, 1976), 180–238.

[25]   Haydon, *Anti-Catholicism in Eighteenth Century England*, 81.

communities, and the trading centres more generally, support for the Jacobite cause was always lukewarm, as it implied insurrection and disruption.
The anti-Catholic propaganda flared up as a means to unify the population
behind the Hanoverian dynasty and against the Stuarts.[26] Only after the
battle of Culloden in 1746 did Jacobitism suffer a decisive blow allowing
legislation to become more lax.[27]

In recent works, documents such as estate records, merchant papers,
and oaths of allegiance have attested to a pervasive Catholic presence.
Furthermore, these sources have shown how in some parts of the country, such as North Yorkshire, Northumberland, the Midlands, and Sussex,
Catholic communities were lively and well-settled. As Caplan argued in
his study of Sussex, wealthy families were the main point of support within
Catholic groups and their estates went untouched throughout the centuries.[28] Moreover, their properties were scattered in other counties, such
as the extensive properties in Yorkshire of the Dukes of Norfolk, which
were each acquired through inheritance. These properties represented a
spiritual and economic centre of the Catholic settlements and the gentry's households were a source of employment as well as offering access
to the Mass or meetings with the priests in private chapels. The younger
sons of these families were often sent to European seminaries, where they
would be educated and prepared for a life in the clergy back at home. The
Catholic nobles acted as patrons, almost independently from the clerical
authorities, and were free to appoint or dismiss chaplains and to sustain
their communities. They kept the Catholic flame burning and practised
their faith undisturbed. There were times when a family would disappear
due to a lack of male heirs or by conforming to the Church of England and
that could mean the vanishing of a community. However, Kinoulty suggests that when a centre was closed, people often moved to another patron
close by and this shift may have led to miscalculations as the Church
would not know where parishioners had moved, instead only registering
the decline. Her extensive study of Sussex analysed the economic situation
of the county, where the population was mainly involved in agriculture.
The community largely made a precarious living with its fortunes bound

[26] Ibid., 91.
[27] Brian Magee, *The English Recusants: A Study of the Post-Reformation Catholic Survival and the Operation of the Recusancy Laws* (London: Burns, Oates, and Washbourne, 1938), 176; Aveling, *The Handle and the Axe*, 366.
[28] N. Caplan, 'The Sussex Catholics, c. 1660–1800' in *Sussex Archaeological Collections*, vol.116 (Lewes: S.A.C., 1978), 19–30: The most prominent Catholic families
in the south were the Carylls in West Grinstead, the Montagues in Easebourne, the
Norfolks in Arundel, and other families along the Sussex–Hampshire border.

by the quality of the harvest. This is why the households of rich families represented the first employers.[29] Poverty was widespread among the community, but this social problem was not directly related to Catholicism and instead was a common feature of the country in general.

It is worth noting that during the eighteenth century, Catholics were not as beleaguered as their ancestors had been decades before. Certainly, a decline in numbers cannot be denied; after years of Jacobitism, penal legislation, and unfair taxation, the landed nobility lost members through conformation or simply a lack of heirs.[30] However, Kinoulty states that this decline occurred across the British gentry as a whole, affecting Protestant landowners as much as Catholics. At this time society was beginning to change as commerce introduced the 'middling sort', a class of professionals enriched by trade.[31] Kinoulty suggests that Catholicism declined because it lacked a middle class capable of ensuring continuity when the landed class was in crisis. However, her work focused mainly on communities in Sussex, which was bypassed by the Industrial Revolution and became a repository of young migrants, Catholics and otherwise. Therefore, her generalisation of a missing middle class is arguably unrepresentative, certainly of the Catholic merchants associated with the Aylwards.

The history of Catholicism is usually a story of emancipation. So, how did this community survive and flourish in practice? Undeniably, common values and interests fostered relationships across religion. Individuals and institutions needed income to survive. European monarchs disregarded the religious affiliation of bankers, and therefore it is plausible to argue that Catholics remained part of British society because of their ability to answer the needs of the fledgling mercantile economy. It is clear that the dwindling of the Catholic community in the face of persecution and the penal laws remains a valid interpretation. However, during the eighteenth century, Catholics were still part of the British scene, despite the hatred they faced.

[29]   Mary K. Kinoulty, *A Social Study of Roman Catholicism in West Sussex in the Eighteenth Century* (Chichester: W. S. R. O., 1982), 28–31: Usually Catholics lived only a few miles from the Mission, though a few people were attested in rural areas or far from the noble families. In the Catholic households, servants were usually Catholics, although Protestants were not altogether excluded.

[30]   Peter Marshall and Geoffrey Scott, *Catholic Gentry in English Society: The Throckmortons of Coughton from Reformation to Emancipation* (Burlington: Ashgate, 2009), 19; Caplan, 'The Sussex Catholics', 19–30; Kinoulty, *A Social Study*, 28: It is interesting that Kinoulty has suggested that the decrease of the Catholic community could be explained by people remaining unmarried, discouraged by the extent of poverty, as well as young workers migrating towards urban centres like London.

[31]   Jonathan Barry and Christopher Brooks, *The Middling Sort of People: Culture, Society and Politics in England, 1550–1800* (London: Macmillan, 1994).

The fierce legislation issued during the seventeenth century had aimed at ousting them from political life and it certainly endangered their role within the country.[32] Nevertheless, their survival and endurance show that they were able to remain part of society. Recent scholarship has very generally hinted at a new role, at the evolution of a community of landowners into one of merchants and businessmen. Glickman, Marshall, and Scott suggest how the community changed while integrating among Protestants.[33] They show that we can assume a certain degree of cooperation and integration and contend that survival was possible through Protestants' support and a process of Catholic self-invention. However, their studies remain linked to the old scholarship which is dominated by religious and political analysis, and their focus is primarily on a body of gentry or lesser nobility. Although economic factors have been briefly surveyed, the overseas economy has been greatly neglected or perhaps avoided. Recent literature has not fully addressed the extent to which this community was marginalised, which strategies ensured survival, and what role Catholics played within the Atlantic trading world.

Indeed, examination of the economic context has the potential to address these queries. Catholic landowners had capital and an income and were certainly involved in economic or financial activity. Their mere existence suggests that they somehow supported themselves and that they might have adopted specific strategies to deal with adverse circumstances. Penal legislation had always been focused on landowners or office-holders, yet there was no precise legislation on the emerging financial activities. The Catholic Church forbade lending money at interest; however, a lack of legal restrictions allowed Catholics to seize the new financial opportunities as potential profits outweighed the religious principles proscribing usury. These factors allowed Catholics to defy legislation and survive. By transforming themselves into merchants, Catholic landowners avoided taxation and imprisonment and their money ensured integration within the Atlantic mercantile economy. Catholics were able to answer the fiscal

---

[32] Bossy, *The English Catholic Community*; J. C. H. Aveling, *The Handle and the Axe: The Catholic Recusants in England from Reformation to Emancipation* (London: Blond and Briggs, 1976); Tony Claydon and Ian McBride, *Protestantism and National Identity: Britain and Ireland, c. 1650–1850* (Cambridge: Cambridge University Press, 1998); Marshall and Scott, *Catholic Gentry in English Society*; Haydon, *Anti-Catholicism in Eighteenth Century England*; Glickman, *The English Catholic Community, 1688–1745: Politics, Culture and Ideology* (Woodbridge: Boydell Press, 2009).

[33] Glickman, *The English Catholic Community*, 59–64; Marshall and Scott, *Catholic Gentry in English Society*, 1–30.

needs of the newly born British state and this ability opened a path into the core of British society. Therefore, a new research agenda about Catholicism is possible.

The domestic horizons of the Catholic community have previously been investigated. Bossy's pivotal study *The English Catholic Community* deals with a group of landowners and lesser gentry and argues critically against Magee's *The English Recusants* and Hughes' *The Reformation in England.*[34] Both Magee and Hughes assumed the theory of a depleted and dwindling community; however, Bossy states that this assumption is true only for the late seventeenth century. He found that overall the size of the community was static and was neither eroding nor increasing. Bossy's study tells the story of the community from the Reformation towards the Emancipation, focusing on how it was sustained by a body of missionaries and priests.[35] He introduced the concept of a Catholic community instead of a Catholic minority. There were many varied religious denominations in England during the early modern period and Catholicism was just one facet of English non-conformity.[36] Certainly, Bossy did not focus on politics, as his approach examined mainly religious issues, and he presented this community as a body of priests, missionaries, and gentry. This same pattern has been followed by Aveling and by Norman, who support the notion of a decrease in the community but at the same time stress its endurance.[37]

A different approach has been adopted by authors such as Colley, Johnson, and Power and Whelan, who have each emphasised how Catholic penal laws excluded Catholics from civil and political life, namely through the Corporation Act (1663) and the Test Act (1673), which required office-holders to repudiate the Catholic faith and instead take the Anglican Sacrament and Communion.[38] Penal legislation has been interpreted as part of a wider process of nation-building that took place in Britain during

---

[34] Bossy, *The English Catholic Community*; Brian Magee, *The English Recusants: A Study of the Post–Reformation Catholic Survival and the Operation of the Recusancy Laws* (London: Burns, Oates and Washbourne, 1938); A. O. Meyer, *England and the Catholic Church under Queen Elizabeth* (London: Kegan, Trench, Trubner & Co., 1916); Philip Hughes, *The Reformation in England* (New York: Macmillan, 1951).

[35] Bossy, *The English Catholic Community*, 194.

[36] Ibid., 1–7.

[37] Aveling, *The Handle and the Axe*, 253, 291, 325–326; Edward Norman, *Roman Catholicism in England: From the Elizabethan Settlement to the Second Vatican Council* (Oxford: Oxford University Press, 1985).

[38] Linda Colley, *Britons Forging the Nation 1707–1837* (New Haven: Yale University Press, 1992), 326; T. P. Power and Kevin Whelan, *Endurance and Emergence: Catholics in Ireland in the Eighteenth Century* (Dublin: Irish Academic Press, 1990; Bernard Ward, *The Dawn of the Catholic Revival in England 1781–1803* (London:

early modern times. Protestantism seemed to have been fundamental in constructing the identity of the nation and so, in turn, Catholicism was perceived as an ideological threat and a perverted version of Christianity.[39] This anti-Catholicism proved to be a fundamental element of cohesion, helping to identify everything which was not essentially British. It helped build a nation. Unsurprisingly, these hostile feelings were stronger in times of war and political turmoil, and in 1715 and in 1745, during the Jacobite rebellions, threats of a Stuart restoration and possible French invasion fuelled the persecution.[40] Usually, disorder was more common in the coastal regions where a possible invader would have landed and it was in times of war that hostile legislation was issued. During the last decades of the seventeenth century, England found itself in the throes of conflict with France and Spain with twenty years of fighting and it was at this time that Catholic-targeted penal laws were enforced throughout the three Kingdoms of England, Scotland, and Ireland.[41] Nevertheless, despite this legislation, Catholics and Catholicism endured, suggesting a certain degree of public suppression and private connivance at play. In fact, Haydon has pointed out that threats of popery were always directed against remote and distant stereotypes of Catholics, while those who were close, such as neighbours or friends, were not perceived as dangerous.[42] Gentry families, Catholic or otherwise, shared the same values and social habits as their Protestant neighbours, so fear remained stronger in areas where there was no proximity with the group.[43] The overall result was a far less rigorous application of the penal laws during this century.

Anti-Catholicism was based on perceptions and mainly linked to political exigencies. Certainly, being part of a community helped foster a sense of protection from intolerance, but religion during the early eighteenth century, despite still being divisive, was no longer as crucial in policy-making as in the previous years. Recent scholarship supports a grim picture of decades of persecution, but at the same time hints at a new trend, a turning

---

Longmans, Green & Co., 1909); Johnson, *Developments in the Roman Catholic Church in Scotland.*

[39]   Haydon, *Anti-Catholicism in Eighteenth Century England,* 4.

[40]   Ibid.; Claydon and McBride, *Protestantism and National Identity,* 36.

[41]   Power and Whelan, *Endurance and Emergence,* 23. In 1700, in Scotland the 'Act for Preventing the Growth of Popery' attempted at depriving all Catholics of their land. It also banished Catholic priests and imposed Protestant education. In 1704, Queen Anne compelled Irish Catholic landowners to choose between conformity or fragmentation of the estates among the heirs, whether male or female.

[42]   Haydon, *Anti-Catholicism in Eighteenth Century England ,* 1–21.

[43]   Marshall and Scott, *Catholic Gentry in English Society,* 1–30.

point dictated by the new national and international scenes.[44] Glickman's *The English Catholic Community* emphasises how the community was more integrated at home than previously thought. He argues in the same terms as Haydon about the disjuncture between representations of Catholics and local tolerance.[45] But he disagrees with the idea that Catholics were a shattered group, noting how some Catholic landowners could flaunt large estates and vast incomes and how, when danger loomed, they resorted to strategies such as safely assigning their lands to Anglicans. He highlights how Catholics became part of Protestant social circles; they attended hunts and meetings, and shared the same hopes and anxieties about a changing society. Glickman, like Scott and Marshall, introduces the concept of social integration. Moreover, he hints at the rejuvenated role of Catholics as businessmen who, when landowning was no longer profitable, financed projects in agriculture, mining, and industry, and became professionals or traders. However, his study focuses on the religious and political aspects of Recusancy or Jacobitism and, like Marshall and Scott, primarily looks at the gentry.[46] His work has the merit of identifying a new economic role for the Catholic community, although still disregarding the Atlantic and Mediterranean economy.

Catholicism in the Irish Kingdom

In June 1541, Henry VIII declared himself King of Ireland. Everyone acknowledging his authority would now be protected by English law and able to become an English subject. The plan of the government was to transform Ireland into a Protestant and English kingdom, in order ultimately to create a Tudor 'Britain'.[47] Henry VIII was the first of a series of monarchs who tried to subjugate Ireland, ultimately failing. Both the Tudors and the Stuarts concerned themselves with the Irish problem, implementing foreign

---

[44]   Ibid., 9-17; Thomas McLoughlin, *Contesting Ireland: Irish Voices against England in the Eighteenth Century* (Dublin: Four Courts Press, 1999) 113.

[45]   Glickman, *The English Catholic Community*, 59–64; Haydon, *Anti-Catholicism in Eighteenth Century England*, 1–21. Marshall and Scott, *Catholic Gentry in English Society*, 1–30.

[46]   Ibid.

[47]   C. Brady and R. Gillespie, eds, *Natives and Newcomers: The Making of Irish Colonial Society, 1534–1641* (Dublin: Irish Academic Press, 1986); M. Kishlansky, *A Monarchy Transformed: Britain 1603–1714* (London: Penguin, 1996); N. Canny, *Making Ireland British, 1580–1650*; B. Bradshaw and J. Morrill, *The British Problem, c. 1534–1707: State Formation in the Atlantic Archipelago* (London: Macmillan Press, 1996).

reforms that were more or less coercive. Yet they were either unaware or uninterested in understanding Irish culture and society. Ireland was in fact a kingdom of multiple identities where Old English lived alongside the Gaelic Irish and, after the sixteenth century, New English settlers. If originally differences had been simply ethnic, with the sixteenth-century Reformation they also became religious. The Old English were the original English settlers who had crossed the Irish Sea in the twelfth century. By the second wave of conquest, the community had adopted many of the native Gaelic customs, making it difficult to differentiate the two groups. The Old English were culturally English, speaking the language and having loyalty to the Crown. But, they were Catholic and the Counter-Reformation gave them a sense of belonging and proximity with Catholic Europe. They were involved in trade and developed links with Spain, France, and the Flemish ports. By the second decade of the seventeenth century, the pace of political and cultural change had quickened and was apparent in increased English control in the localities and in Counter-Reformation influences from the continent. Throughout the sixteenth and seventeenth centuries, reckless English policies and a second wave of English conquest brought the emergence of a new group known as the New English, whose identity has since been constantly debated. Were they Irish Protestants? British subjects? How to define them? There is still debate around the appropriateness of the term Anglo-Irish, but what is certain is that this new community were torn in their allegiance. They felt themselves to be subjects to the English Crown and implemented its policies, but as time went on, their new 'Irishness' meant they began to have many privileges limited. They were not represented at Westminster and were forced to accept economic policies that affected their interests such as the Woollen Act (1699) which prohibited the export of Irish wool to England. In the early eighteenth century, they asked to be recognised as British and part of the United Kingdom, but as they had nothing to offer in economic terms, the request was denied.[48]

The position of the Gaelic Irish Catholics was another matter altogether. They had always been seen as political rebels and enemies, and religion only

---

[48] J. Smyth, 'Like Amphibious Animals: Irish Protestants, Ancient Britons, 1691–1707', *The Historical Journal*, 36, 4 (1993): 785–797; D. W. Hayton, *The Anglo-Irish Experience, 1680–1730: Religion, Identity and Patriotism* (Woodbridge: Boydell Press, 2012). B. Bradshaw, 'The English Reformation and Identity Formation in Wales and Ireland' in *British Consciousness and Identity: The Making of Britain, 1533–1707*, ed. B. Bradshaw and P. Roberts (Cambridge: Cambridge University Press, 1998), 43–111; N. Canny, 'Identity Formation in Ireland: The Emergence of the Anglo-Irish' in *Colonial Identity in the Atlantic World, 1500–1800*, ed. N. Canny and A. Pagden (Princeton: Princeton University Press, 1987), 159–212.

added another dimension to the rivalry. The Gaelic world was in fact a society divided in lordships and where loyalty was personal, directed towards the immediate family, which represented a political and religious universe of any locality. Any reform implemented from above disrupted this social order where the people were mainly illiterate and pledged allegiance only to their own local lord. The native Irish did not speak English and because they rarely saw preachers or felt the presence of the church, its authority, both religious and political, was also distant. Indeed, the main shortcoming of the English reforms was their foreignness; their Englishness, which impeded their assimilation from the Gaelic population. In fact the reception of the Protestant Reformation was hindered by the fact that Ireland had never experienced a Renaissance and was not so receptive to the cries of anti-clericalism. A further problem was the crucial role of the state in implementing reforms. In Ireland, the central authority of Church and State was almost non-existent. The government had authority only within the Pale, an area around Dublin, and had no strong influence outside that area. The Church of Ireland was in serious financial trouble and found itself unable to supervise the spiritual life of the flock or coordinate preaching. Clergymen were not highly educated, and often those who were moved to the continent. Some Irish or Anglo-Irish clergy, as well as Scots and English ministers, tried to preach the new reformed ideas, but were met with a hostile environment, opposition from the local laity, and no support from the state. Any reform, whether political or religious, needed to be accepted first by the local lords, who represented the only recognised authority in vast areas of the country. Any attempt at reform without their consensus would have led to rebellion, something of which the Dublin government was always wary. Ultimately, English monarchs failed as they never had a clear vision of how to rule this kingdom.

After the early attempts of her father to gain control in the country, Mary Tudor later tried to steer the process Henry VIII had inaugurated, but her short reign brought no significant changes. When Elizabeth I took the throne, however, she introduced a new programme and was resolute in continuing and completing her father's reforms. She addressed the problem of introducing the Reformation all over again, but her policies were extremely short-sighted and doomed to failure. She saw Ireland as an unwelcome inheritance and disregarded native Gaelic cultures and society, with their traditional factional divisions and cultural differences.[49] Ireland at this time was regarded as a society of savages, formed by fiefdoms and lordships. The plan of the government was to force Irish

---

[49]   Bradshaw and Morrill, *The British Problem*.

lords to surrender their lands which would be then re-granted to them with new English titles. The aim was to turn the lords into English subjects and extend English authority across the entire kingdom. Ireland was seen only as a means to protect England from continental Catholic forces, but ultimately Elizabeth I only stirred violence and created deep religious divisions.[50]

James I, although adopting a less aggressive attitude in domestic and foreign policy, continued to implement English reforms in Ireland. If Elizabeth had been responsible for deepening religious divisions, James can be credited for creating what would become Northern Ireland. He dreamed of a British colony in Ulster and promoted immigration from both England and Scotland. Because of their common Gaelic heritage, the Scots integrated far more easily in the north of the country, where English settlers were put off by the harsh natural conditions. Here, Catholic landownership visibly declined as Catholics were dispossessed and forced to leave. James' dream was perhaps not realised, but his legacy would be felt for centuries. Ulster became neither Protestant and British, nor Catholic and Irish. In the rest of the kingdom, the King's policies were no different from Elizabeth's.[51] He wanted peaceful coexistence, but still enforced penal laws, forcing the Catholic clergy to leave the island. The many Irish who refused to take the Oath of Supremacy, and recognise the authority of the English Crown, fled, and cities like Waterford were disenfranchised. By the 1620s, the New English settlers held most of the offices in the Kingdom of Ireland. James I believed in spreading Protestantism, which he viewed as a moral and religious enterprise, and although he proclaimed himself *rex pacificus*, towards Ireland he made an exception.[52] His son, Charles I, was perhaps even more ambivalent, and his biggest mistake was in trying to implement religious reforms that the Irish would not accept. In early 1641 the Irish and the Old English rose in revolt against Charles I, coming together as confederates, fighting for their faith and lands. Their rebellion was the beginning of the Civil War across the three Kingdoms, yet when Charles I was executed in 1649, the Irish Catholics had received few concessions and the Catholic question was still unresolved. It was Cromwell perhaps

[50] *Conquest and Union: Fashioning a British State, 1485–1725*, ed. S. G. Ellis and S. Barber (London: Routledge, London, 2013).

[51] Robert Emmett Curran, *Papist Devils: Catholics in British America, 1574–1783* (Washington DC: The Catholic University of America Press, 2014),1–18.

[52] C. Brady and R. Gillespie, *Natives and Newcomers*; J. Ohlmeyer, 'Driving a Wedge within Gaeldom: Ireland & Scotland in the Seventeenth Century', *History Ireland* (1999).

who sounded the death knell to the Irish question. The Interregnum (1651–1660) vanquished the nation as Cromwell indeed felt as though God had sent him a mission of removing the Catholic threat. Papists were declared guilty of treason, the Catholic clergy was dispersed, and Catholic properties confiscated. In this time, Catholic land ownership fell from 22 per cent to 5 per cent or less and in 1653 marriages between Catholics and Protestants were banned.[53]

During the Restoration, penal legislation was not necessarily reinforced but the position of Catholics in the British Isles remained problematic. Charles II believed in restoring order between the State and the Church, and after witnessing the death of his father, knew that unrest was to be avoided. He was pragmatic and more interested in the taxes the Kingdom would provide than in tackling religious differencess. Yet despite Charles' Catholic leanings, Catholics did not fare much better during his reign. In 1669, he restored the Catholic hierarchy, but penal legislation remained in place. The scene changed again when his brother James II became King in 1685. Expectations mounted, but ultimately were not met as James, although sharing their religion, did not do much for his Catholic subjects. There was some element of freedom under the new monarch but the Irish Church was required to support its own clergy and still no Catholics sat in the House of Commons or held a political role.[54] James II tried to rehabilitate Catholics by restoring them to positions of power, but his reign was too short and his small achievements were swept away by the Williamite Revolution of 1688 to 1691. Again, what was seen as an English Revolution badly hit the Irish Kingdom, where most of the fighting took place.[55] After 1691, Ireland was once again a conquered nation, where the position of Catholics became even more problematic. Ethnic and religious divisions became strained by political allegiance as all Irish Catholics were seen as potentially Jacobites, seditious subjects, and supporters of James II. The 1690s represented the end of any Catholic political influence and a disconnection between English politics and Jacobitism, and many members of the gentry and those in trading centres were killed, exiled, or converted.

---

[53] J. Morrill, *Oliver Cromwell and the English Revolution* (London: Longman, 1990); Kishlansky, *A Monarchy Transformed.*

[54] P. J. Corish, *The Catholic Community in the Seventeenth and Eighteenth Centuries* (Dublin: Helicon, 1981), 18–72.

[55] D. W. Hayton, 'The Williamite Revolution in Ireland, 1688–91' in *The Anglo-Dutch Moment: Essays on the Glorious Revolution and its World Impact*, ed. J. I. Israel (New York: Cambridge University Press, 1991).

The Maritime Narrative

In their analysis of mercantile communities, recent historians have paid limited attention to the links between religion and trade, and even less to Catholics.[56] Recent literature has either disregarded or eschewed a possible connection between Catholics and the Atlantic–Mediterranean communities,[57] and historians have seen *either* a Catholic *or* a business person. So, how did religious minorities place themselves within the commercial world? There is a Protestant answer. Huguenot and Quaker merchants' activities across the Atlantic have been studied, so we know that these two religious groups defined themselves through strong family relationships and a shared faith. They disregarded nationality, but dealt primarily within Protestant circles. Bosher and Tolles argue that economic partnerships were based on religious beliefs, and although these communities acted across national borders, they interacted mainly with other co-religionists: 'Only in a network of relatives and fellow Roman Catholics, fellow Protestants or fellow Jews did a merchant normally feel that his contracts and funds, ships and merchandise, were in good hands.'[58]

[56]   Nuala Zahedieh, 'Making Mercantilism Work: London Merchants and Atlantic Trade in the Seventeenth Century', *Transactions of the Royal Historical Society,* 6th series (1999): 143–160; Nuala Zahedieh, 'Overseas Expansion and Trade in the Seventeenth Century' in *The Oxford History of the British Empire: The Origins of Empire,* vol. I, ed. Nicholas Canny et al. (Oxford: Oxford University Press, 2011), 398–421; R. C. Nash, 'Irish Atlantic Trade in the Seventeenth and Eighteenth Centuries', *The William and Mary Quarterly Journal,* 42 (1985): 329–356; Xabier Lamikiz, *Trade and Trust in the Eighteenth Century Atlantic World: Spanish Merchants and their Overseas Networks* (Woodbridge: Boydell Press, 2010); Nuala Zahedieh, *The Capital and the Colonies: London and the Atlantic Economy, 1660–1700* (Cambridge: Cambridge University Press, 2010); Gauci, *The Politics of Trade*; Stanley Chapman, *Merchant and Enterprise in Britain from the Industrial Revolution to World War I* (New York: Cambridge University Press, 1992); Sheryllynne Haggerty, *'Merely for money'? Business Culture in the British Atlantic, 1750–1815* (Liverpool: Liverpool University Press, 2012); Hancock, *Citizens of the World*; Sheryllynne Haggerty, *The British Atlantic Trading Community, 1760–1810: Men, Women and the Distribution of Goods* (Leiden: Brill, 2006).

[57]   Zahedieh, *The Capital and the Colonies*; Zahedieh, 'Making Mercantilism Work', 143–160; Nuala Zahedieh, 'The Merchants of Port Royal, Jamaica, and the Spanish Contraband Trade, 1655–1692', *The William and Mary Quarterly,* 43 (1986); Hancock, *Citizens of the World*; Haggerty, *'Merely for Money?'*.

[58]   S. Marzagalli, 'Trade Across Religious and Confessional Boundaries in Early Modern France' in *Religion and Trade: Cross-Cultural Exchanges in World History, 1000–1900*, ed. F. Trivellato, L. Halevi, and C. Antunes (Oxford: Oxford University Press, 2014), p. 172.

Furthermore, Bosher asserts that it is not possible to talk about a mercantile and international Catholic community because Catholics were mainly clergymen, gentry, and lesser nobles. He contends that Catholics were not entrepreneurs, did not create consistent trading zones, and did not form partnerships beyond their national borders.[59] Indeed, Catholicism and mercantile communities are rarely discussed together. The pivotal studies of Hancock, Zahedieh, and Haggerty offer thorough analyses of the mercantile world, but Catholicism does not enter their narratives. However, the actions of Catholic merchants at this time suggest that they could indeed be any of Hancock's Citizens of the World or Haggerty's Atlantic Men. They fit perfectly into the merchants' profiles offered by this literature. Indeed, like any of the subjects of Hancock's work, the Aylwards and their associates started their business by tapping into networks of traders that belonged to the same counting-house. A good firm was vital because it was able to ensure good account keeping, cash flow, and provide networks. These partners introduced new players, and often, as Zahedieh argues, merchants would resort to family; however, dealing with relatives was not necessarily the most profitable strategy as nephews and brothers could be unreliable and unsuitable for the profession.[60] In fact, the few complaints received by the Aylwards in their vast correspondence were mainly about their relatives.

Nevertheless, beyond the family and the firm there was always the wider mercantile community.[61] Indeed, Haggerty highlights how merchants sometimes dealt with next of kin or co-religionists. In the Atlantic, exchanges were slow and highly unregulated; resorting to family was easier, especially when one was new to the business and family and religion offered the opportunity to tap into strong and tested networks. However, the vastness of the Atlantic trade made acting only within one religious group unprofitable. The exchanges required the involvement of many agents and knowledge of everyone's religion was not possible. Within the community, merchants were extremely skilled and astute, well educated in accounting and writing. They kept accurate records of their

---

[59]   Bosher, 'Huguenot Merchants and the Protestant International in the Seventeenth Century', 99–100; Frederick B. Tolles, *Meeting House and Counting House: The Quaker Merchants of Colonial Philadelphia, 1682–1763* (New York: Norton & Co., 1963).

[60]   Lamikiz, *Trade and Trust in the Eighteenth Century Atlantic World*, 9–14; Haggerty, *'Merely for Money'?*, 66–131: Good behaviour was fundamental because reputation was based on actions and the ability to fulfil obligations; Zahedieh, *The Capital and the Colonies*, 55–136.

[61]   Haggerty, *The British Atlantic Trading Community, 1760–1810*.

vast transactions which spanned impressive numbers of commodities and countries. They always copied their letters so as to secure references in case of the loss of correspondence, used bills of exchange, and resorted to trustworthy partners.

Haggerty is one of the few Atlantic historians to assume that merchants did not act only within their religious circles, though this is secondary to other interests pursued in her work and she notes that the theory of non-communality does not extend to all religious minorities. In fact, in her analysis of the Quaker merchants of Pennsylvania, she agrees with Tolles that this community traded across national boundaries, although only with other 'Friends'. Other historians have surveyed religious minorities, notably the Presbyterians in England and the Catholic *conversos* in France.[62] Each of these groups moved across national boundaries but acted mainly with co-religionists. At times, however, both groups established contacts within the dominant society, facilitated by being within the same religious denomination. The Presbyterians acted within a Protestant country, whereas the Spanish *conversos* were simply foreign Catholics in France.

Recently, research on inter-faith relations has seen an important contribution with Trivellato's *The Familiarity of Strangers* and its concept of selective trust.[63] This analysis of the Western Sephardim diaspora has introduced the theory that Jewish merchants worked within different circles of co-religionists but also with non-Jews. The work is part of a broader historiography on trade across cultures, in particular between Christians and other religious groups. Trivellato's work inspired a similar line of inquiry to examine the trading rationale of British Catholics. Religion and trade have been widely studied, but the story of Catholics and their part in the Atlantic–Mediterranean economy remains unexplored.

As mentioned in the Introduction, in recent historiography the analysis of Catholicism and its part in trade focuses mainly on the Irish expatriate communities. During the mid-seventeenth century following the Cromwellian wars, Irish Catholics – mainly merchants – fled their country to

---

[62] Gayle Brunelle, 'The Price of Assimilation: Spanish and Portuguese Women in French Cities, 1500–1650' in *Women in Port: Gendering Communities, Economies, and Social Networks in Atlantic Port Cities, 1500–1850*, ed. Douglass Catterall et al. (Leiden: Brill, 2012) 155–182; Pamela Sharpe, 'Gender in the Economy: Female Merchants and Family Businesses in the British Isles, 1600–1850', *Social History/Histoire Sociale* 34 (2001): 291.

[63] Francesca Trivellato, *The Familiarity of Strangers: The Sephardic Diaspora, Livorno and Cross-Cultural Trade in the Early Modern Period* (London: Yale University Press, 2009).

settle on the continent and overseas.[64] It is clear that although Irish Catholic merchants in Europe have been researched, further analysis of Catholicism within the Atlantic–Mediterranean trade is still needed. The literature on mercantile communities has somewhat neglected Catholics, yet the Aylwards and their associates fit perfectly into each of the various analyses offered by recent historiography: they worked in transatlantic and European trade and they tapped into the communities of British expatriates based in Spain, France, the Dutch territories, and London. They also worked with Protestants and moved beyond the Catholic community because the new global economy required wider networks in order to be profitable. Their dynamics and their strategies show little difference compared with those of other merchants of the time. As for the Irish expatriates, their Catholic contacts were crucial in securing safer strategies in times of international warfare and political turmoil. Like Haggerty's or Zahedieh's merchants, the Aylwards acted merely for profit and were not affected by their beliefs. They were citizens of the world, who at the beginning of the eighteenth century based themselves in London, the epicentre of Atlantic commerce. Hancock presents a group of businessmen who, after enriching themselves, merged into the old gentry.[65] Indeed, the Aylwards bought country retreats and spent springtime in Bath, which had become a fashionable city at the time.[66] They prospered in a Protestant commercial world, suggesting that it is not entirely correct to talk about sectarianism when referring to the Catholic community. So, were the Aylwards and their associates atypical? Recent literature has highlighted how politics and social change affected English Catholicism, and political interactions between Catholics and Protestants have already been suggested. Therefore, is it possible to also assume a certain degree of economic co-operation?

This book opens in the 1670s, when the first business accounts of the Aylward family are recorded, and concludes in 1714 with the death of Mrs Helena Aylward and her last correspondence with various partners across Europe. It is undeniable that the Catholics studied to date often intermarried

---

[64] Lamikiz, *Trade and Trust in the Eighteenth Century Atlantic World*, 133–134; L. M. Cullen, ed., *Economy, Trade and Irish Merchants at Home and Abroad, 1600–1988* (Dublin: Four Courts Press, 2012): Agreeing with Cullen, Lamikiz further argues that the families of these merchants and businessmen intermarried with each other.

[65] Hancock, *Citizens of the World*, 279–382.

[66] Gauci, *The Politics of Trade*, 233: Gauci affirms that wealthy traders did not necessarily aim to merge into the aristocracy, but they were certainly interested in preserving power in their urban world. MS, Lett. C. 192 Bodleian Library, Letter of Mr Hill to John Aylward, from Priory, 1700. Hill commented on the country house bought by Aylward in Hampstead.

or socialised among a close-knit circle of coreligionists. However, their economic activities show no regard for Catholic partners. The Aylwards and their associates resorted to family and friends on occasions, but the most profitable deals were carried on with Protestants. They were astute merchants and their community both assured the survival of their business and promoted inter-faith interaction. Through the Aylwards it is possible to reconstruct the Catholic mercantile communities in Cadiz, St Malo, and London. The family sheds light on dozens of merchants and extensive networks operating in Atlantic and Mediterranean trade from the 1570s well into the nineteenth century, as testified by the literature on Catholic expatriates in various European ports. Indeed, Croft, Bailey, Bergin, and Truxes each show how extensive Catholic networks began to operate in Atlantic–European ports from Elizabethan times until the nineteenth century.[67] Therefore, the Aylwards provide a case study on a much wider phenomenon; and it is precisely the integration of this primary material with the studies available that adds an important new dimension to the history of the Catholic community. British Catholics' economic actions offer a new insight into the Atlantic–Mediterranean world, in which the merchants acting 'merely for money' moved beyond their religious communities.[68] Ultimately, they complement the new theory offered by Glickman that Catholics saw themselves as an integral part of the nation, both socialising and working with Protestants.

Political and Economic Context

In order to understand the Aylwards and their associates, it is crucial to contextualise their careers. In the British Isles at this time, Catholics had witnessed the economic change in old Europe. From the new overseas lands, these merchants imported bullion, dyes, and new foods and drinks in exchange for European manufactured goods. This trade was not monopolised and the transactions were on merchants' accounts. As Zahedieh notes, many traders participated but only a few survived because skills, money, and good luck were all essential to success.[69] Due to colonial and political interests by the end of the century, Europe found itself in the throes of both the Nine Years War and the War of the Spanish Succession.

---

[67] Bergin, 'Irish Catholics and their Networks in Eighteenth Century London'; Truxes, *Irish American Trade*; Craig, *Irish London*.

[68] Haggerty, '*Merely for Money*'.

[69] Zahedieh, 'Overseas Expansion and Trade in the Seventeenth Century', 398–421.

During two decades of war, the Aylwards and their partners moved between France and England. Their movements were certainly dictated by economic strategies as it was safer to export French goods to Spain when the former was at war with England. Meanwhile, during the War of the Spanish Succession, the Aylwards lived in London, from where it was easy to co-ordinate the smuggling of French and Spanish goods from Portugal. The decades in which they lived saw epochal economic and political evolutions, with only a few years of relative peace from 1698 to 1701. This was the age of mercantilism, in which English foreign trade boomed and global dynamics emerged. The role of the merchant became crucial as European society adapted to this new wider world and new concepts of sociability emerged together with new classes and new opportunities. The merchants of the time, like their governments, believed in a national commercial policy which pursued wealth, disregarding and exploiting other countries in a zero-sum game.[70] The Atlantic–Mediterranean economy offered these new opportunities and the Catholics seized them.

British Catholics were involved in the Anglo-Spanish trade according to mercantilist tenets. They maximised English exports and imported Spanish bullion and raw materials on English vessels because of the widespread belief that economic resources were finite and competition among the states was harsh. Trade was an exchange of the products of the land and certainly this view also supported the trading monopolies, including the East India and Royal African Companies, which were strongly backed by James II's policies. The Tories sided with the English king, whereas the Whigs fostered labour, manufacturing, and commerce as important sources of wealth. They introduced the idea that resources were infinite and the state needed to promote their exchange by importing raw materials for manufacturing and not only for re-export, to prevent profits only being for the merchants. The Tories believed in imperial expansion, territorial aggrandizement, and the war against the Dutch, whereas the Whigs supported the manufacturing sector and a war against France, the main economic rival in Europe. Essentially, the political debate was one between war and free trade, and as a result the Crown's commercial monopolies were attacked, the manufacturing sector was fostered, and the war was with France. However, the political economic tenets promoted by James II once again became popular towards the end of the War of the Spanish Succession, when the newly born British government opened negotiations with France. The time of the Aylwards witnessed the first possibility of a transfer of power from a landed elite to a new mercantile class, although

---

[70]   Pincus, 'Rethinking Mercantilism'; Pincus, *1688: The First Modern Revolution*.

whether or not this shift actually happened is still open for debate.[71] What is certain is that the Aylwards lived at a time in which there was no mercantilist consensus, as Pincus put it. Possibly the marriage of their daughters into the landed nobility was part of this political climate, but if anything, it proves Bossy's theory that Catholics were in transition and adapting to the new society and did not utterly reject the old values and traditions. Nonetheless, it is clear that these traders acted in virtue of mercantile principles and had mercantile and pragmatic minds.

The late seventeenth century also saw the birth of the stock market as a result of international unrest as European governments needed funds to support their wars. The financial system came as a response to the commercial revolution; when entrepreneurs started gathering resources through trade they then had liquidity to invest in related financial activities. The Financial Revolution mainly began after 1688 and evolved during the Nine Years War. The conflict proved longer and more expensive than expected, meaning costs were extremely high.[72] The new financial system was a main feature of the new Atlantic world that emerged in the late seventeenth century, and Catholics fitted perfectly into this new scene. Indeed, in the early years of the eighteenth century they invested trading profits into the sea companies. It seems as if the new economic and financial system born in the age of mercantilism provided them with an opening, since the British government needed money and disregarded the religious affiliation of its lenders. During this age, economic policies were more pressing and religious issues were not a political priority. It was a time in which the importance of commerce was highlighted by the political involvement of traders who, by becoming members of Parliament, could influence business policies.[73] Economic issues were transversal, encompassing traders' and the gentry's interests. As a result, political economy started to dominate the English and then British political debate. The fiscal needs of the 1690s led to the creation of new policies and a new sense of coordination between

[71]   Ibid., 24; J. Hoppit, 'The Landed Interest and the National Interest, 1660–1800' in *Parliaments, Nations and Identities in Britain and Ireland, 1660–1850*, ed. J. Hoppit (Manchester: Manchester University Press, 2003), 83–102.

[72]   Anne Murphy, 'Financial Markets: The Limits of Economic Regulation in Early Modern England' in *Mercantilism Reimagined: Political Economy in Early Modern Britain and its Empire*, ed. Philip J. Stern et al. (Oxford: Oxford University Press, 2014), 264–265; Jeremy Black, *European Warfare, 1660–1815* (London: Yale University Press, 1994), 107–110.

[73]   Gauci, *The Politics of Trade*, 209–272. Traders did not necessarily look to be part of the gentry by becoming politicians. During the reign of Charles II, new economic policies were issued, such as the Navigation Laws. The 1680s showed a lack of interest in the economy, revived a decade later, during the Nine Years War.

state and trade. Economic growth inevitably affected British society and its politics and the Aylwards and their associates could be deemed figureheads of a community that adapted. As with other non-conformists, exclusion from public offices shifted their interest towards economy and finance.

This study rethinks the usual assumptions about how Catholic communities are thought to act in commerce, moving within circles of co-religionists and relying mainly on networks of kinship. This chapter has examined the most recent debates on trade, Catholicism, and nationality, as well as the political and economic context in which the narrative lies. Work on the Catholic community in Britain has until now been dominated by John Bossy's characterisation of Catholicism as simply another form of dissent. This formulation, while useful from the perspective of British religious history, includes limited research on British and, especially, English Catholics. Recent work by Gabriel Glickman has begun to address a new narrative of Catholics. He recovers the threads in intellectual Jacobitism which led English Catholics back into the mainstream of eighteenth-century debate. However, the social and economic lives of Catholics are almost entirely neglected in his research. Catholics at this time enjoyed access to international networks that gave them real advantages in trading within France and Spain, as well as their colonial dependencies. Work by scholars such as David Hancock has already illuminated how merchants relied on pre-existing links of ethnicity or religion to establish the relationships of trust that facilitated long-distance trade. Other than a few studies of the banking and commercial houses in London, there is no extensive research on Catholic entry into the commercial life of the emerging British Empire. This book hopes to address a sizeable hole in the literature and offers a profound revision to the history of Catholics within the British Isles.

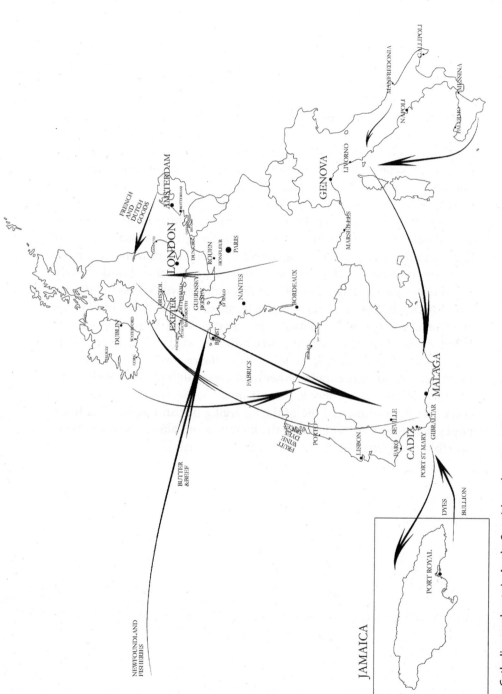

1: Catholic merchants in Anglo-Spanish trade, 1670–1687

Chapter 2
Catholic Merchants in Anglo-Spanish Trade, 1670–1687

In 1672, the merchant John Aylward moved to Spain – 'the Darling and the Silver Mine of England' – with the aim of establishing himself within Anglo-Spanish trade.[1] There, he joined the British community of expatriates which had been settling in Iberian ports since the late Middle Ages.[2] English, Scottish, and Irish merchants had been operating in Spanish ports for many centuries and possibly since before the Norman conquest. The number of Catholics living in Spanish ports, particularly those from Ireland, increased after the Cromwellian conquest of their kingdom (1649–1653). The English soon turned to commerce when landowning was no longer viable due to heavy taxation and so, with the new ability to buy and sell properties and engage in commerce, thousands of foreign Catholics began to establish themselves in Spain, particularly in the port of Cadiz,[3] the most important harbour in the peninsula due to its access route to colonial trade.[4] For centuries, Cadiz's position on the Atlantic had fostered successful exchanges between the north of Europe, the Maghreb, and the Western Mediterranean ports. The North African coasts were now a gateway to the Saharan and Sub-Saharan trading routes, and trade along these was 'immemorial and ancient'; thus throughout the sixteenth

---

[1] Jean O. McLachlan, *Trade and Peace with Old Spain, 1667–1750: A Study of the Influence of Commerce on Anglo-Spanish Diplomacy in the First Half of the Eighteenth Century* (Cambridge: Cambridge University Press, 1940), 6.

[2] Pauline Croft, 'Trading with the Enemy, 1585–1604', *The Historical Journal*, 32, 2 (1989): 281–302.

[3] Ciaran O'Scea, 'Special Privileges for the Irish in the Kingdom of Castile (1601–1680): Modern Myth or Contemporary Reality?' in *British and Irish Emigrants and Exiles in Europe, 1603–1688*, ed. D. Worthington (Leiden: Brill, 2010), 108; Patrick O'Flanagan, *Port Cities of Atlantic Iberia, c. 1500–1900* (Burlington: Ashgate, 2008). O'Flanagan estimates that there were around 40,000 foreigners in Cadiz at the end of the seventeenth century.

[4] Steve Pincus, 'Rethinking Mercantilism: Political Economy, the British Empire, and the Atlantic World in the Seventeenth and Eighteenth Centuries', *The William and Mary Quarterly*, 69 (2012): 10.

century, Cadiz became part of a redistribution network of North European fabrics and American goods.[5]

In the 1670s and 1680s, British Catholics saw life in Spain as an excellent opportunity to initiate new career paths through which – as this chapter will assess – their economic strategies, abilities, and the fortuitous circumstances before them might allow them to flourish as traders. The survey of their papers offers the possibility of a thorough analysis of the places, contacts, and goods which featured in their deals, suggesting that although Catholic contacts facilitated initial settlement, in trade, Catholics showed no religious communality, but only a desire to profit. The Atlantic economy promoted new religious and social orders and it seems that Catholics seized these new opportunities and promoted the national interests by working alongside their Protestant neighbours.

Context

In order to assess British Catholics in commerce, it is fundamental to explore their economic, religious, and political environment. In the British Isles, seventeenth-century commercial expansion was dominated by the ideology of mercantilism. England adopted strict protectionist policies that affected not only foreign powers but also its domestic relations with Scotland and Ireland. The English government saw Scotland as a supply of cheap labour and staples; however, Ireland was seen almost as a conquered colony, whose commerce was at times forced to English ports or hindered so as not to compete with English production. In the Atlantic, both kingdoms competed with each other for trade with the English colonies; Irish merchants were not allowed to trade with colonies that England possessed in the Caribbean and North America. In the 1670s, English foreign policy and economic security were subject to further threat from Holland, while diplomatic relations with France and Spain were relatively peaceful. England saw Holland as the main enemy, the interloper to be weakened in order to strengthen its own trade in a zero-sum game.[6] As a result of the threat of rising Dutch commercial power, European rulers, particularly in England and France, resorted to protectionist laws. England started introducing this legislation in the 1650s and 1660s by requiring all imports of colonial products to be carried on English *bottoms,* or the ships of the country of origin. These navigation laws were further enhanced in the 1670s and 1680s. They

---

[5]   O' Flanagan, *Port Cities of Atlantic Iberia.*
[6]   Pincus, 'Rethinking Mercantilism'.

were an open attack on the Dutch as their power was based on carrying other nations' trade across the Atlantic and the Indian Oceans. The result would be three decades of almost uninterrupted warfare in which the United Provinces' supremacy inexorably faded, opening up opportunities for England's dominance of the Atlantic. After the third Anglo-Dutch War in 1674 and the end of the prohibition of trade with France in 1678, English trade prospered.[7]

In the second half of the seventeenth century, Europe's protectionist policies jeopardised its commerce instead of supporting it. New policies and duties endangered trade, and in times of political turmoil new laws affected economic transactions. In England, the economy's rising wealth soon became the priority of the political agenda, replacing the question of religion as its prime concern. After tackling the Dutch rivalry, England needed France and Spain for its trading balance, and as a consequence an attitude of public complicity was shown towards Catholicism. Indeed, during the previous decades, English politics had focused on fierce Catholic persecution; penal legislation had been issued in the late sixteenth century and constantly re-enacted throughout the following century, banning Catholics from civil and political careers and forcing them to conform to the Anglican Church. However, during the Restoration, England's economic needs and foreign relations affected its religious policies. Charles II acted with ambivalence towards Catholics; he did not repeal any restrictions against them but he did not encourage or enforce their persecution. In 1685, with the accession of his Catholic brother James, the situation profoundly changed.[8] In April of the same year, the business partners Caunter & Howe enthusiastically reported that King Charles II had died and his brother James II had been proclaimed as King 'without disturbance'.[9] Disturbance, however, would soon follow. Since the late 1670s, English politics had been disrupted by the Exclusion Crisis, an attempt to exclude the Catholic prince from the succession. Only a few months after his accession to the throne, a rebellion ensued. The Duke of Monmouth, the illegitimate son of Charles II, led a rebellion claiming to be the lawful Protestant heir to the throne. He did not meet with the support he hoped and ultimately, at the hand of the executioner, he 'received the due desert [sic] of his unnatural rebellion'. The

---

[7]   W. E. Minchinton, *The Growth of the English Overseas Trade in the Seventeenth and Eighteenth Centuries* (London: Methuen, 1969), 12.

[8]   Joseph Bergin, *The Seventeenth Century: Europe 1598–1715* (Oxford: Oxford University Press, 2001), 133.

[9]   AY 21, f. 12, Business Correspondence. Letters to John Aylward from [Samuel] Caunter and [John] Howe at Alicante [first 5 letters signed, Warren, Caunter and Howe]. Feb. 1684–Dec. 1686.

Aylwards' partners had anxiously followed the unfolding of the events after the landing of the Duke at Lyme on 11 June and they were pleased that one of his opponents, the royalist Duke of Albemarle was 'alive to see it [the execution] performed' in July.[10]

The year 1685 was a profound turning point in the politics of the British Isles. James II was a controversial figure and his policies never met with large consensus in the English government. He believed in modernising his three kingdoms and in strengthening their power and wealth. In terms of the economy, James considered trade to be a zero-sum game in which the British Isles would be enriched by weakening their competitors because of the limited natural resources available. He promoted imperial expansion in both England and Scotland and strongly backed the mercantile monopolies that would have protected English merchants.[11] However, his foreign policy stance contradicted this rationale as he strengthened relations with France, both diplomatic and commercial. In terms of propaganda, James' evident admiration for Louis XIV gave scope to the opposition to mount protests against him, but the most pressing issue was the King's attempt to restore Catholics to a position of power. The threats of absolutism and Catholicism could no longer be accepted. In 1688, James II was overthrown and forced to flee the country. It was the beginning of a political revolution that would hugely redefine the three kingdoms, and trigger twenty years of European warfare. It was also a turning point in British national history. After James II's deposition, no Catholic monarch would be allowed to sit on the British throne. The Protestant religion became a symbol of British national identity, making the position of Catholics even more problematic, associated with the old regime and the new forces of Jacobitism. In terms of foreign relations, this firm anti-Catholic stance meant rivalry with France, a struggle that would influence the discourse on British identity up to the beginning of the nineteenth century.

Besides political turmoil, those decades also saw profound economic change and the birth of the fiscal-military state. It was an age of profound crisis but also of new opportunities. The flourishing Atlantic trade

[10]   AY 21, f. 13, Business Correspondence. Letters to John Aylward from [Samuel] Caunter and [John] Howe at Alicante [first five letters signed, Warren, Caunter, and Howe]. Feb. 1684–Dec. 1686. The Duke of Albemarle fought the rebels led by the Duke of Monmouth during the summer of 1685. The latter claimed to be the rightful Protestant heir to the throne, being the natural son of Charles II. AY 79, f.2. Business Correspondence. Letters to John Aylward from John Searle in Exeter on 13 June 1685. John Searle worked with Wyse and Brooking and was associated with the firm Power & Hill.

[11]   Pincus, 'Rethinking Mercantilism'.

triggered epochal economic and social changes. Most of all, it introduced a new commercial era and new social values. The Aylwards and their partners found themselves in a period both fitting and beneficial for Catholic entrepreneurs.[12] Particularly in England, landowning was no longer able to answer all the economic and fiscal needs of the government. As a consequence, political attention shifted towards commerce where revenues were potentially high. Catholic landowners, as well as their fellow Protestants, reinvented themselves in these new activities in which anyone able to dispose of vast capital was welcome. Money had no religious denomination.[13]

Although Europe still played an important role, either as supplier of exports or as an outlet for colonial products, the incredible expansion of trade in the Aylwards' times increasingly focused on the Americas. The expanding Atlantic world demanded more capital, but at the same time, the merchants requested more protection and new trading policies.[14] This change was underpinned by the ideas that the wealth of a nation could be based on commerce and not necessarily just on land. The merchants' community was amassing great capital, and its role within the society was acknowledged. Commerce was still organised into monopolies, controlled by individual companies, but these companies were losing their various privileges and a vast number of them were being abolished due to their lack of competitive reputation. According to modern economic theories, the growing influence of the commercial elites certainly influenced the new 'politics of trade'.[15] This new approach could also be explained by the new role of the Parliament and the decreasing influence of the Crown that traditionally supported the companies.[16] Until the late 1670s, the English

---

[12]   Perry Gauci, *The Politics of Trade: The Overseas Merchant in State and Society, 1660–1720* (Oxford: Oxford University Press, 2010).

[13]   Pincus, 'Rethinking Mercantilism', 10. There was no consensus on the British economy. Trade and manufacturing were becoming prominent in the political agenda and merchants moved closer to the political circles. Catholics seized the opportunity of this fluidity by working with Protestants, meanwhile exploiting their ties with Catholic countries, especially at times of political tension.

[14]   David Hancock, 'Atlantic Trade and Commodities, 1402–1815' in *The Oxford Handbook of The Atlantic World, c.1450–c.1850*, ed. Nicholas Canny et al. (Oxford: Oxford University Press, 2011), 324–340. Throughout the seventeenth century, the British government supported trade; however its measures had just taken the forms of chartered companies.

[15]   Avner Greif, 'Coercion and Exchange: How did Markets Evolve?' in *Essays in Economic History and Development*, ed. A. Greif, L. Kiesling, and J. V. C. Nye (Stanford: Stanford University Press, 2012), 28.

[16]   Gauci, *The Politics of Trade: The Overseas Merchant in State and Society, 1660–1720* (Oxford: Oxford University Press, 2003), 127–137. In the 1650s, during the Cromwellian regime, trade attracted new attention and new commercial policies were of

government did not enact consistent trading legislation and commerce was monopolised by these chartered organisations. All traders outside these monopolistic ventures had to rely on their own strengths, or on other associational or familial structures. Nevertheless, it is worth noting that monopolistic policies were not necessarily unproductive, since being part of a company could assure constant capital, access to precious information, and financial guarantees. The drawbacks were the inability to protect trade from other foreign competitors. Therefore, the merchants sought different regulations and more freedom.

In the late seventeenth century, the already burgeoning Atlantic commerce began to change further. With the decline of the mercantile companies, the Atlantic markets became more flexible and the system of monopoly was slowly replaced by independent ventures.[17] A singular entrepreneurial approach was deemed more profitable and large merchant companies were taken over by small partnerships where costs and gains were divided among a few individuals, usually members of the same family. The decades in which the Aylwards started their business witnessed this transition, particularly in the 1680s, when new coherent commercial policies were issued. Merchants asked for various forms of insurance and protection, but they did not seek strict supervision that could have curbed competition with other rivals.[18] Indeed, the strength of British Catholics also lies in the fortunate circumstances in which they found themselves. This new economic environment was beneficial for those who could not be part of the company's committee, yet were flexible and able to elude controls. In those decades, Catholics profited because they could act in various European countries almost undisturbed. As Catholics they could settle in Spain and access Catholic ports, and as Britons they could move within the British Isles. They could arrange and undo partnerships at their choosing, adapting trading strategies that under strict regulation would not have been possible.

This flexible environment favoured their economic tactics. Slowly, the chartered companies were supplanted by more associational and familial structures.[19] Family firms and small partnerships became the most common organisational forms. Merchants, instead of buying a share in a company, started to share the costs of single vessels. They set out the differing terms

---

consequence. However, it was with Charles II and his Council of Trade that English commercial policies profoundly shifted.

[17]   Hancock, 'Atlantic Trade and Commodities, 1402–1815', 324–340.

[18]   Perry Gauci, *The Politics of Trade*, 128: the Caribbean, North American, and Mediterranean trades were still highly unregulated.

[19]   Hancock, 'Atlantic Trade and Commodities, 1402–1815', 335–336.

for each new single journey, and the Aylwards' accounts show a different partnership for each shipment. This practice was certainly safer, avoiding the input of vast initial capital to buy stock and offering the opportunity to re-think the associations if partners proved unreliable. By negotiating the specific terms of particular collaborations, it was possible to diversify the business and to tap into different circles of partners. This practice was perfect for merchants who needed to carefully plan their actions and select their associates. Indeed, in the transactions between Spain and England, the Aylwards' accounts registered various partners of different nationalities, such as Spanish, British, French, Italian, and Dutch, as well as different religions. When their business expanded to involve other European ports, their associates were in all likelihood not all Catholic. Merchants, brokers, porters, and agents were introduced by friends and acquaintances.[20] Each associate was chosen based on whether they could be deemed trustworthy. The Aylwards were not members of a company, and knew that the Atlantic trade offered them the best opportunities, since it was mostly unregulated. Unsurprisingly, they noticed that many merchants participated in such trade, but few survived because certain skills and competences were fundamental.[21] However, they were aware that the new economic policies and trading organisational forms favoured them as traders and allowed them to be part of the scramble for the Atlantic riches.

The vast amount of goods being exchanged across the Atlantic Ocean redefined the dynamics of European commerce; colonial products were cheap and in high demand, and the European nations able to re-export them would dominate the markets. England soon emerged as the dominating trading power. It slowly established its monopoly in the Atlantic and its mercantile community thrived. The merchants initially focused mainly on the import and export of textiles. London turned itself into the financial and economic heart of the Empire, because the majority of trading goods produced in the colonies were registered there. All the products were subsequently shipped towards Europe or back again to the West Indies where manufactured goods were highly requested.[22] At the time, the main route towards America was through Spain, at least officially. The English govern-

---

[20] AY 5, f. 1, Business Correspondence. Miscellaneous letters to John Aylward, Jan.–Dec. 1686. In late 1685, Martyn, associated with the firm Power & Hill, wrote to the Aylwards wishing to strengthen their acquaintance and to discuss a future profitable partnership in the Anglo-Spanish trade.

[21] Nuala Zahedieh, *The Capital and the Colonies: London and the Atlantic Economy, 1660–1700* (Cambridge: Cambridge University Press, 2010), 55–136.

[22] Ralph Davis, 'English Foreign Trade, 1660–1700', *The Economic History Review*, 7 (1954): 150–166; James Walvin, *Britain's Slaves Empire* (Gloucester: Tempus, 2000),

ment and its merchants therefore cherished this collaboration, particularly as the area also offered access to other Mediterranean markets.

In fact, while based in Spain, Catholic interests spanned an impressive assortment of goods and locations. Their deals embraced an eclectic range of commodities, from women's thimbles to wine and fruit. In the first years of the settlement, they mainly dealt in fabrics and provisions. Their exchanges involved France, Italy, Ireland, Holland, and the Levant, although the balance of trade was in favour of England. English trade was fuelled by American bullion, silver, and gold imported by the Spanish. The West Indies also supplied dyes, and this flow of precious metals and raw materials promoted English manufactures, fishery, and agriculture whose products were the 'fundamentals of trade'.[23] Silks and spices came from the East, whereas France and Italy provided luxury goods, such as velvets, oils, and wines, and Spain gave fruit. These products were exchanged for North European manufactured goods, particularly English tin and lead, and Baltic hides, timber, and iron. English politics responded to mercantilist precepts and trade as an exchange of finite resources was seen as a stimulus for home production and a wealthier system. By re-exporting colonial commodities, England was able to acquire all the continental products not produced domestically. Ultimately, European merchants working in Cadiz shipped European goods to the Americas, and trade would come full circle.[24] Through the Mediterranean and across the Atlantic, global markets emerged; these economic contingencies offered opportunities for integration to Catholics. The Aylwards found perfect circumstances for prospering in the Anglo-Spanish trade. As Catholics, they were able to work and move undisturbed in Iberian ports. Their ability to access south European ports offered great advantages against other competitors. They were players in the British mercantile community and countered civil and political impairment with economic inclusion.[25]

21–34; F. J. Fisher, 'London's Export Trade in the Early Seventeenth Century', *The Economic History Review*, 3 (1950): 151–161. Gauci, *Emporium of the World*.

[23]   Pincus, 'Rethinking Mercantilism', 18.

[24]   Davis, 'English Foreign Trade'.

[25]   Edward Norman, *Roman Catholicism in England: From the Elizabethan Settlement to the Second Vatican Council* (Oxford: Oxford University Press, 1985), 38; H. Roseveare, *Market and Merchants of the Late Seventeenth Century: The Marescoe–David Letters, 1668–1680* (Oxford: Oxford University Press, 1987).

Anglo-Spanish Trade

The British cherished their relationship with Spain, despite the outbreaks of war and the threat of Catholicism to the Protestant faith. Indeed, trade with southern Europe was fundamental in balancing an export of English fabrics with Irish and Scottish dairy products, meat, and fish. It allowed for a maximising of exports from the British Isles as well as imports of raw materials and bullion. The overarching aim was to increase national wealth, with traders disregarding their partners' Catholic identities entirely. Although Seville officially had the monopoly of colonial trade until 1717, Cadiz had already informally assumed this role by the 1680s due to its geographical position. It soon became the most important European–Atlantic port and in turn attracted a more significant community of British expatriates who saw the potential profits as Spain was unable to provide for its own vast colonial empire. Indeed, despite the Spanish colonies at this time being banned from producing any goods, the country lacked a competitive manufacturing sector and its own agriculture was not productive enough to meet demands at home and abroad. Cheap textiles, in high demand to clothe the colonists, were instead produced in England or the Netherlands. Foreign merchants also provided various staples and provisions, primarily beef, butter, fish, and maritime stores. As a result, the Spanish economy stagnated and the country acted as a bridge, brokering American bullion and European goods, but not producing anything itself. Its trade was in theory its monopoly; however, in actuality the Spanish market merely supplied wines and fruit. High corruption and protectionist policies led to its inexorable decline: its gold and silver enriched the other European merchants, its wools and dyes enriched the manufacturing sector of England and the Netherlands, and England increased its wealth upon association with Spain. For European traders, these circumstances were extremely profitable, and Spain offered many opportunities to reap great rewards.

The major problem of the Spanish market was the persistence of commercial monopolies. In the Iberian ports, *consulados* merchants' guilds did not facilitate free enterprise, whereas the North European trades flourished as the French, Dutch, and English governments assured greater freedom of movement to their businessmen. In Cadiz, the *consulado* protected commerce, controlled the traders, and coordinated the American fleets. However, although officially managed by Spanish authorities, the sailing of these fleets was monitored by European merchants due to their incredibly precious cargoes. Thanks to the Spanish officials' connivance, foreign traders were able to load their merchandise, evade all taxes, and ultimately defy the rules. To avoid trading duties and tariffs they would load unregistered goods onto the American *flotas* directly from their own vessels floating in the bay of Cadiz.[26] Once these colonial cargoes returned, to avoid controls and conceal their illegal trades, the products would be dropped in other Iberian ports or handled publicly by Spanish factors on behalf of English or Dutch merchants who 'stayed quietly in the background'.[27] Perhaps contraband could have been tackled through different economic policies. Smuggling seemed to have been the only profitable option left to merchants at this time as the colonial trade was highly taxed with export duties of five per cent and import taxes as high as ten or twenty per cent. For instance, in 1683, one English partner, John Wyse, complained about this Spanish taxation. He briefed the Aylwards about a shipment of goods worth £150 which was to be sent to Exeter but warned them that the introduction of new taxation had raised the duties on fruit by four per cent; according to their accounts, the traders were indebted by £75 and were expected to pay this sum within sixty days.[28] It was likely because of these policies and the heavy taxation that the Spanish monopoly on the Atlantic trade was undermined in various ways.

During their time in Spain in the 1670s and 1680s, the Aylwards were introduced to a vast group of associates which supplied the transatlantic vessels and had contacts with many European ports. Their actual contacts were numerous and of many and varied nationalities. It is likely that there was also a similar variety of religious denominations among them. For Spanish, Italian, and French merchants, it is possible to assume their Catholicism, but the same cannot be claimed for the English or the Dutch. In actuality, some of them were certainly Protestant, such as the Londoners Charles Peers and Thomas Brailsford who would go on to play a crucial role during the Glorious Revolution. During these years, the Aylwards' associates travelled between the continent and Britain where each of their firms were based. In particular, Power & Hill kept their accounts from as far back as the early 1670s and there is no evidence of any blood or religious ties to them.

In Cadiz, Power & Hill offered a foothold in the business community. Through them, the Aylwards were soon introduced to other companies

---

[26]   C. H. Haring, *The Spanish Empire in America* (New York: Harcourt, Brace & World, 1952), 306–307. Once a year, usually in April or May, the *flotas* would sail towards the Gulf of Mexico, touching first at the Canary Islands. The galleons, mainly war vessels directed towards South America, would sail in July or August. Both fleets would spend the winter in the Americas and would meet the other homebound vessels in Havana.

[27]   Croft, 'Trading with the Enemy', 286.

[28]   AY 2, Business Correspondence. Miscellaneous letters to John Aylward, 1683.

such as Ambrose & Upton and Enys & Aldrington, as well as many associates working in the English ports of Exeter, London, and Bristol. The possibility of business links with English ports meant the ability to supply the Spanish market with all the manufactured goods needed in exchange for provisions which were coming from Mediterranean and Levantine ports. In fact, the merchants in England provided access to the British markets as well as the Baltic commodities, whereas Catholic contacts allowed easy access to various south European countries – such as Italy or the Venetian possessions – and multiple transactions meant greater chances of survival. When a market turned difficult, there was always the opportunity to deal with other ports and other people. Moreover, in order to trade successfully it was essential to have a timely supply of high quality merchandise available for a competitive price, and so having contacts based in various locations was undoubtedly the best strategy as chances were greater to find the most lucrative deals.

Right from the early years of their careers, the Catholic associates were already aware of how their religious contacts would be crucial in sustaining British commerce. Catholicism was important in establishing networks across European borders. Through their community they had the opportunity to work with co-religionists in different countries and through various firms to link with any associates in the British Isles. In Britain, many partners were based in Exeter, a port bustling with French, Dutch, and German merchants. The decision to work out of this English port was dictated merely by the relevant role played by the city in the Anglo-Spanish trade. Exeter certainly had the most lucrative exchanges with the Netherlands, from where Dutch and Baltic products would reach England, before being re-exported to Spain and Portugal. In the late seventeenth century, the focus of Exonian merchants on the Netherlands was forced by the high duties in the import and export of French goods; yet the decrease in direct Exonian–French trade should not be over-stated. In fact, particularly from London, a significant quantity of Exonian fabrics was not only moved to Spain, but also reached France.[29] It was because of the role of this port as an international hub that the partnerships between British Catholics in Spain and Exeter were so frequent. From there, the Wyses – often associated with the Brookings – worked with the Aylwards in Spain for more than twenty years. They were part of Power & Hill's network and by the 1680s had been working in the Spanish trade for more than two decades, with associates based in Iberian ports and England, and with involvement in the

[29] W. B. Stéphens, *Seventeenth Century Exeter: A Study of Industrial and Commercial Development, 1625–1688* (Exeter: Exeter University Press, 1958), 101–108.

West Indian trade. They were now among the most prominent merchant families operating in that market.[30]

Indeed, the Wyses introduced the Aylwards to the firms of Doliffe & Radbourne and Humphrey & Boden, and to many independent traders such as the Watkins and the Searles. Each contact would introduce them to other merchants or factors so as to create a continuous expansion of a thriving network. Searle in fact introduced the Gramars and the Sitwells in London, and the Brookings introduced the Aylwards to partners in Bristol. The exchanges made with Bristol were not as numerous as the ones with London or Exeter, but nevertheless, the port was rising in importance in the Atlantic trade and many contacts with the Iberian ports were strengthened. Working among these conditions, the Catholic merchants in Spain shared both high profits and high risks. The costs of commerce were incredibly high and managing their exchanges, which involved multiple transactions, was certainly no easy task. The Wyses seemed to have offered the right skills, training, and experience, although religion does not appear to have been part of this relationship. Perhaps due to the nature of their conversations, they never disclosed personal beliefs or opinion on politics. They don't feature in the scholarship on the Irish diaspora and their faith is therefore not clear. Nevertheless, they introduced the Aylwards to numerous new circles of merchants through which the couple expanded their correspondence to include agents based in the English ports of Bristol, Weymouth, and Topsham, and those across other European cities in which merchants offered partnerships and provided commodities for export.[31]

The records show that the Exonian Sardner, an associate of the Wyses, had significant interests in the Italian markets, and brought these precious contacts into his partnership with the Aylwards.[32] From these South English ports, various exchanges were also closed with the Netherlands, although during the 1680s, the Aylwards' exchanges with the country's traders were infrequent, mainly involving correspondence with Amsterdam and in scant exchanges primarily regarding 'Rein wine' and manufactured goods that would complement the English trade.[33] The trading relations of British

---

[30] AY 101, Business Accounts. Bills, accounts, and receipts for merchandise to Dec. 1687.

[31] AY 2, f. 14, f. 7, Business Correspondence. Miscellaneous letters to John Aylward, 1683. AY 1, f. 5 and f. 3, Business Correspondence. Miscellaneous letters to John Aylward, 1672–1676.

[32] AY 4, f. 11, Business Correspondence. Miscellaneous letters to John Aylward, Jan.–Dec.1685.

[33] AY 98, Business Accounts. Accounts, receipts, and bills of exchange for merchandise to Dec. 1684; AY 100, Business Accounts. Bills, receipts for merchandise to

Catholics with these territories would go on to increase in the 1690s as a result of commercial strategies during the Nine Years' War (1688–1697), and in the early 1680s the Aylwards were introduced by Power & Hill to the Catholic Creaghs, based in Holland, whose role would be prominent during the conflict which was to follow.

But for the meantime the Aylwards used their base in Cadiz to forge new connections across the French ports. French trade was important for British Catholics despite France being England's main competitor in the market, being the most populous European country with a flourishing foreign trade. When England signed the commercial treaty with Spain in 1677, its merchants hoped to affect the French economy by trading more with Spain and thus decreasing French exchanges with the British Isles. The Spanish treaty allowed English merchants to export bullion and assured lenient policies: ships were not inspected, factors were not questioned, and goods were not detained.[34] The balance of trade was advantageous for both countries. However, despite this preferential treatment, the merchants from Power & Hill continued to deal with France for the high quality products that maintained the country's competitive edge. Through this frequent collaboration, the firm was able to introduce the Aylwards to new partners in France: the Porters and Woulfe & Trublet. These merchants had created contacts that spanned the country, from Marseilles to St Malo, and although their partnership would be more significant in the 1690s, it was in the early 1680s that the Aylwards first began collaborating with them in Spain.

Besides their French contacts, during these years the Aylwards were beginning to establish contact with traders in Italian ports such as Livorno, Genoa, Palermo, and Naples. Transactions of Mediterranean goods during the 1680s were infrequent but were being gradually introduced to a network of merchants affiliated to the firms of Ambrose & Upton and Harper, Cross & Parker. Again, the intermediary utilised was Power & Hill which shared a vast network of traders operating in Italian ports, and through them, also trading in Levantine goods. Indeed, through Italy, the associates accessed the Levantine ports of Alexandretta, Smyrna, and Aleppo. Thanks to their religion, British Catholics had easy access to Italian ports as well as commercial networks across Livorno, Genoa, Naples, and Gallipoli. From there, they could rely on extensive networks of native traders as well as English Protestants. In fact, English merchants had been settling in Livorno

December 1686. With one of Power & Hill's associates, the Londoner Gramar, the Aylwards invested in the Netherlands. Their interests were many and varied. AY 13, f. 4, Business Correspondence. Letters to John Aylward from Aaron Atkins at Amsterdam and Port Royal, Apr. 1684–July 1688. Seven letters.

[34] McLachlan, *Trade and Peace with Old Spain*, 14.

since the early seventeenth century, and in just a few decades had become the most important of the mercantile communities, controlling the majority of Mediterranean exchanges from north to south of the peninsula.[35] Livorno was soon established as the English headquarters in the Mediterranean. Because its trade was not subject to the English Levant Company which controlled the traffic between England and Venice, it proved to be an attractive base for any merchant who did not want to be constricted by government regulation, in turn allowing for competition with Venice in redistributing colonial and northern European goods. The Aylwards and their associates worked extensively in this area, procuring goods and information for their Protestant partners in England. British Catholics established partnerships with local dealers, particularly in Italian ports as is evident with the Pincettis in Genoa and Costa & Sanguineti in Livorno – merchants who had associations with Ambrose & Upton, Warren, Caunter & Howe and indirectly with Power & Hill. Warren & Caunter, in particular, never hid their support for the Catholic monarch in England, often reporting political news and constantly briefing the Aylwards with updates about the unfolding of the rebellion of the Duke of Monmouth.[36]

It was in these thriving cities that Italian and British firms coordinated shipments of corn and wheat from Sicily and Sardinia as well as olive oil from Gallipoli.[37] Through Cadiz, they introduced fabrics, as well as tin and lead, which were both highly sought after commodities in the war-ridden Mediterranean. Trade exchanges with these ports would intensify in the 1690s and in the 1700s, but the transactions were not insignificant even during the 1680s. From the south of Spain, Mediterranean goods would be diverted either to the north of Europe or the colonial markets, usually Jamaica, where Power & Hill worked with Aaron Atkins. However, the British Isles was the main focus for merchants. The Aylwards frequently went to London and exchanged commodities with the Irish ports of Dublin, Belfast, and Waterford. Nicholas Lincoln and Peter Knowles corresponded from Dublin and Belfast, and it was from Ireland that they shipped provisions including butter and salmon while also re-exporting fruit and wine to Iberian ports. These successful commercial links between Irish and

---

[35] H. Koenigsberger, 'English Merchants in Naples and Sicily in the Seventeenth Century', *The English Historical Review*, 62, 244 (1947): 304–326.

[36] AY 21, f. 13, Business Correspondence. Letters to John Aylward from [Samuel] Caunter and [John] Howe at Alicante [first 5 letters signed, Warren, Caunter and Howe]. Feb. 1684–Dec. 1686. The Duke of Albemarle fought the rebels led by the Duke of Monmouth during the summer of 1685.

[37] AY 3, f. 16, Business Correspondence. Miscellaneous letters to John Aylward, Jan.– Oct. 1684. In Italy they frequently worked with the Pincetti family.

Iberian ports had been established in the late Middle Ages, but had become problematic in the late seventeenth century. Due to the vast community of Catholic expatriates in Cadiz, Irish ports such as Waterford, Dublin, or Belfast intensified their exchanges with Spain; however, these deals drew a fine line between legal and illicit trade, disregarding protectionist policies and institutional arrangements. Since the 1670s, Ireland's status had shifted from that of a colony to a potential rival for English exports, and as a result Irish provisions sometimes needed to be re-exported from England – if not being altogether banned from English ports. Due to these difficulties, it was common for English vessels to instead be used in exchanges in an attempt to evade seizure, although the merchandise did not stop in any English port. British Catholics strove to diversify their interests in order to mitigate potential losses, but these Irish–Iberian exchanges defied English navigational laws, and prompted the community towards resorting to illegal deals – practices that would become common in the subsequent decades.[38]

As illustrated in Figure 2, during the 1670s and 1680s the Aylwards began to build their network across Europe. A variety of merchant houses (or firms) introduced them to associates working in Atlantic and Mediterranean ports.[39] The Aylwards started in Cadiz in the early 1670s and by the end of the 1680s had contacts in twenty-three port cities from the Baltic region to the south Mediterranean. A group of almost forty merchants of both Catholic and Protestant religions moved between a wide range of countries, diversifying trade and offering more chances of surviving in commerce. Catholic contacts had proved crucial in strengthening commercial networks in Spain France and Italy, but religion was not a priority in choosing associates. The Aylwards knew that the best deals could ultimately be closed only in the English market. Indeed, each of the firms had their headquarters in London and the most solid partnerships were formed with Protestant traders in English ports.

In the Anglo-Spanish trade, Catholic merchants worked closely with non-co-religionists. The Aylwards and their partners thrived in commerce, and for the sake of business, disregarded religious affiliations. The analysis of the Aylwards' trading networks, the goods dealt, and the places accessed aids understanding of their commercial strategies. Their partners operated across all major European Atlantic ports from Spain to Hamburg and from Lisbon to Livorno. Their rationale was akin to that of any merchant:

---

[38]   AY 2, f. 8, Business Correspondence. Miscellaneous letters to John Aylward, 1683.
[39]   The merchant counting-house was the physical place where merchants discussed business as defined by Hancock. In Zahedieh's work they are more often referred to as firms.

maximising profits. Their religion helped them to settle in Spain and to establish contacts in Catholic countries. Their Protestant English and Dutch ties, on the other hand, clearly exemplify the ability to diversify the business and to go beyond their close-knit religious group. Their strategy became necessary in order to trade successfully and these contacts testify a certain degree of toleration, or perhaps pragmatic acceptance, within the Atlantic-mercantile world.

The Dynamics of Trade

The Catholics' trading networks in Spain spanned many European countries and, although tapping into circuits of religion and nationality, were ultimately based on trust. Its merchants were aware of the hazards of trade, which is why they looked carefully at various mercantile networks and judiciously selected the best partners. Their economic rationale was common to anyone involved in commerce at the time when everyone looked for skilled traders with a clear knowledge of the market and its policies. During the 1670s and 1680s there was not yet a strong enough legal system to support the recovering of debts because institutionalised guarantors in the form of trading or insurance companies were not yet fully developed. The only protection for merchants was to choose reputable partners. The decision to work with any particular merchant was based on reputation which spread around the merchant houses, at exchange meetings, and through introductions from other associates.[40] The Aylwards were always up-to-date with the latest gossip regarding fellow merchants' dealings and the reputations of their partners centred on their ability to remit payments and pay off debts. Only certain 'friends and acquaintances' were recommended; commerce was full of 'slanderous tongues' and a constant assessment of the dependability of others was crucial.[41] Therefore, strong assurances came from resorting to men from a reliable circle of traders, whether Catholic or not.[42] Particularly, in the 1680s, the number of Power & Hill's associates

[40] Zahedieh, *The Capital and the Colonies*, 55–136; Gauci, *The Politics of Trade*, 128; Sheryllynne Haggerty, *'Merely for money'? Business Culture in the British Atlantic, 1750–1815* (Liverpool: Liverpool University Press, 2012), 17, 198–236.

[41] AY 3, Business Correspondence. Miscellaneous letters to John Aylward, Jan.–Oct. 1684; AY 13, f. 3, Business Correspondence. Letters to John Aylward from Aaron Atkins at Amsterdam and Port Royal, Apr. 1684–July 1688.

[42] The Protestant associates were aware of the Aylwards' Catholicism. The next chapter will argue that Protestant merchants looked for Catholics because of their religious contacts. Catholicism was not at all detrimental in establishing commercial partnerships.

increased;[43] each merchant seemed to have been in contact with more than one merchant house at the same time and the Aylwards themselves exchanged letters with at least six firms. Among the most prominent were Power & Hill, Radcliffe & Doliffe, Warren, Caunter & Howe, and Harper & Cross; firms which owned branches in Livorno, Cadiz, Exeter, and Bristol.

Although they spanned various networks, these firms became crucial for British Catholics in the 1680s. Judging by the vast number of partners cited in the letters and recorded in the firm ledgers, they were well-established merchant houses, offering large groups of partners who exchanged commodities in the Mediterranean and across the Atlantic. These esteemed firms were fundamental in times of economic depression, securing credit availability and financial stability. Trading circuits could last years, and the issues faced were varied and went far beyond merchandise costs and shipping. Merchants were exposed to the whims of the weather, shipwrecks, and the threats of pirates. Harvests might not be as profitable as expected, and relief was expressed when unseasonable showers would 'enliven the dull fields'.[44] Bad weather could hinder shipping or the arrival of colonial cargoes, and could deter people from 'going to town and buy[ing] the merchandise'.[45] Threats also came in the forms of privateers who always loomed around the coast, especially in times of war. Sometimes, there was also just simply bad luck, as evident when in 1700, a ship from Portsmouth bound for the East Indies was wrecked just off the coast of Cadiz in Chipiona as it touched 'upon a rock'.[46] In order to minimise losses and protect against these threats, merchants operated in small partnerships of one or two families. These partnerships were short term, usually covering only a single shipment, and were renegotiated over each new deal. Under these arrangements, each partner promised to share costs of the freight, *Primage* and *Avarage*, and to send the merchandise in good condition. In each contract, the sender promised to ship the merchandise 'by the grace of God in good order'; and the receiver, to pay the charges while expecting the 'danger of the seas only'. They waited religiously for the 'good ship to [reach]

---

[43]   AY 100, Business Accounts. Bills and receipts for merchandise to December 1686.

[44]   AY 4, f. 11, Business Correspondence. Miscellaneous letters to John Aylward, Jan.–Dec.1685. Sardner added: 'God be praised the weather should continue very seasonable' [...] 'hopefully the wheat will be good as well. God grant to animate this poor [Spanish] people.'

[45]   AY 93, f. 31, Business Correspondence. Patrick Woulfe writing from Puerto Santa Maria.

[46]   AY 93, f. 20, Business Correspondence. Patrick Woulfe writing from Puerto Santa Maria.

her desired port in safety', with 'no remedy but patience'; 'Amen'.[47] Agents outside the company could be utilised to expedite all the transactions, although the final decision lay always in the hands of the merchants who completed the forms and ultimately signed them off. These transactions and their associated costs required a vast amount of capital and strong partnerships were essential. Aware that 'the dangers of the seas' could be many and unexpected, a partnership with a trustworthy and reputable firm was paramount in ensuring the survival of the enterprise.

Indeed, Table 1 highlights the losses faced between 1684 and 1686. One transaction which opened and closed within these three years spanned an impressive number of goods and ports. Initially, 85 butts of sherry were consigned to London, together with 43 chests of oranges and lemons, 15 chests of indigo, 30 butts of oil, and also raisins. Before reaching London, the vessel docked at Cadiz where it was loaded with 250 soldiers directed to Finale, a small town next to Genoa under Spanish control. The captain, Goulding, was commissioned to deliver the troop and 'take the receipt from the chief minister in the place unto whom they are committed'.[48] After unloading the soldiers, Goulding would load corn and wheat. He would look for them in Genoa, Livorno, for as much as will 'well loade the ship', which should have been 3,200 *fanegas* (55.7 litres) of which 100 *fanegas* were then bound for Spain, stopping at Gibraltar, Cadiz, and Sanlucar. Hence to Bristol, London, and Plymouth.[49] In 1685, Power & Hill paid Captain Goulding for this shipment; but the men of the crew had been paid with 68 pieces of eight each, instead of 78, as initially agreed. John Aylward, who commissioned the deal, did not provide enough credit and Power & Hill covered the rest.[50] The transactions conducted had not been profitable and failed to cover all the expenses incurred – as suggested in the harsh terms set by John Aylward when he decreed that time spent in the Italian ports would be deducted from the captain's monthly pay 'being his own responsibility to cover'. This lengthy exchange of corn, wheat, and soldiers did not prove lucrative,[51] and

---

[47]   AY 93, Business Correspondence. Patrick Woulfe writing from Puerto Santa Maria; Devon Record Office, 42102/2198c.

[48]   AY 4, Business Correspondence. Miscellaneous letters to John Aylward, Jan.–Dec.1685.

[49]   *Fanega* is a Castilian measure which varied. It could be 4.4 *arrobas* or 110 *libras* (*libra* is a Castilian pound). Trade in the Iberia Empires.

[50]   AY 4, f. 28, Business Correspondence. Miscellaneous letters to John Aylward, Jan.–Dec. 1685.

[51]   This operation was part of a group of businesses carried out in Italy during 1684–1686. The merchandise was mainly bought in Palermo and Livorno. The bills of exchange were mainly drawn on Amsterdam.

when the account was closed at the end of 1686, the balance recorded was negative. The transactions had faced high insurance charges and running costs and the agents involved had proved to be unreliable – so money was spent for prosecution. In 1684, 48 *maravedis* were spent prosecuting a certain Andrez Aragone and another agent. Yet the highest expenses were paid out for duties such as 'freighting' or 'Anchoridge': salaries for the captains, the crew, and the men involved in loading, landing, and distributing the goods.[52] In another instance, expenses were registered for John Aylward's horse, who suffered from *muermo*, an infection in the lungs. The partners were dissatisfied with the horse's physical condition, claiming that 'He is rotten' and that the animal was worth less than the amount they had spent to cure him.[53] Goulding also met with unfavourable weather and had to pay for men looking for the lost cargo of grain. After remitting the bills of exchange, it was clear that the profits did not cover the initial capital invested (see Table 1). Power & Hill were crucial in covering losses and fulfilling outstanding payments. They offered credit for new transactions that, if successful, would repay the lent capital. Despite registering initial losses, the Aylwards subsequently accounted for profitable exchanges, exemplifying how a firm provided support and insurance for its men.

Table 1: Account book for a transaction, 1684–1686

	1684		1685		1686		Total
	Rs	*mds*	*Rs*	*mds*	*Rs*	*mds*	
Debit First book	218,816	10	396,221	19	58,220		−281,989 *Rs* 13 *mds*
Credit First book	166,766	16	160,293	2	64,208	8	

Note: The sum is accounted in Spanish money, in *reals* (*Rs*) or pieces of eight, and *maravedis* (*mds*). The Spanish *real* or piece of eight was a silver coin, initially worth 34 *maravedis*. During the seventeenth century its value was halved in silver and *vellon*, therefore the *real* was valued at 68 *maravedis*. Source: Haring, *The Spanish Empire in America* (New York: Harcourt, Brace, and World, 1963), p. 286. Source: the account book of the AY 100, Business Accounts, Bills, receipts, etc., for merchandise to Dec. 1686.

---

[52] AY 111, Business Accounts. Account book of John Aylward at Malaga, 1674–1686, with notes to 1703. AY 112, Business Accounts. Rough account book of John Aylward relating to cargoes sent to and from Cadiz, c. Apr. 1689–Jan. 1693.

[53] AY 111, Business Accounts. Account book of John Aylward at Malaga, 1674–1686, with notes to 1703.

The associates were aware that their business needed reputable firms and would not have survived by solely relying on help from either family or the religious community. Relatives were not always skilled traders, but the advantage of dealing with family was in the flexibility of not being burdened by a company's legal documents and regulations. In the Aylwards' papers, nephews, cousins, and sons-in-law all stood out as sources of great concern.[54] More lucrative deals were closed through the associations with Power & Hill and certainly they proved crucial in supporting the Aylwards' business and in providing logistical and financial help for difficult transactions. As mentioned above, in the mercantile world, trust was based on perceptions and these feelings were not necessarily experienced only within blood ties or among co-religionists. Nonetheless, in times of political turmoil or economic downturn, or when Power & Hill experienced financial depression, the associates' families ensured financial security and the survival of the business. Furthermore, it was possibly the family who provided the Aylwards with their initial capital and who introduced the couple to the French market. It is clear that next of kin were not disregarded; however, the transatlantic world required a range of different skills that a small pool of men could simply not provide.

Working with wider circuits and various firms provided invaluable training and knowledge of the markets. For instance, in 1684, the associates purchased Newfoundland fish on credit from England, having been advised that the 'French bacalau man be [sic] denied admission into the Spanish ports'.[55] Around the same time, they were advised not to buy *raisins solis* as in England they were selling 'soe [sic] dully' and the duties were so high that 'they turne to soe poore an acc[ount] as give no incouragem[nt] at all'.[56] However, although advising the associates on the deals was the main role of a merchant house, the long associations and the tone of the letters tell that somehow these firms were successful in fostering a sense of belonging among their merchants. The Aylwards often exchanged warm greetings, wishes of 'joyful holidays', and excellent wines with various partners.[57] Once an associate proved reliable, they would

---

[54]   Family members were often involved in mismanagement, delays, gossip, or imprisonment.

[55]   AY 3, f. 22, Business Correspondence. Miscellaneous letters to John Aylward, Jan.–Oct. 1684.

[56]   J. M. Price, 'What Did Merchants Do? Reflections on British Overseas Trade 1660–1790', *The Journal of Economic History*, 49 (1989): 267–284; AY 5, f. 16, Business Correspondence. Miscellaneous letters to John Aylward, Jan.–Dec. 1686.

[57]   AY 4, f. 26, Business Correspondence. Miscellaneous letters to John Aylward, Jan.–Dec. 1685.

work with them more consistently, and during the 1670s and 1680s, many transactions were closed with the same circle of partners. Associates were chosen for their commercial skills and relevance in the Anglo-Spanish market. Their prompt remittances and strong abilities ensured successful outcomes. The extent of the transactions and all implied costs required a vast amount of capital, and partnerships were fundamental to distributing the costs between them. In fact, when working with Power & Hill's group of associates, the Aylwards' account books show profitable gain, especially during the first years of the 1680s. In 1686, the books recorded a credit of 44,447 *reales de vellon* plate, and 25 *maravedis* plate (roughly 2,000 pounds sterling) whereas the debt was only 13,667 reals plate (see Table 2). This profit was registered after almost three years. In 1686, only '19 merchants exported English goods worth over £1,000 to North America and 22 to the West Indies', whereas, in terms of imports, fewer than ten merchants imported goods 'over £5,000 value from North America and 28 from the West Indies'. The significance of the amount is further highlighted by the fact that the entire value of the English trade with New Spain through Cadiz was roughly £400,000 per annum in the 1690s.[58]

This transaction was opened on 24 August 1684, but no money was seen until 15 May 1686. The exchange comprised of wheat, corn, lemons, and oil, and cost and profit were calculated only at the end when it was possible to judge what the deal had been worth. All costs were met in advance and the expenses faced were wide-ranging. During the first year, they paid for freighting, ensuring the cargoes, for 'anchoridge', and for prosecuting disloyal partners.[59] Before the vessels departed, the first bills of exchange had been drawn up. These initial costs were inflated by the continuous journeys, and throughout the three years, the costs of shipping increased significantly. But the shipments were the least of their concerns, because once the vessels landed, they faced the costs of unloading the merchandise and bringing it ashore. This service involved paying both the crew and

---

AY 23, f. 8, Business Correspondence. Letters to John Aylward from Messrs Champneys and Pitts at Seville, July 1684–Apr. 1686. 1 bundle. Champneys and Pitts thanked the Aylwards for warning them that French privateers were off the coast of Cadiz; AY 3, Business Correspondence. Miscellaneous letters to John Aylward, Jan.–Oct. 1684. Papers relating to John Aylward's dependence with Mr Thomas Lambert. The correspondence is between Mr Willmott and Mr Lambert, Malaga, 1684. There were other associates involved in the transactions, such as Thomas Brailsford.

[58] Nuala Zahedieh, 'Making Mercantilism Work: London Merchants and Atlantic Trade in the Seventeenth Century', *Transactions of the Royal Historical Society*, 6 (1999): 143–160, 146.

[59] AY 100, Business Accounts. Bills, receipts, etc., for merchandise to Dec. 1686.

agents that would dispatch the merchandise. Fortunately, in this exchange the partners involved remitted punctually, and at the end of 1686, the transaction proved lucrative.

Table 2: John Aylward's debts and credit accounted by the firm Power & Hill for the period 1684–1686

	1684		1685		1686		Total
	Rs	mds	Rs	mds	Rs	mds	
Debit **Second book**	188,181	12	225,467	98	83,319	6	−13,667 Rs
					26,732	34	
Credit **Second book**	213,090	15	215,947	9	23,985	6	+44,447 Rs 25 mds
					23,416	31	

Note: Spanish money in *reals de vellon plate* (Rs) and *maravedis plate* (mds); AY 100, *Business Accounts*, Bills, receipts, etc., for merchandise to Dec. 1686.

The transaction examined yielded profitable financial gain that provided capital for the next deal and was a good sum considering that 25 pipes of wine were worth 7 *reals de vellon*, 16 *maravedis* were enough for a prosecution, and 736 *maravedis de vellon* were paid for a black male child sent from Jamaica by Henry Hall.[60] Despite this latter example, there is little engagement of the Aylwards in the slave trade. Cadiz was never a slave port as the trade had been already monopolised by the Portuguese and later by the British and the French.[61] From 1684 to 1686, the Aylwards made profits in almost all of their transactions. Costs and the gains were usually calculated after a period of three years, which was fairly common in the Atlantic trade as only after the end of that cycle would it have been possible to judge the deal's worth.[62]

[60]   Ibid.

[61]   O'Flanagan, *Port Cities of Atlantic Iberia*.

[62]   All the arrangements of buying and selling goods were made on credit and the accounts were kept accurate and then compared to cover differences in cash. Sometimes they resorted to the courts as not all of the partners promptly fulfilled their obligations; AY 112, Business Accounts. Account book of John Aylward relating to cargoes sent to and from Cadiz, c. Apr. 1689–Jan. 1693; Nuala Zahedieh, 'Making Mercantilism Work'; Nuala Zahedieh, 'The Merchants of Port Royal, Jamaica, and the Spanish Contraband Trade, 1655–1692', in *William and Mary Quarterly*, 43, 4 (1986): 570–593, 584.

A successful exchange provided capital for the next deal and only by tapping into numerous trading circuits would the continuity of the business be ensured. The trading engagement of the Aylwards was extensive and with the support of Power & Hill, they carried out many transactions simultaneously. All deals were conducted through bills of exchange which began to overtake coins and commodities as forms of payment.[63] During the early modern centuries, silver coins had been the most accepted form of currency; however, in the unregulated Atlantic trade, these new bills started to spread as more secure forms of credit. The banknotes could be paid to the bearer and also transferred to another party or be negotiated. Easy credit facilitated the exports, and long-term credits were given to correspondents or buyers to cover the ventures. In the Atlantic trade, it was easy to fall into debt if the correspondent did not remit in time.[64] All bills of exchange were remitted at the end of the trade, which is why merchants could calculate their profits only after the circuit was closed. Losses were possible, as clearly examined by Atkins, who stated 'it has been an unprofitable ship, for I never see a penny as yet of my money'.[65] Therefore, trust and reputation of the payer were crucial in the process.[66] Indeed, the Aylwards usually drew bills on their merchant house of Power & Hill, or on a few other trustworthy partners. Their bills were remitted in Amsterdam and London. Bills from Amsterdam had become the universal instrument of transfer throughout northern and western Europe, yet gradually the bills in London became discountable and a negotiable instrument during the last decades of the seventeenth century. In 1686, remitting in London already seemed more common and profitable, as suggested by one of the Aylwards' partners in Exeter.[67] Sometimes, if not remitting the bills, the partners would have accepted bartered goods, but the idea of remitting the payment in fruit over the years, instead of cash, was not always a welcome practice as Thomas Wyse once promptly replied: 'I wonder you are not

---

[63]   Hancock, 'Atlantic Trade and Commodities, 1402–1815', 333. The Aylwards' world was changing. Commerce not only demanded new policies, but also introduced substantial changes in the economy as well as in society. Among others, the Aylwards adapted to the new process of dematerialisation of money which developed during the second half of the seventeenth century.

[64]   AY 2, f. 2, Business Correspondence. Miscellaneous letters to John Aylward, 1683. Mr Watkins was asking Mr Wyse to remit in three years.

[65]   AY 13, f. 1, Business Correspondence. Letters to John Aylward from Aaron Atkins at Amsterdam and Port Royal, Apr. 1684–July 1688.

[66]   Sheryllynne Haggerty, *The British Atlantic Trading Community, 1760–1810: Men, Women and the Distribution of Goods* (Leiden: Brill, 2006), 150–159.

[67]   AY 5, f. 16, Business Correspondence. Miscellaneous letters to John Aylward, Jan.– Dec. 1686

ashamed to make such a [sic] offer to me.' 'For no matter how distressed anyone's condition', Wyse himself would have confidence to write such an 'unreasonable expression' [to propose bartered goods instead of money].[68]

In trade, the costs faced were substantial and duties were high, particularly in the Spanish market, due to excessive regulation and corruption. Taxes varied from province to province and although foreign merchants were granted certain privileges by the Anglo-Spanish treaty of 1667, bribes were not unusual. Resorting to contraband was common and a good relationship with the officials was desirable. In Spain, the Aylwards and their associates were close to the mercantile authorities of the *consulado* in a friendship that would consistently prove beneficial. The consuls were representatives elected annually by the merchants. This institution managed all the merchants' civil suits and also issued all financial and commercial policies. During the seventeenth century the *consulado* became a corporation of a few merchant houses and its commercial power allowed the institution to soon monopolise the transatlantic trade.[69] However, this situation of monopoly benefited only a few and, as a consequence, smuggling spread. The Spanish Crown attempted to implement a monopoly that never fully existed and contraband flourished as everyone wanted to partake in Spanish riches. To compensate for the losses, the Spanish crown repeatedly imposed heavy fines. For instance, in 1681 Power & Hill briefed its associates about new charges of four per cent due to a Spanish law to enforce higher payments. This measure was ultimately detrimental to commerce, but it would have been hard to foresee the effects. However, they must have paid and obliged with their duties;[70] they had the desire to profit and abided as much as possible to the rules. Their rationale undeniably proved correct as in the 1680s, despite all the potential problems in trade, they successfully closed profitable exchanges.

The thorough analysis of their trades shows how Catholic merchants operated according to universal rules. Merchants moved in networks of trust within the circle of their merchant houses or within their own partnerships. A firm was fundamental in training and establishing valuable contacts

---

[68]   AY 2, f. 6, Business Correspondence. Letter of 12 August 1683. During the early 1680s, barter still featured in the exchanges and it did not seem unusual. At times, the Aylwards paid for oil and drapes from Rotterdam half with money and half with other goods. At the same time, the fabrics might have been exchanged for wine and fruit; likewise iron and money for tobacco.
[69]   Haring, *The Spanish Empire in America*, 305–308.
[70]   AY 111, Business Accounts. Account book of John Aylward at Malaga, 1674–1686, with notes to 1703.

and thus the merchant's ability to profit would benefit from expanding his circles. The Aylwards clearly acted within this pattern. Their firms were necessary in order to survive in commerce, particularly at the beginning of their careers. Their ability was in using these initial contacts, their community, and their national identity to expand their networks and to establish themselves in the mercantile world. Besides their personal abilities, their economic rationale was standard practice. They sought out trustworthy partners because this practice was fundamental for carrying on business; trust was crucial in transactions which could face many difficulties in such an unregulated environment. This period is significant because of how Catholics abided by universal mercantile values irrespective of religion. Their ability to work effectively assured integration in the mercantile community and their contacts allowed diverse economic strategies that helped building successful careers. The network is representative of the system in which British Catholics integrated into the Atlantic mercantile community and worked beyond national and religious borders, furthering British commercial interests. Furthermore, Catholics defied stereotypes of communal exclusivity and instead worked for economic inclusion.

In Spain, British Catholics continued to trade through their private companies and the breadth of their enterprise required working with a diverse group of tradesmen in order to attain a competitive edge. In the unregulated commercial world, they knew that tapping into a narrow circle of partners would not suffice or lead to success, and their dealings show no evidence of limiting their trading partners to their community. Although often working with family and co-religionists, they were not sectarian and, unlike other religious minorities in trade, chose partners based on their reputation and reliability in trade, and not because of their faith.[71]

During their years in Spain, from 1672 to 1687, the Aylwards were able to establish themselves in the mercantile world thanks to their religious community and national ties. The former, at times, secured access to markets and enhanced trust with other Catholic traders, but it was not sufficient to preclude Catholics trading easily and frequently with Protestants. The latter also meant an advantage in the religion of their associates. Catholic contacts were advantageous as they allowed certain privileges in Spain and

---

[71] Frederick B. Tolles, *Meeting House and Counting House: The Quaker Merchants of Colonial Philadelphia, 1682–1763* (New York: Norton & Co., 1963), 89: this religious minority was not parochial, and its trading networks covered the all the North Atlantic world, from Nova Scotia to Lisbon. J. F. Bosher, 'Huguenot Merchants and the Protestant International in the Seventeenth Century', *The William and Mary Quarterly*, 52 (1995): 77–102.

profitable exchanges within the Mediterranean. Moreover, their national identity secured a share in the trade with the British Isles, and good fortune or contingencies turned them into successful traders. The Aylwards had partners in the most important European ports, and this assured the survival of their business as they were constantly updated with what the various markets needed and where it was possible to find particular commodities.[72] In order to avoid disappointment and a loss of profits, the Aylwards needed to be highly competitive. They profited in the Anglo-Spanish trade, while also investing in other European markets. In Spain, through the British firms with which they associated, they established a partnership with their future in-laws, the Porters, prominent merchants in Cadiz who had vast interests in French trade. How and when they met is not clear; however, in the mid-1680s the Aylwards were already keeping account of various transactions with them.[73] Through this collaboration, the prominent John Aylward met Helena Porter, and they married in 1687. These family networks assured entrance into a wider mercantile community in France, which will be the subject of the next chapter.

In Spain, these merchants created their own luck, astutely choosing partners and tapping into various groups in order to maximise their profits and boost British trade. Their religious and ethnic ties facilitated their beginning, but by the end of the 1680s their networks were so vast that they probably did not know all the agents involved and their religious affiliation. They could not be acquainted with all the brokers, porters, suppliers, or seafarers, suggesting that their rationale was 'merely for money'.[74] They moved beyond their religious community and they diversified their contacts to access new networks as the only way to success. In Spain, Catholics integrated into the British mercantile community and reaped the profits of the Anglo-Spanish trade. This ability to resort to religious identity and nationality when necessary developed during this decade in the Spanish ports and would prove vital in subsequent years.

It is possible that as expatriates, Catholics did not act as outsiders in the commercial world. British merchants had been working for centuries in Cadiz and Seville; from the late sixteenth century, Catholic merchants strengthened the British presence in the area. Their ability to access

---

[72]   AY 5, f. 16, Business Correspondence. Miscellaneous letters to John Aylward, Jan.–Dec. 1686. For instance, in 1686, in one of his letters, John Aylward was assured by a partner that their goods were as good as any 'whatsoever of that sort' that were going out of England.

[73]   AY 101, Business Accounts. Bills, accounts, receipts, etc., for merchandise to Dec. 1687.

[74]   Haggerty, *'Merely for Money?'*

Catholic countries ensured acceptance in the mercantile community. Their strategies would become more evident during the following decades of European warfare. Nonetheless, even during the 1670s and 1680s, it was clear that these Catholic entrepreneurs, in managing their businesses and disregarding political and religious affiliation, moved intrepidly within the Atlantic trading community. In the 1670s and 1680s, the Aylwards and their associates were mainly based in Cadiz and in the province of Malaga. From 1687, the major partners moved to St Malo. They did not abandon the Anglo-Spanish market, thus they became its most sought-after suppliers. In French ports, through smuggling and privateering, the Aylwards and their associates would keep the cogs of British commerce spinning and ensure its survival during a decade of European warfare.

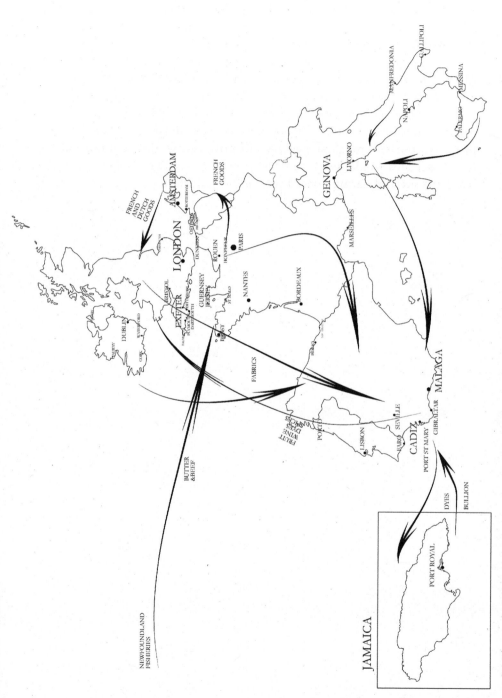

2: British merchants in St Malo during the Glorious Revolution and the Nine Years War, 1688–1698

Chapter 3

British Catholic Merchants in St Malo during the Glorious Revolution and the Nine Years War, 1688–1698

On 26 May 1687, John Aylward and his 'sweet consort', Helena, arrived at their country house in St Malo[1] – marking the start of what was to be a decade of great prosperity for the newlywed couple. More than ten years in the south of Spain had allowed the Aylwards and their associates to flourish as traders, and by the late 1680s business was thriving. In Cadiz, as part of its British mercantile community, the Aylwards had reaped the profits of the Anglo-Spanish trade, in providing supplies to the transatlantic fleets and to England. There had likely been multiple personal and economic reasons for this move to France, and religious ties and past loyalties ensured that vital contacts with the Iberian ports would not be severed. The Aylwards stayed in St Malo for eleven years, eventually settling in another community of Catholic expatriates and beginning a period which would not only introduce new players into their correspondence, but reinforce already well-established partnerships.

But things would not always run smoothly for the couple. It was after less than a year in France, in the summer of 1688, that John Aylward received a letter from long-term London associate, Walter Ryan, fearing a Dutch invasion as soon as the wind proved favourable. He warned that every merchant was in great consternation due to 'these juncture of times … making money very skarse'. In his view, trade would be greatly disrupted 'and there was nothing to be done'. [...] 'Wee trust in God will not last long. But that wee are with God's grace in a capacity to oppose them.'[2] The international scene had become bleak, as had the prospects for European commerce, and there was no way that Aylward as a Catholic merchant could have predicted what the year of 1688 would come to mean for British history.

[1] AY 37, Business Correspondence. Letters to John Aylward from Richard Enys and Eustace Power, who congratulated them on their safe arrival.
[2] AY 101, Business Accounts. Bills, accounts, receipts, etc., for merchandise from Dec. 1687. Letter of 8 October 1688 from Walter Ryan in London.

The year marked the beginning of a turbulent decade – to say the least – in the British Isles. After James II was overthrown, the country was forced to rethink its political and religious identity while continuing to assert its commercial power against continental forces. Nobody could have predicted that the Glorious Revolution would in fact lead to great instability and a period of nine years of European warfare where France fought the League of Augsburg, formed by Spain, Holland, Austria, England, and Savoy. Crucially, for Catholic subjects of both Britain and Ireland, this crisis was more than just political and threatened to completely regress their status as citizens by erasing significant progress made under the rule of James II. Their loyalty to the new regime of William and Mary was now being questioned. Anyone was a potential Jacobite plotting to re-enthrone the Stuarts, and Catholicism was now perceived as a threat all over the three kingdoms. In Ireland, in particular, these years were particularly turbulent as they were the time when most of the fighting took place. In fact, the Williamite War (1688–1691) was a turning point in Irish history. It saw the beginning of a second English conquest that ushered in another difficult time for Catholics. In the 1690s, penal laws across the Isles became more restrictive. Catholics were barred from legal or political careers, and enforcing conformity to the Protestant churches became a pressing concern. For Catholic families, it meant a new struggle and many were torn, worrying about securing their properties as well as their children's future.[3] While many remained in their countries, many others chose exile on the continent, forging contacts within major European communities and the extensive networks across France. But ultimately they never severed ties with their mother country and continued to swear loyalty to both their faith and their land. Indeed, in 1690, during the escalation of the Williamite Revolution, the Fitzgeralds, in a letter to John Aylward, wrote of hope that the Irish Jacobites 'may defend themselves and keep the country'.[4] Some months later, in 1691, after the Irish had refused the conditions offered by William III, they wrote again of how 'deplorable the situation was [...] nothing but our loyalty would ever hinder us from embracing liberty of conscience to be established by law'.[5]

---

[3]   Eoin Kinsella, 'In Pursuit of a Positive Construction: Irish Catholics and the Williamite Articles of Surrender, 1690–1701', *Eighteenth-Century Ireland*, 24 (2009): 11–35.

[4]   AY 20, f. 36, Business Correspondence. Letter from Robert Butler in Cadiz to John Aylward, 26 September 1689.

[5]   AY 6, f. 20, Business Correspondence. George Fitzgerald writing from Nantes, 14 August 1691.

This chapter situates the life and work of the Aylwards into these international scenes where political and religious allegiances were being renegotiated. It aims to offer an insight into how Catholic merchants contributed to the survival of British commerce during the Glorious Revolution (1688–1689) and the Nine Years War (1688–1697), when commercial conflict between England and France raged across the continent, endangering their most profitable links.[6] In St Malo, John Aylward was introduced to his wife's family – the Porters – bringing him into a circle which allowed for involvement in the Irish trade and where Catholic contacts were increased. Catholic merchants would coordinate the smuggling of French goods into England, relying on their contacts in Iberian ports, which meant that, ultimately, French goods would make it to England either directly via the Channel or indirectly through Spain. It was this ability to tap into French, English, and Spanish imperial networks which ensured the survival of British businesses and during this decade, the audacity of the Catholic associates showed no bounds. Walter Ryan was right in his assumption about the difficult 'juncture of times', but was wrong in his concern as Catholic merchants showed that they could indeed 'oppose' these forces. These war years would go on to be profitable for the Aylwards and their associates, each amassing significant fortunes which would later allow them to retire to country retreats and enjoy the luxury of the springs in Bath.[7]

Catholics in St Malo

In St Malo, the local mercantile community had extensive networks across the Atlantic, reaching not only the Caribbean, Newfoundland, and South America, but also the East as far as Arabia, and even China. In the Channel, Malouin traders carried out constant exchanges with London and Bristol of English tin and lead, cod, Irish provisions, and Breton linens – and when trade was disrupted by warfare they would resort to the fishermen in Guernsey and Jersey.[8] For the Aylwards, the move to St Malo was also influenced

[6] M. Kishlansky, *A Monarchy Transformed: Britain 1603–1714* (London: Penguin, 1996); A. McFarlane, *The British in the Americas, 1480–1815* (London: Longman, 1992).

[7] MS, Lett. C. 192 Bodleian Library, Letter of Mr Hill to John Aylward, from Priory 1700. Hill commented on the country house bought by Aylward in Hampstead.

[8] J. S. Bromley, 'The Trade and Privateering of St Malo during the War of the Spanish Succession' in *Corsairs and Navies, 1660–1760* (London: Hambledon Press, 1987), 280–281; Regina Grafe, *Distant Tyranny: Markets, Power and Backwardness in Spain, 1650–1800* (Princeton: Princeton University Press, 2012), 52–79.

by considerations of personal networks that facilitated mercantile ones. In Spain, they had begun to work with the Porters, a merchant dynasty established in Cadiz and St Malo. In fact, it was through the collaboration with Matthew Porter that John Aylward had met his future wife, Helena Porter. Helena was an English Catholic, and so in this case the marriage followed a pattern common to men within a religious group and the mercantile community, where it often established or consolidated a business partnership.[9] Family partnerships would thus expand the business network and indeed, the Aylwards seized the opportunity to expand their contacts and work in France. Their business would benefit greatly from the marital deal with the Porters; not only were they introduced to a wider network of merchants in various French ports, with many and varied interests in European and Atlantic markets, but these new acquaintances also introduced the Aylwards to new lucrative opportunities. Furthermore, being based in France would save their business from the disruption of the War.

In Cadiz in the 1670s and 1680s the Catholic associates had already established contacts with French ports to supply the Anglo-Spanish vessels with French goods. However, from the late 1680s, living in France meant the ability to more carefully coordinate the movement of French commodities to England or Spain which would prove crucial at a time in which France replaced Holland as England's main commercial enemy.[10] In the 1670s and the 1680s, England had avoided a war with France as the court had been concerned with the Dutch. In July 1688, the Aylwards' Catholic associates rejoiced in the birth of the Prince of Wales, James Francis Edward, and recounted how a great Council was held with the '43 people present at her [Queen Mary of Modena's] delivery... for the satisfaction of any who should doubt about the truth' – yet probably not so much for the satisfaction of Mary.[11] Catholic merchants were pleased by this event, as James's son ensured the Catholic succession for the three kingdoms. However, the Protestant court feared a return to Catholicism, and the Dutch dreaded the possibility of an Anglo-French alliance which would have affected the European balance of power. Skirmishes between France and the Netherlands had already begun in the previous decades when Charles II needed France to fight the Dutch power. On 5 November 1688, William landed at

---

[9] Nuala Zahedieh, *The Capital and the Colonies: London and the Atlantic Economy, 1660–1700* (Cambridge: Cambridge University Press, 2010).

[10] McFarlane, *The British in the Americas.*

[11] AY 72, Business Correspondence. Letter from Mr Power in London, on 11 June 1688. Power writes the Queen 'fell in labour at 4 in the morning, had some respite till 6 when she began to be worse …[the Prince was born] at ¾ past 9'.

Torbay to prevent a possible new alliance between James II and Louis XIV.[12] The flight of James II and the accession of William III went on to change English foreign policy. William went to war with France in an effort to stem its rising power on the continent and in the New World as the country's flourishing trade, booming population, and aggressive foreign policy were raising great concerns back in England.[13] Furthermore, in the 1660s, Louis XIV had set his mind to a grand imperial vision which inevitably meant competition for the English in the Caribbean and the West Indies as both nations were lured by Spanish riches and the great potential of the North American wilderness. The French, with their settlements in Canada (1650s) and in Louisiana (1682) threatened English colonial expansion. Inevitably, the Nine Years War was not just a European affair and had many different stages, mainly in the Channel but also in the Caribbean and North America ('King William's War'). To justify the fighting, England used anti-Catholic propaganda and the threat of Jacobite rebellion, or, as the Protestant Charles Horde put it, of a Stuart 'reinthroning'.[14]

Nevertheless, and despite all efforts, French products continued to retain their value in European and colonial trade and the ability of the Catholic networks to provide them only strengthened their commercial skills. Once in France, the Aylwards put old and new contacts to use; in the Iberian ports, they could count on relatives and agents to manage their Spanish accounts. The associates that had previously proved reliable, such as the Watkins, the Ryans, and the Wyses, continued their collaboration. Working in France provided the traders with further access to significant capital and credit, while introducing them to wider mercantile networks. Thanks to such new relationships, the Aylwards had less need to rely on contacts within the family, who often were not reliable or fit for the job. In France, as previously in Spain, successful deals would mainly be closed with non-Catholic partners.

Among the partners in London, the most influential were Thomas Brailsford, Charles Horde, Charles Peers, and the Halls. All skilled traders, they introduced the Catholics of St Malo to new markets and strategies, and it was through this collaboration, that the Catholics' business in the British Isles would reach new heights. Thomas Brailsford never hid his aversion for the Catholic monarch James II, 'who endeavoured to subvert the Constitution of the Kingdom, [...] by the advice of the Jesuits and other

---

[12] Kishlansky, *A Monarchy Transformed*, 477.

[13] Benjamin, *The Atlantic World*, 476–482.

[14] McFarlane, *The British in the Americas*, 119–122. AY 51, f. 13, Business Correspondence. Letter from Charles Horde in London, 13 May 1692. Most of the letters are counter-endorsed from Amsterdam by Philibert Brothers.

wicked persons' – possibly referring to the Commons' resolution of 1689.[15] He would eventually be buried in Lothbury parish church in London, a place that suggests his 'Reformed' faith, and being right beside the Bank of England could not have been more apt for a merchant.[16] The Halls, William and Francis, were Brailsford's nephews and mainly based in Port Royal, in Jamaica.[17] They never openly discussed religion but it is feasible to assume they were not sympathetic to the Catholic cause as they had a distrust of any merchandise coming from Ireland. Finally, Charles Horde, also based in London, shared Brailsford's views on James II. In one letter to the Aylwards he discussed his political position, stating that the French probably thought James II would have had many supporters in England, but that in reality the only supporters were 'his party, the women parsons' and some gentry of broken fortunes'. Moreover, he added, a 'man who could not keep 3 kingdoms […] can never conquer them'.[18] Despite sharing these remarks with their Catholic trading partners, they frequently urged mercantile collaboration with them. Indeed, the most significant deals came as the result of Catholic–Protestant partnerships among merchants who helped each other defy wartime policies and secure the survival of Britain's trade through smuggling and privateering.

In the 1690s, resorting to privateers was possibly the only option offered to the Aylwards and their associates. Since the twelfth century, privateering had been the practice commonly used by the European governments against each other at times of war.[19] Privateers were private actors who had government sanction for their actions in the form of a commission allowing them to keep some portion of whatever goods they captured. The only difference between privateers and piracy lay in this state sanction. During the war in the 1690s, the main privateering centres were on the French coast at St Malo and Dunkirk, and various ports in Sussex and Kent on the English. The peak of privateering in the Channel came between 1689 and 1697. With the Treaty of Ryswick in 1697, which ended the Nine Years War,

[15]   AY 18, f. 2, Business Correspondence. Letters to John Aylward from Thomas Brailsford and Richard Holder in London, 28 January 1689.

[16]   AY 111, Business Accounts. Account books of John Aylward at Malaga, 1674–1686. With notes to 1703.

[17]   Zahedieh, *The Capital and the Colonies*; CO 110–152, Brailsford Papers, Letters to John Aylward from Thomas Brailsford and the Halls, 1688–1690.

[18]   AY 51, f. 13, Business Correspondence. Business letters to John Aylward, from Charles Horde in London, 13 May 1692.

[19]   Janice Thomson, *Mercenaries, Pirates and Sovereigns: State Building and Extra Territorial Violence in Early Modern Europe* (Princeton: Princeton University Press, 1994), 22–25. In 1708, privateers were allowed to keep all their prizes and also paid a bounty based on the number of prisoners taken.

both English and French governments attempted to reduce these commercial practices, but were unsuccessful and privateering continued both in Atlantic and European waters.[20] Since the war had disrupted commerce in the Mediterranean and in the Atlantic, the associates in St Malo considered investing in privateering as a potentially lucrative business opportunity. Historiography agrees that privateering was the main practice adopted by merchants in times of warfare, and acknowledges also the role of Catholics in this business. Monod argues that Catholics had a political motive behind their involvement, as, along with the merchandise, they exchanged seditious information. However, the Catholics associated with the Aylwards make no mention of political or religious motives, suggesting their actions in the business were solely for profit, as this chapter will soon show.

In the 1690s in St Malo, trading patterns and practices changed, although the main focus was still on Cadiz and the supply of the *flota*. The best deals were closed when the transatlantic fleets were about to sail and needed supplies for the Spanish American colonies; usually then all sorts of fabrics and manufactures were in high demand.[21] The merchants operated between London and Cadiz, supervising all the Atlantic deals[22] and during this decade, their transactions widened to include France. The exchanges that had previously been concentrated on England and Spain were now expanded to include French ports, facilitating access to the Mediterranean and the Atlantic, particularly St Malo, La Rochelle, Nantes, and Marseilles. In England, Catholics' trading partners were mainly based in London, but also in the minor ports of Dartmouth or Falmouth, and in the Channel Islands.[23] It was a time of transformation which offered new opportunities and the Catholics seized them. Although always in accordance with the rules and values of their community and mercantile class, they ultimately worked for profit.

Trade during the Nine Years War

During the summer of 1687 and the early months of 1688, the associates in St Malo traded with relative ease while forging inter-imperial connections. From the north of France they closed profitable exchanges of English

---

[20]   McFarlane, *The British in the Americas.*

[21]   AY 37, f. 7, Business Correspondence. Letter from Power & Hill on 21 July 1687. Chapter 5 will examine in great detail the goods traded.

[22]   AY 103, f. 9, Business Accounts. Accounts, bills for merchandise to Dec. 1689

[23]   Renaud Morieux, 'The Fisherman, Friend of All Nations?' and 'The Game of Identities, Fraud and Smuggling' in *The Channel: England, France and the Construction of a Maritime Border in the Eighteenth Century* (Cambridge: Cambridge University Press, 2016), 211–247 and 248–282.

fabrics, Spanish dyes, Mediterranean fruit, and French cloth. Merchandise arrived from the Mediterranean, the Baltic region, or French imperial possessions before being directed to Spain, England, or westward to the West Indies. These international transactions ran smoothly until the winter months of 1688 when part of the *flota* anchored in the Cadiz waters while other ships were provisioned in the Americas. In the European ports this was the time to explore the markets and see what the new season offered. Fruit, wine, and fabric should have supplied the *flota* over the late spring. Catholic merchants in St Malo planned their deals and looked forward to the departure and arrival of the American vessels. From Brittany, the Catholic community could procure merchandise from all over the country as the partners travelled in the north of France with frequent journeys to Paris, Rouen, and Nantes, and also to Marseilles, Lorient, or Bordeaux. From the Mediterranean, they worked extensively in the port of Genoa where the main firm was Harper & Cross. In England they corresponded mainly with London, and in Ireland with Waterford. Partners in those hubs discussed the merchandise and potential deals. However, the scene changed when 'the Prince of Orange and Parliament declared wars with the French', closely followed by Spain's declaration against France by 'command of the Emperor'.[24] French goods had been embargoed and exports were suspended. From then on, merchant ships would run at great hazard, causing the associates to stop and ponder; 'when there are these wars is better you sit still awhile'.[25] But, were they willing to see their trading stall?

As early as May 1689, the Catholics in St Malo had begun to prepare new schemes for French imports into Spain. The trust, or perhaps pressure, invested in the agents in Spain was immense as they were responsible for both introducing illegal French goods in Spain, and managing them 'with safety and advantage'.[26] Initially the Aylwards and their associates continued to introduce goods into England, often moving them first through Hamburg, Amsterdam, or through the island of Guernsey. In Hamburg, French partners would have handled the merchandise making sure the goods would 'turn to the best account'.[27] Another option would have been to resort to Italian vessels or move the goods through Amsterdam with the help of the Creaghs, a renowned family of smugglers established in the

---

[24] AY 20, f. 31, Business Correspondence. Letters to John Aylward from Robert Butler at Malaga and Cadiz, May 1687–Dec. 1692; AY 20, f. 33, Business Correspondence. Letter to John Aylward from Robert Butler on 20 June 1689.

[25] AY 20, f. 33, Business Correspondence. Letter to John Aylward from Robert Butler on 20 June 1689.

[26] Ibid.

[27] AY 20, f. 32, Business Correspondence; AY 20, f. 33, Business Correspondence.

Netherlands. Possibly of Anglo-Irish heritage, they helped the Aylwards in the Dutch market.[28] From Guernsey, the associates resorted to fishermen who were keen to continue a trade that the war had disrupted.[29] Ultimately however, Cadiz was the port from where the American fleets loaded, and to where all the European merchants looked.

From May to October 1689, the agents in Spain hustled and bustled along the docks, writing many letters and worrying about the transactions. They anxiously waited for instructions and for supplies from France, while also taking care of merchandise ready to be shipped to the Indies. The letters were, at times, confusing. Various pieces of correspondence had probably been 'miscarried' and the authorities sifted through the mail in search of information.[30] The associates exchanged a vast amount of correspondence with documents and orders coming from Paris and London as well as through Waterford. However, some of these were intercepted on their journey, and others were simply lost as there was often a gap of months between them.

Any such delays were detrimental to the business, as letters carried instructions or orders the agents needed to be sure how to proceed. Missing information meant they did not know about any new orders, which commodity was best to keep or sell, and did not have clear information about prices or how much fabric should be sold and to whom. Furthermore, the Spanish authorities controlled the merchandise to forbid French commodities. Despite all of this, goods, especially calicoes and fabrics in general, were in high demand and since the war hindered regular shipments, the prices of English and French goods rose to meet a demand in the colonial markets. If dispatched on the *flota*, the goods would have been extremely profitable and so, they were worth the risk.

The first years of war had been a training ground for the Aylwards and their associates. They honed their skills and over two years, the tone of their correspondence changed. In the early 1680s, their letters were mainly a form of account books in which goods were listed together with their prices, partnerships, debtors, and creditors. In contrast, from the late 1680s

---

28   L. M. Cullen, 'The Smuggling Trade in Ireland in the Eighteenth Century', *Proceedings of the Royal Irish Academy. Section C: Archaeology, Celtic Studies, History, Linguistics, Literature* 67 (1968/1969): 149–175; *Irish and Scottish Mercantile Networks in Europe and Overseas in the Seventeenth and Eighteenth Centuries*, ed. David Dickson et al. (Gent: Academia Press, 2006).

29   Morieux, 'The Fisherman, Friend of All Nations?' in *The Channel: England, France*, 211–247.

30   S. Pincus, *1688: The First Modern Revolution* (London: Yale University Press, 2009), 143–178.

onwards, they appeared to be more concerned with actually running the business and thinking out the most diverse strategies. The associates here developed tactics that would be refined throughout the years of international war. In the 1670s and 1680s European trade had run more or less smoothly, but in the 1690s only the shrewdest would survive. The fact there was now less of a focus on cost possibly suggests that at this juncture the associates already possessed significant capital to invest. Deals were discussed between the headquarters in St Malo, Cadiz, and London; and in the countryside, in the province of Malaga, agents and porters fetched and handled the goods.

It was during this time of war that religious trading contacts acquired more prominence. The Aylwards and their associates never proved to be particularly religious, perhaps it was simply because of the nature of the correspondence that they did not discuss their faith or show devotion. In actuality, as mentioned in the Introduction, their faith has been reconstructed mainly indirectly through the Protestants' request of the 'Romanist's pass'.[31] However, they were aware of the importance of their Catholic contacts. In Spain, the community operated along religious ties, forging trading networks that spanned from the British Isles to the Indies and the Mediterranean,[32] and in France, the same rationale applied: the Catholic community had established contacts with many ports all over the country. However, just as in Spain, in France, the Catholic community looked beyond itself; in times of war the ability to resort to both religious and non-religious ties became an asset in all operations involving smuggling or recruiting partners who could easily access Spanish, Dutch, and British ports.

In these years it became quite profitable to invest in French goods; they were cheap to buy as officially no one could export them and, although smuggling held risks, it could ultimately prove incredibly profitable. The British Isles and the colonial markets demanded French commodities and it was in fact through the sale of French goods in England and Spain that the Aylwards significantly increased their capital. Through the associates in London, and above all through the Protestant Thomas Brailsford and Charles Peers, this trade could flourish. The Protestant partners were

---

[31] For further discussion see G. Pizzoni, '"A Pass is not Denied to any Romanist": Strategies of the Catholic Merchant Community in the Atlantic World', *Cultural and Social History Journal*, 11, 3 (2014): 349–365.

[32] Thomas Truxes, *Irish–American Trade 1660–1783* (Cambridge: Cambridge University Press, 1988). L. M. Cullen, 'Galway Merchants in the Outside World, 1650–1800' in *Galway: Town and Crown, 1484–1984*, ed. D. O'Cearbhaill (Dublin: Gill and Macmillan, 1984), 63–89.

associates of Power & Hill and had been well acquainted with the Aylwards since the early 1680s.[33] It was over the winter of 1688–1689 that they intensified their correspondence. Their interests were varied, encompassing many ports in the Atlantic and the Mediterranean, and their exchanges involved London, Amsterdam, Bristol, and Port Royal. It was through Brailsford that the Aylwards were introduced to the Halls in Jamaica.[34] Frequently, their exchanges also involved the firm of Charles Peers, a prominent London merchant who would later carry on Brailsford's business after his death.[35] In April 1689, Brailsford and the Aylwards shipped merchandise from Spain and France to the Netherlands using vessels from Denmark, England, and Hamburg. An embargo was in place in London, meaning that no ship was permitted to go to sea, and no fruit was to be brought from any port of France without a 'leave' first being obtained; yet it was permitted that the 'Hollanders have permission to go and come'.[36] The Aylwards were always to give their captain private instructions not to let it be known where he was going. Moreover, because of the war, Brailsford directed that any ship should carry the King of France's pass that the Aylwards as 'Romanists' would not be denied; 'otherwise [Brailsford added] little hopes of safety ... if you see the coast not clear then desist'.[37] Merchandise at this time was also going to the West Indies and in particular to Jamaica, a hub of smugglers and privateers which would become a gem in the British imperial system in the eighteenth century. But it was not yet the prominent sugar-producing colony it would go on to become and despite producing its own livestock and other crops, the settlers there preferred a consistent supply of European food and drink.[38]

It took associates months to organise their deals as the mail was often stopped and precise instructions became almost impossible to obtain so as the months passed they discussed a wide variety of different strategies. The main concern was to procure the required passes so that French privateers

[33] CO 110–152, Brailsford Papers, Letters to John Aylward from Thomas Brailsford and the Halls, 1688–1690. AY 102, Business Accounts. Bills, accounts, for merchandise to 1688.

[34] AY 103, Business Accounts. Accounts, bills for merchandise to Dec. 1689.

[35] In the London Metropolitan archives, it is possible to consult MS 10137, *Day Book of Charles Peers*.

[36] AY 18, f. 4, Business Correspondence. Letter from Thomas Brailsford to John Aylward, 1689.

[37] AY 18, f. 5, Business Correspondence. Letters to John Aylward from Thomas Brailsford and Richard Holder at London on 15 April 1689.

[38] Nuala Zahedieh, 'The Merchants of Port Royal, Jamaica, and the Spanish Contraband Trade, 1655–1692', *The William and Mary Quarterly*, 43 (1986): 570–593; McFarlane, *The British in the Americas*, 131–146.

would not stop the vessels just off the French coast. The partners in London, among them Charles Peers, thought it would have been impossible to procure them, and perhaps desisted from trading with France as many English and Dutch vessels were at sea. Daily reports were heard of French men being carried away by Dutch privateers, and Peers prayed that 'God send John's cargo safe of these hands' and that his ships would sail from London safe from the French.[39] When the associates fell prey to privateers, they resorted if possible to money but also to religion – and not only to pray. In the summer of 1689, Benjamin Bake, a merchant from Exeter begged the Aylwards' help for the release of his nephew Christopher Cary who had been taken prisoner by a privateer off Falmouth. The boy had been carried off in St Malo, and 'by reason is a Catholic [...] may challenge almost a right to a civil treatment in your parts [...]'. Aylward was begged to procure him the liberty 'hee desire and take him in his house'.[40] Bake was willing to provide for the boy's diet and the Aylwards would surely have helped such a reliable partner who controlled the exchange of French wines and fabrics to Exeter and London. Ultimately, what happened to Christopher is not clear, but if anything, this showed that solidarity within the community existed despite religious affiliations.

The year 1689 saw an expansion of the associates' business but also the escalation of political turmoil in Britain. In the correspondence it is clear that they had become very cautious and even began sending two copies of the same letter as those sent from France were regularly being opened. Delayed correspondence could result in missed opportunities, since it was vital for traders to always obtain up-to-date information about the markets and their demands. Accurate correspondence was vital in supplying the fleets for the West Indies and to know which goods would have sold in the Americas as well as their prices 'abord and ashore'.[41] At that time, very high profits were being made from the transactions with the *indianos* and therefore information from New Spain was essential in order to know which 'sorts of goods had been sold there'. Incorrect correspondence could delay the supply of the fleets for the Americas and disrupt the exchanges between the north and south of Europe.

The Aylwards and their associates frequently questioned what would be the safest route for their commodities and during this year goods

---

[39] AY 18, f. 6, Business Correspondence. Letter from Brailsford and Peers to Aylward, 30 May 1689.

[40] AY 16, f. 6, Business Correspondence. Letters to John Aylward from Benjamin Bake, one also from Thomas Hill at Exeter, Aug. 1688–Aug. 1689.

[41] AY 20, f. 30, Business Correspondence. Letter from Robert Butler in Cadiz, 9 May 1689.

were frequently shipped to Italian ports, especially Genoa and Livorno, from where they could be exchanged for Levantine goods. They wondered which ports were better avoided and how best to coordinate their exchanges. From Irish ports, vessels were also going to Iberian ports, Bilbao in particular, after stopping in France. Indeed, it had been off the Basque coast that one of their vessels was seized on suspicion of carrying French goods. This time of war disrupted trade, not only because of the threat that vessels might be seized, but because conflicts meant the creation of new policies and new taxation to support military efforts. In Spain, an *indulto* had been imposed on all French merchants, and apparently, all traders were demanded by the Spanish King to contribute to the six million ducats requested – four million in pieces of eight and two million in 'ready money'.[42] The merchants did not know on which goods these new duties would be imposed; possibly French products would be taxed more, but there was no certainty on the other commodities. The Spaniards themselves invested in French goods and, according to Butler, so did 'those [the authorities] who adjusts the *indulto*'.[43] That being the case, it was possible that the duties would not be extortionate.

A heavy fine was frequently imposed by the Spanish crown on the merchant communities to finance the war effort. This was paid by the *consulado* through high taxes imposed on various items of merchandise and collected half in Spain and half in the Indies. The tax usually amounted to a million ducats and would go on to become common policy during the War of the Spanish Succession.[44] Besides heavy taxes, inspections also became commonplace. In August 1689, the King of Spain ordered his ministers in the kingdom to see all nations' account books in order to know if anyone had any 'French concerns' in their hands.[45] The Spanish authorities were rigorous about their controls. According to Butler, this practice of extreme control was destroying business: 'The commerce is molested every day with one new thing or other', he complained, and for months did not know how to proceed or where to keep his registers.[46] Any French 'indication' was to

---

[42] AY 20, f. 49, Business Correspondence. Letter from Robert Butler (Van Holstein) in Cadiz, 31 December 1691.

[43] AY 20, f. 52, Business Correspondence. Letter from Robert Butler (Van Holstein) in Cadiz, 14 January 1692.

[44] C. H. Haring, *The Spanish Empire in America* (New York: Harcourt, Brace & World, 1952), 307–308.

[45] AY 20, f. 37, Business Correspondence. Letter from Robert Butler in Cadiz on 1 August 1689.

[46] AY 20, f. 62, Business Correspondence. Letter from Robert Butler (Van Holstein) in Cadiz on 2 June 1692.

be avoided as the country's merchants were not even allowed to reside in Cadiz after a *pragmatica* issued by the government declared that they must all move at least twenty leagues from the harbour.[47]

Inevitably, politics had a direct influence on business and the merchants needed to accurately observe the scene. Even the death of a queen could be an issue for the trade since a new consort meant new alliances and policies; but with them, new business opportunities. Indeed, on 28 February 1689, Butler reported, with some delight, the death of the Queen Regent of Spain, Marie Louise d'Orléans, who died from indigestion of 'china oranges, pickled oysters, chocolate and frozen milk'.[48]

> After eating all that stuff she went and ride out in the fields where her horse had a little stumble and put her body out of order. She felt the approaches of death she erred out she was poisoned and two days after dyed she was opened and her *matrice* was found dried up so that she could not conceive by any man whatsoever.[49]

Her unfortunate death meant business as the event had caused a rise in the price of the black *bayes*[50] and knowing the goods would sell well, Butler wished their cargo of the English fabrics would arrive quickly. Again in 1692, the associates monitored the health of Maria Anne of Neuburg, second wife of the Spanish King Carlos II. She was very ill and had been 'given over' by the doctors. In the event of her death, the price of 'black bayes' would have once again seen a 'somewhat considerable' increase,[51] and the associates' business in the fabrics would have profited much from the event. Unfortunately for them, the Queen survived.

Despite all the problems, the 1690s would eventually prove to be a profitable decade in which the Catholic associates' business expanded and their interests became varied. As already noted, in the 1680s Catholic merchants responded to the needs of the Anglo-Spanish trade; the Catholic contacts

---

[47] AY 20, f. 50, Business Correspondence. Letter from Robert Butler (Van Holstein) in Cadiz on 17 December 1691.

[48] AY 20, f. 28, Business Correspondence. Letter from Robert Butler in Cadiz to John Aylward on 28 February 1689. R. Oresko, 'The Glorious Revolution of 1688–89 and the House of Savoy' in *The Anglo-Dutch Moment: Essays on the Glorious Revolution and its World Impact*, ed. J. I. Israel (Cambridge: Cambridge University Press, 1991), 365–388. Marie Louise d'Orléans died on 12 February 1689. At the Court of Charles II, she supported the French faction, despite being the granddaughter of Charles I of England.

[49] AY 20, f. 28.

[50] Ibid.

[51] AY 20, f. 65, Business Correspondence. Letter from Robert Butler in Cadiz.

allowed access to Mediterranean markets, whereas English traders closed the deals in the north of Europe. In the 1690s the merchandise remained the same but the commercial network had become much more extensive and its strategies more diverse. Catholic ties, familial networks, and business partners across Europe made this all possible. From St Malo, letters were exchanged with England, Spain, Ireland, and Jamaica and these were the years in which the Catholic associates established themselves as transatlantic traders, corresponding directly with Port Royal and exporting goods from the Levant. The most challenging aspect of the business at this time was in procuring supplies from continental ports, and the Aylwards and their associates began to deploy all possible tactics. For instance, they wrote to Peter Power requesting use of his name or the name of any other English friend to ship the goods to England by the 'most secure and best conveniency he can get', saying that whatever would be done they would assume the risks and run the hazard.[52] The strategy seen as 'most secure' was in working with Protestant partners; in fact, during this decade the Catholic merchants worked with co-religionists as well as non-Catholics. These dynamics suggest that they could rely on any businessman who would prove useful and well-connected in a certain trade. Through this they forged wider connections beyond their group and their correspondence shows constant discussion about which strategies to adopt or which men to rely on, with at times disregard for religious or national affiliation.

Catholic–Protestant Partnerships

During the Nine Years War, privateering remained a constant threat for the Catholic community and their associates as it was the main strategy used by France and England. A simple letter of marque would be enough for any captain to act as a privateer and introduce the seized vessels into their own ports in the type of assaults which inflicted significant losses and provided lucrative rewards for the captors. The main centres for privateering were in ports facing the Channel: Dunkirk, St Malo, and Brest, and on the English side, coastal hubs such as Falmouth, Dartmouth, Weymouth, and the Channel Islands of Guernsey and Jersey.[53] Documented in the Aylward papers are a few cargoes which were taken as prizes and then released

---

[52] AY 104, f. 13, Business Accounts. The partners involved were Cruice, Murphy, and Thomas Hease.

[53] David. J. Starkey, *British Privateering Enterprise in the Eighteenth Century* (Exeter: Exeter University Press, 1990), 35–84.

through personal contacts. Ships would be usually seized 'a mile off Dover Castle' or from San Sebastian.[54] These assaults affected the merchants' transactions from French and Spanish ports; but despite this, privateering also offered the Catholic associates opportunities to smuggle their own goods into the European ports. At the beginning of the hostilities in 1689, all English imports of French goods were banned. However, from 1692 it became possible to bring them in as privateering prizes with a percentage of the profits then going to the Crown.[55] This new legislation offered splendid opportunities to British Catholics to introduce French goods into English ports by faking seizure. The English partners were themselves privateers and with forged passes obtained through friends or bribes, were able to easily exchange such merchandise.[56] Families including the Butlers, the Goolds, and the Lynchs were among the most renowned owners of privateer vessels at the time, having operated similar business in the Channel for years.[57] Therefore, it is possible that the legislation simply acknowledged a *de facto* situation since the associates, like any other merchants, had long been employing these tactics –since before they were state sanctioned in the early 1690s.[58]

At the time, the Catholics from St Malo adopted these practices mainly thanks to help from the community in London, particularly from Charles Horde and Thomas Brailsford, with a minor role being played by their own families. The relationship with the London merchants had been well established since the 1680s, but it was in late 1688 that the partnership strengthened. In fact, it was with the eruption of the Glorious Revolution that the Aylwards fully realised the importance of their English partners to help introduce French goods to London. The goods in which they invested were numerous and diverse, however the most striking aspect of their correspondence is how they dealt with this merchandise. They knew that with the landing of Prince William of Orange, hostilities would soon begin. In London, an embargo had been issued on foreign ships; officially, goods

---

[54] AY 6, f. 20, Business Correspondence. Miscellaneous letters to John Aylward, Jan. 1687–Dec. 1691; AY 19, f. 4, Business Correspondence. Letters to John Aylward from Andrew Browne at Ostend and Bruges, Aug. 1691–July 1692, Jan.–Mar. 1701.

[55] Bromley, *Corsairs and Navies*.

[56] AY 20, f. 56, Business Correspondence. Letter from Robert Butler in Cadiz.

[57] Bromley, 'The Jacobite Privateers in the Nine Years War' in *Corsairs and Navies*, 139–166: The Butlers were active Channel privateers and they were also involved in military operations during the Nine Years War.

[58] Paul Monod, 'Dangerous Merchandise: Smuggling, Jacobitism, and Commercial Culture in Southeast England, 1690–1760', *The Journal of British Studies*, 30 (1991): 150–182.

were stopped at the custom house and French linens could not be sold.[59] In order to avoid the blockade and introduce French goods, the partnership instead helped ship goods to Flanders and move northward, landing at Scotland or the north of England.

In the first months of 1689, the associates agreed to trade French goods through Dutch privateers or English men-of-war.[60] Brailsford and Peers deemed it impossible to obtain passes for French or Irish goods. It was, however, possible to fake a seizure, or to send the French linens first to Amsterdam and Rotterdam and then on to London, although they knew problems 'might still incur with the admiralty'.[61] They insured all cargoes and were confident that this strategy would prove successful, knowing 'the Hollanders still have permission to come and go' in all English ports.[62] Officially, French vessels or French goods at this time could only reach English ports with a leave from the Lords of Treasury – something Brailsford was confident he could obtain. The strategy became that the Aylwards were instructed to procure passes from the French King and to use either a Danish, Hamburger, or English vessel, and to give secret instructions to the captain to ensure that nobody knew he was going to Holland. From there, the French merchandise could be moved to England. The King's pass was necessary to prevent the ship being taken by a French privateer in the Channel and ensure it could still reach London. Under 'an old act of Parliament called the Act of Navigation' which required English colonial trade to be carried out only using English vessels and crewmen, their ships needed to be English or have a crew of trusted 'mates'.[63]

During the summer of 1689, the English government intensified the attacks on French commerce and even neutral vessels such as those of the Danish or Portuguese were seized by English and Dutch men-of-war if they were coming from France. English vessels too would be taken if crossing the Channel when the prohibition was ratified, making the situation even more difficult for the Aylwards and their associates. To combat the risk, Brailsford informed the Aylwards that it was possible to obtain licences

---

[59]   AY 20, f. 33, Business Correspondence. Letter from Robert Butler in Cadiz on 20 June 1689.

[60]   AY 18, f. 6, Business Correspondence. Letter from Thomas Brailsford, from London on 30 May 1689; AY 20, f. 5, Business Correspondence. Letter from Robert Butler in Malaga on 23 September 1687.

[61]   Ibid.

[62]   AY 18, f. 4, Business Correspondence. Brailsford to Aylward, 1689.

[63]   AY 18, f. 7, Business Correspondence. Letter from Thomas Brailsford from London, 20 June 1689; AY 18, f. 10, Business Correspondence. Letter from Thomas Brailsford from London, 11 July 1689.

through 'friends' – although the authorities would still control the validity of the commodities in the custom house. Certainly, he knew that money 'may blind the eyes of some clarks and prevent too much examination'.[64] For such a tactic, it was necessary to offer at least 100 guineas per pass, a significant amount given that Peers complained that the insurance of 20 or 30 guineas against 'Pirates, Thieves and Suprizals' was extremely expensive.[65] Once these licences were obtained, the merchants in St Malo would change the name of the vessels in English and then inform the partners in London of the new name and how many men would be covered by the pass. The best strategy proved to be to go from France to Faro in Portugal where the goods could be unloaded and moved to a fishing boat directed to Spain. Since the goods were contraband and at risk of seizure, the fishing *barca longa* would have gone to Malaga, where the London associates would register them under their names.[66] The cargo from Spain would then have been freely admitted to England. The Aylwards and Brailsford adopted many different strategies to exchange commodities between England and France at this time, and in August 1689, considered exchanging goods together with prisoners. This tactic was adopted frequently and usually proved successful; the idea being to seek permission to return a number of English prisoners from France and to pay around 100 crowns for each man. In return, they would have sent to Calais twelve French prisoners held in England.[67] They sought permission from the King's Commission for Exchange of Prisoners, confident the petition would be accepted. Once in St Malo, the traders would buy an English vessel which had been taken as a prize, and together with the imprisoned men, use it to send back all sorts of goods and anything they deemed 'a penny worth'.[68] The merchants created a ring of security around the scheme by also arranging to have the

---

[64] CO 110–152, Brailsford Papers, 1688–1692.

[65] CO 110–152, Brailsford Papers, National Archives. The cost of assurance was shared among the partners, to cover the ship until it would have eventually landed in the port of destination and in order to avoid all the vagaries of: 'the Seas, Men of war, Fire, Enemies, Pirats, Rovers, Thieves, Fettezones, Letters of Mart and Counter mart, Surprizals, Taking at Sea, Arrests, Restraints and Detainments of all kings, princes and people of what nation, condition or quality soever, Barratry of the Master and Marriners and of all other perils, losses and misfortunes that have or shall come to the hurt, detriment or damage of the said goods and merchandizes or any part thereof'.

[66] AY 18, f. 13, Business Correspondence. Letter from Brailsford to Aylward, 27 June 1689 and f. 9, Business Correspondence. Letter from London on 1 August 1689.

[67] AY 18, f. 11, Business Correspondence. Letter from Brailsford to Aylward, 18 July 1689.

[68] Ibid.

King of France's passes and all bills of loading under Brailsford's name; the latter would assure safety from English assaults, whereas the former would have ensured protection from the French. They knew that if permission of the authorities was not granted, the vessel could have gone to Holland or Hamburg in the first assurance against the possibility of being 'blew up'.[69] In order to smuggle French goods either from Spain or directly from France, they thought carefully about all likely scenarios and how they might respond to them. In the meantime, despite these consuming efforts in northern Europe, the merchants did not fail to consider the potentially lucrative West-Indian trade. During the early stages of the Nine Years War, many associates moved between Port Royal and London, and despite not knowing how the military expeditions would develop, they still intended to organise cargoes for the Caribbean. A shipment could consist of 1,000 to 1,200 barrels of beef and 200 to 300 half barrels of pork.[70] In London, Brailsford procured passes for Jamaica. With Irish vessels they had to be extremely cautious because usually these ships were forced to pass through London. The answer was to avoid Irish crews and resort instead to English ships and crews. They frequently discussed the transatlantic fleets as it was possible their sailing would soon be stopped because of the war, and 'if the suspencion would be two years, as everybody feared, there would be no good deals anymore'. Nevertheless, despite the odds, their resolution was to 'hitt the naile while it is hot' and their instinct proved right; especially at the beginning of 1689, when they reaped good profits.[71]

In the summer months of 1691, goods were being exchanged from the British Isles on board privateer vessels, the method by which goods were moved in and out of France. Between 1691 and the summer of 1692, the partners in London and the Catholics in St Malo exchanged a vast amount of correspondence in which they discussed policies, vessels, and from whom to seek protection. Horde was based in London and, with the Aylwards, dealt in French goods and provided English vessels. Occasionally Danish ships would be used with all the necessary French passes. The partners also thought about supplying vessels for the Levant as Horde had been informed that the English government was organising 'something extraordinary' for the East.[72] In the meantime, they continued to supply the Jamaican fleet as a place where they could dispose of vast amounts of prize goods.

---

[69] AY 18, f. 13, Business Correspondence. Letter from Brailsford and Richard Holder from London, on 1 August 1689.

[70] Ibid.

[71] CO 110–152, Brailsford Papers.

[72] AY 51, f. 3, Business Correspondence. Letters to John Aylward, from Charles Horde at London, Nov. 1691–July 1693. Most of the letters are counter-endorsed from

For the Aylwards and their associates, solidarity and excellent net-
working skills were fundamental in these circumstances due to the great
need for caution not only about the commodities, but also the vessels
being employed. The correct documents and passes were vital for smooth
transactions and Charles Horde seems to have been close to the Lord of
Treasury officials, mentioning them on various occasions. It was through
permission from their offices that Horde and the Aylwards were able to
introduce merchandise from France by using a boat carrying prisoners.[73] In
the early months of 1692, they had to be cautious as the English Parliament
had increased controls on the import of French goods. The Parliament was
'sitting until is adjurned or prorogued', and in the meantime the Aylwards
were advised to keep their goods and not 'to venture in a hazardous enterprise'.[74] They worked through influential friends to obtain permissions or
hoped to prove through the insurance that their goods belonged to Horde.
A 'great friend' worked to get the licences and the trade was profitable as
they resorted to any strategy in order to exploit the deals. However, the
situation soon got out of control when in the early months of 1692 many
French vessels were taken up as prizes and brought in front of the Lord of
Prize Council where they would be heavily charged. Furthermore, members
of the English Parliament proposed legislation stating that corresponding
with France would be an act of treason. Charles Horde fervently hoped that
act would not be issued.[75]

In July 1692, the precarious situation for the Aylwards escalated when
James II threatened England with a possible 'reinthroning' and won
the support of 'the great army of Louis XIV'. It was rumoured that the
King would be opposed by an army of 200,000 armed men in England,
and it seemed that at that moment James II was moved to a 'religious
port in Italy'.[76] Meanwhile, the English army threatened to land in
France and in the summer of 1692, 20,000 men departed Portsmouth.
Horde wrote to the Aylwards hoping to secure their goods inland by
at least twenty or thirty leagues. They also thought to move them to

---

Amsterdam by the Philibert Brothers.

[73]   AY 51, f. 4, Business Correspondence. Letter from Charles Horde, in London, on 29
       December 1691.
[74]   AY 51, f. 5, f. 6, Business Correspondence. Charles Price was 'the friend' providing
       the passes.
[75]   AY 51, f. 10, Business Correspondence. Letter from Charles Horde, in London, and
       the Philibert brothers, in Amsterdam, on 21 July 1692.
[76]   AY 51, f. 13, Business Correspondence. Letter from Charles Horde, in London, and
       the Philibert brothers, in Amsterdam, on 13 May 1692.

Amsterdam[77] but when the associates realised the English soldiers were descending from Flanders, it was agreed to keep the goods where they were. The privateering activity became the only option but certainly came with hazards. The Catholic associates had a duty to inform the London partners about the vessels brought to France as prizes, and asked for any small 'toole' that could be bought reasonably.[78] They had to know details about the content, the marks and numbers, the names, and from where they had departed; and in London, they wanted to know if the vessels when taken were full or empty. When a boat was full they used 'friends' to obtain a grant and bring it back to England complete with French goods, a scheme being used by other merchants at the time.[79] After 'much pain' and 50 guineas, Horde obtained a grant from her Majesty with the help of the 'Lords of Treasury and Commissioners of the Customs' for a few tonnes of merchandise to be imported and exchanged for prisoners.[80] The associates then had to pretend these tonnes had been lost in a prized vessel and exchange the letters via Amsterdam.

During the early 1690s, the British associates worked on their tactics. Each exchange needed a different strategy and in each letter, the partners mapped out all the different possibilities offered to them. They meticulously considered all the different routes, how to procure the goods and which vessels to deploy. Any trade, illegal or legal, was allowed, and resorting to privateering was probably one of the safest plans in these times of warfare. Privateering was often confused with piracy, and it was certainly difficult to distinguish between the two since both implied the assault and seizure of commercial vessels. Officially they both targeted the enemy's cargo, but in times of turmoil any vessel and crew very easily became prey for another. All of their plans and use of personal contacts proved well worth the risk as during the first years of the hostilities when the Aylwards' business was extremely lucrative. During this time, the English partners proved vital as they allowed for illegal but profitable exchanges. Charles Horde was one of

[77] AY 51, f. 12, Business Correspondence. Letter from Charles Horde, in London, on 29 July 1692; and f. 13, Business Correspondence. Letter from Horde on 13 May 1692.

[78] AY 51, f. 11, Business Correspondence. Letter from Charles Horde in London on July 1692.

[79] Bromley 'The Jacobite Privateers in the Nine Years War', 139–165; Bromley, 'The North Sea in Wartime, 1688–1713'; Bromley, 'The Trade and Privateering of St Malo During the War of the Spanish Succession', 339–388; Bromley, 'The French Privateering War, 1702–1713' in *Corsairs and Navies, 1660–1760* (London: Hambledon Press, 1987) 213–242. Starkey, *British Privateering Enterprise in the Eighteenth Century*; Morieux, *The Channel: England, France.*

[80] AY 51, f. 20, Business Correspondence. Letter from Charles Horde, in London, on 23 September 1692.

the main architects of these strategies and when reading his correspondence and scornful comments about James II, it is reasonable to assume that he was neither a Catholic nor sympathetic to the Catholic cause. Nevertheless, the presence of religion did not hinder a highly successful collaboration with the Catholics in St Malo.

Surprisingly enough, during these years even previously difficult family members proved helpful. Until then, nephews and in-laws seemed to have proved only to be a source of great concern, but during the early 1690s they seemed to show some abilities. For more than a year the Aylwards and their family exchanged correspondence under false names, adopting the Dutch–sounding identities of *Van Holstein* and *Jacob Van Angracht*.[81] Van Holstein (alias Robert Butler) was based in the Spanish city of Cadiz, from where he supervised the shipping of Spanish fruit and wine. In May 1692, he became extremely worried as the French were about to attack the port of Cadiz and merchants' correspondence was being opened in Madrid. A squadron from Marseilles was poised to bombard Cadiz and several English merchants had burnt their vessels to prevent capture. Many families were leaving the port city, and many members of the firm Power & Hill had already gone, fearing the war and all the difficulties of running the business it would bring. The merchant Eustace Power had no fixed lodging since he moved from Hill's'; it was written that 'He sleeps in one place and eats in another' and he was going back to London.[82] However, Butler was determined to stay, or perhaps he was waiting for his uncle's orders.[83]

In the last months of 1691, 'Van Holstein' dealt with English and Dutch ports. When shipping goods there was a constant threat of attack from French privateers, although if convoys were seized on the way to London, the Aylwards could have relied on their French contacts to free them. On the other hand, the Spanish agents supervised the arrival and departure of the fleets to protect their precious cargoes, particularly when the American bullion was to be moved ashore.[84] English and Dutch privateers were

---

[81]   AY 20, f. 60, Business Correspondence. In the back of the letter there is this caption: letter written to Aylward on the 3 May 1692 by Robert Butler. Answered on 2 June. AY 20, f. 54, Business Correspondence, again we can read: letter written to Aylward on 11 February 1692 by Robert Butler. Answered on 10 March; AY 20, f. 51, Business Correspondence. Letter written on 3 December 1691, answered on 31 December.

[82]   AY 20, f. 34, Business Correspondence. Letter from Robert Butler in Cadiz, 4 July 1689.

[83]   AY 20, f. 60, Business Correspondence. Letter from Robert Butler in Cadiz, 5 May 1692; AY 20, f. 49, Business Correspondence. Letter from Robert Butler (Van Holstein) in Cadiz, 31 December 1691.

[84]   AY 20, f. 49, Business Correspondence. Letter from Robert Butler (Van Holstein) in Cadiz, 31 December 1691.

a constant threat off the coast of Cadiz, and being able to deal with both parties gave the Catholic merchants a significant advantage. During the spring of 1692, transactions were hindered by the fear of a French invasion whilst taxation rose enormously. The Spanish authorities considered taxes of 32 per cent, although this information was not yet official. The *indulto* would in the end be set at 20 per cent which, although lower than expected, was still detrimental.[85] Therefore, from St Malo, the associates became concerned about shipments of fruit that, if taxed at the new rates, would not have made any profit. Their answer was to ship the commodities in different vessels so as to minimise the risks. Usually they also relied on north European vessels to move the products, whereas Italian ships were more commonly used for sending invoices to the partners. They would ship part of their goods on Swedish vessels and the other half on Danish or Polish in a measure of precaution which evidently proved successful since, in March 1692, their deal of Spanish fruit was worth a total of 38,000 *reals*.[86]

As Figure 2 [or Fig. 3?]illustrates, all of this scheming was invariably also directed at the American fleets. In the summer months of 1692 there was hope that the *flota* would sail, but while waiting for any news, the associates also invested in the Levantine trade. They juggled various transactions at the same time so as to reduce risks, with the aim of carrying on and concluding the deals. It was in times of great upheaval that merchants could test both their skills and their ability to survive in the market and to profit. They resorted to false identities and avoided mentioning the partners involved. When briefing about the dealing, they only referred to their initials so as to avoid major problems should the letters be opened. The strategies adopted by these men in the first years of war is a testament to their creativity, resilience, and willingness to resort to any means in order to continue to work. Despite the political turmoil, they knew that French products remained in high demand; therefore, they needed to trade them. In these difficult times, it was essential to work with trusted and skilled partners, regardless of their being either Catholic or Protestant. The associates were carefully chosen for being competent, reliable, and also somewhat audacious as every step in the transaction process had to be accurately planned and there was no room for error. The Catholics in France worked primarily with Protestants in London interested in organising illegal but potentially lucrative deals. However, the network also involved co-religionists and even family

---

[85]   AY 20, f. 50, Business Correspondence. Letter from Robert Butler (Van Holstein) in Cadiz, 17 December 1691; AY 20, f. 57, Business Correspondence. Letter from Robert Butler in Cadiz, 24 March 1692.

[86]   AY 20, f. 62, Business Correspondence. Letter from Robert Butler (Van Holstein) in Cadiz, 2 June 1692.

members who at the times proved reliable. The decisions were based on the ability of these family members to move undisturbed in Spain, and once again testify as to how the Catholic community did not disregard religious or familial networks, but simply prioritised trustworthy and reliable traders. The aim of the Aylwards and their Catholic associates was to answer the markets' needs, and to do so they worked with anyone they deemed capable. Collaboration choices were driven only by the quest for profit.

Community, Family and Trade

Within the mercantile world, family was at the base of most partnerships. Family members usually provided the initial capital and offered the foothold in commerce needed for a fledgling business. Grassby suggests that the services of kinsmen were needed in distant overseas trade where it was more comfortable to deal with family than strangers; it was perhaps easier to reconcile differences within the family network, rather than resorting to litigation that was time-consuming and costly.[87] However, working within the family could cause problems as 'kin could be a liability because of fraud and dispute.'[88] Indeed, from the Aylward papers it is clear that feuds within families strained commercial relations and at times their letters could barely provide information on what the market asked and how the deals proceeded. When the traders in St Malo left their family in Spain to act as agents, the men constantly bickered instead of procuring the goods. It was not unusual for family members to fail to meet expectations or to fight over management: kin could be financially unreliable and often become a burden.

Analysing the family relationships of the Malouin community sheds light on the intricacies of international trade where the disruptions caused by warfare seemed to have been the least of their concerns. From St Malo, the Aylwards and their partners considered what could affect their exchanges. Important factors were the quality of the merchandise, the skills of the agents deployed, and the weather. They feared disruptions, but more than anything they were frustrated about the conduct their agents were reporting in the correspondence since, above all, they wanted them to work properly and uphold a certain reputation. Merchants of any faith followed a universal code of conduct that overcame religious differences and favoured

---

[87]   Richard Grassby, *Kinship and Capitalism: Marriage, Family and Business in the English-Speaking World, 1580–1740* (Cambridge: Cambridge University Press, 2001), 269–311.

[88]   Ibid.

exchanges among groups operating over large distances.[89] Whether it was in the Atlantic, in London or in the Mediterranean, the only assurance in such an unregulated environment was to make sure that the partners would behave, stick to the rules, and not spend too much money. Reputation and trustworthiness were built on universal rules which combined interest and religion, reason, and honour, so that any deviants would be responsible before God. The cardinal virtues of a good trader were wisdom, prudence, and justice. Business networks were built with family and co-religionists, but inevitably with strangers too, as family did not always uphold these values. Unfortunately, in the winter months of 1688 and 1689, for almost an entire season the correspondence was tainted by a dispute between Robert Butler, James Porter, and Paul Den, members of influential families who bickered over table linens, gossip, and bedding. They were supposed to be supervising the exchanges in the south of Spain, but could not stand working with each other. The Aylwards and their firm worried for weeks about how to manage the exchanges, having to deal with the childish behaviour of their agents whose attitudes and unwillingness to follow their orders meant delaying transactions and hindering the outcome.

Indeed, among the agents left in Spain, the immediate families of both the Porters and the Butlers eventually caused disappointment. The associates expected them to be knowledgeable about their business, diligent, careful with their domestic expenses and able to keep the accounts in order. The Aylwards needed them to move between Malaga and Cadiz and to minimise costs and, in fact, initially they were probably encouraged to share living quarters, but this arrangement seemed not to work. Butler blamed Paul Den for the high living expenses they faced in Malaga where Den had liked 'to live great and high and eat and drink well at another's cost just as when he was at the consul'.[90] This was all at the expense of John Aylward. Apparently, Paul Den had taken advantage of Butler by living in his home without any payment or offers to cover his expenses there. Furthermore, Butler had been cheated by Den regarding his new accommodation in Cadiz. Butler was assured that Porter's residence would be full of household

---

[89] Zahedieh, *The Capital and the Colonies*; Sheryllynne Haggerty, *'Merely for money'? Business Culture in the British Atlantic, 1750–1815* (Liverpool: Liverpool University Press, 2012) 17, 198–236; Francesca Trivellato, *The Familiarity of Strangers: The Sephardic Diaspora, Livorno, and Cross-Cultural Trade in the Early Modern Period* (London: Yale University Press, 2009); Grassby, *Kinship and Capitalism*; S. D. Aslanian, *From the Indian Ocean to the Mediterranean: The Global Trade Networks of Armenian Merchants from New Julfa* (London: California University Press, 2011).

[90] AY 20, f. 33, Business Correspondence. Letter from Robert Butler, in Cadiz, to John Aylward, 20 June 1689.

items but when he moved to Cadiz from Malaga, found the house empty and regretted having sold everything to Den. However, Butler assured his uncle – John Aylward – 'you wanted to send me sheets, but I have [them] and also brought table linens'.[91] While in Cadiz, he swore he would spend a great deal less because Den would not be with him anymore. In Cadiz, Butler assured his uncle that he lived in a little house, 'a hole wherein I lye and dine, a warehouse, kitchen and another room where the boy lyes in'.[92] The house was on New Street, in an area safe from robbery, with people and passers-by around all day and night. Butler and Porter had probably been chosen since in Cadiz they could work undisturbed and integrate fairly easily in the community of expatriates thanks to their religion. The associates thought that Catholic family members could be useful as agents in Spain, asking only that they be just in their dealings, demand fair prices, pay their debts promptly and provide merchandise of good quality.[93]

For the Aylwards and their associates, it was important to build and maintain their own reputation but also to assess others. The major source of commercial loss came from misplaced trust and so information about character and reputation was constantly sought. Wives, children, apprentices, and servants might meet and exchange gossip at regular meetings or at church to keep everybody informed. Monitoring across the Atlantic was difficult and much was left to the discretion of the agents, so the only solution became to establish strong relationships with trustworthy agents.[94] Perhaps because of the dispute over bedding, Butler showed considerable resentment towards Porter. He saw that Porter was 'taking away' his credit, and was 'such a crossgraine strange sort of a humour man … there is not speaking or having to doe with him.[95] Apparently, Butler had been accused of not respecting his colleagues and spreading gossip both about Watkins – another Power & Hill associate– whom he labelled 'a broken man', and also about his uncle John.[96] In the merchant house, while discussing the exchange of certain goods with an agent in Guernsey, Butler did not miss the opportunity to deny all the gossip about him as 'pure forgery'.[97] He was concerned about his reputation and relished recounting how Porter was

---

[91]   Ibid.

[92]   Ibid.

[93]   Zahedieh, *The Capital and the Colonies*, 90–102.

[94]   Ibid.

[95]   AY 20, f. 36, Business Correspondence. Letter from Robert Butler in Cadiz sent to John Aylward, 26 September 1689.

[96]   AY 20, f. 47, Business Correspondence. Letter from Robert Butler in Cadiz sent to John Aylward in February 1690.

[97]   Ibid.

beaten 'black and blue' at night while with a 'whore'. Porter accused a rival merchant, Hacket, of having sent someone to have him beaten over an issue regarding business in French linens between the two.[98] There had been disagreement about the price, the goods were revealed to the justice, and in the end they lost; 'to save a penny they lost a pound'.[99] However, there was no evidence of Hacket being the mind behind this attack and Porter made all the town 'laugh heartily'.[100] '[...] Even though he had a sword he did not use it, and was beaten just by one man. He is so pusillanimous [...] He is a strange man, very morose and reserving of his words'.[101]

The worst part of this affair was that Porter accused someone who turned out not to be guilty, conduct which caused him serious discredit in the mercantile community and perhaps prevented future collaborations. Butler continued his story, talking about envy in the profession and he assured his uncle that he only hoped the best for his own business. However, Porter told people that Butler had a 'scandalous foolish tongue', apparently in a meeting with other merchants at the firm the only topic was how John Aylward had been cheated in his marriage, in terms of the marital deal. 'This are lies from him or someone that envy me and wants my destruction'.[102] Butler thought of Porter 'He is a man, my aunt [Helena Aylward] pardon me, which God or Devil will never be the better'. At the end of the letter Butler begged his uncle not to mention anything to Porter, urging him to safeguard his own business. 'He is a newsmonger so do not tell who are your correspondents or your businesses'.[103] He reassured his uncle that he was behaving; not only had he chosen a house belonging to a convent but always went home before 'the Oration'.[104]

The merchants in St Malo soon realised their relatives were unfit for the job. They grew wary of their family in Cadiz and Malaga as they continued bickering and mistrusting each other. The two opened each other's correspondence; indeed more than once, Porter had opened Butler's personal letters 'by removing the principle seal [...] and nibbling with the other

[98] Ibid.

[99] AY 20, f. 36, Business Correspondence. Letter from Robert Butler in Cadiz sent to John Aylward, 26 September 1689.

[100] AY 20, f. 47, Business Correspondence. Letter from Robert Butler in Cadiz sent to John Aylward in February 1690.

[101] AY 20, f. 10, Business Correspondence. Letter from Robert Butler in Cadiz sent to John Aylward, 3 January 1688.

[102] AY 20, f. 34, Business Correspondence. Letter from Robert Butler in Cadiz sent to John Aylward, 4 July 1689.

[103] Ibid.

[104] AY 20, f. 33, Business Correspondence. Letter from Robert Butler in Cadiz sent to John Aylward, 20 June 1689.

two, thinking they were letters for the company'; but Butler thought that 'only an excuse'.[105] However, even Nicholas Aylward 'broke the chief seal' of Butler's letters when they were under the cover of the Lynchs, recognising the name of John Aylward upon them. The pair also failed to complete the most basic tasks such as keeping the associates in France up to date with information, always blaming each other for the failure. Indeed, in 1689 John Aylward did not receive the letter that Butler had given to 'Porter's boy to be put in the post house'; Butler suggested that this young agent was as inept as Porter, so he was not surprised 'why they should miscarry'.[106] Unsurprisingly, Harper & Cross did not particularly enjoy working with the Aylwards' family and over the spring of 1688 exchanged 'saucy impudent letters' with them.[107] Apparently, Robert Butler blamed them for having accused him of not promptly selling the fruit he had received.[108] The Londoner Charles Peers thought Butler to be a 'good ingenious, careful yung gentleman' but added that 'to be playne' he preferred to do business with Hill.[109] Indeed, the role of Power & Hill was crucial for the successful outcome of the Spanish deals as they monitored the behaviour of the associates left behind. For a business based on reputation, Power & Hill ensured safe book-keeping, honoured the obligations, and paid the debts, whilst reporting the gossip among the associates and supervising the legal suits.[110] Furthermore, they made sure, the agents would not be acquainted with all the details of the transactions.[111]

Power & Hill then had the daunting task of supervising the exchanges, the agents, and of protecting the interests of John Aylward from fraud or other accidents. In fact in 1688, they informed Aylward that John Searle, the partner working with Robert Butler, was causing trouble and smearing

[105] AY 20, f. 28, Business Correspondence. Letter from Robert Butler in Cadiz sent to John Aylward, 28 February 1689.

[106] AY 20, f. 21, Business Correspondence. Letter from Robert Butler in Cadiz sent to John Aylward, 24 October 1688.

[107] AY 20, f. 11, Business Correspondence. Letter from Robert Butler in Malaga sent to John Aylward, 20 January 1688.

[108] AY 20, f. 13, Business Correspondence. Letter from Robert Butler in Malaga, 30 March 1688.

[109] AY 18, f. 7, Business Correspondence. Letter from Thomas Brailsford in London, 20 June 1689.

[110] David Hancock, *Citizens of the World, London Merchants and the Integration of the British Atlantic Community, 1735–1785* (Cambridge: Cambridge University Press, 1995), 383; Zahedieh, *The Capital and the Colonies*.

[111] AY 37, f. 6, Business Correspondence. Letters to John Aylward from Richard Enys and Eustace Power and one from Power, Hill, Enys & Company, one account for freight charges, all from Cadiz. Aug. 1682–Jul. 1687.

his reputation, proving 'so inveterate that he spares you to none in his tongue and pen and hath written us two long charterpiece that we have not thought to answer [...] but you are above the reach of his malice'.[112] Apparently, Aylward was accused of having not met his payments and of forging his partner's signature after Searle could not recall certain agreements. Searle abused Aylward's credit and held his commodities; he had 'lost his shame and is grown desperate'.[113] In reality, Searle had been fired, after working for the Aylwards for seven years when they discovered he had been stealing from them. However, instead of resorting to the justice and punishing the offender with 200 lashes, the Aylwards decided to pardon him out of the respect they felt for his family. They granted a pardon, as Searle's family had returned the goods.[114] Unfortunately, Searle was a 'knave' and 'the greatest villain that ever was', and reacted by writing ill of Aylward to other partners as well as supporting other merchants involved in lawsuits against him. Power & Hill tried to bring him to 'as favourable an agreement and conclusion'[115] as possible, as Hill was disgusted of his 'evil and crooked ways' and the trouble caused by the legal procedures.[116] A trial could last for months causing annoyance but also slowing trade. The loss of money could be significant because a merchant would have not only paid for the legal procedures, but their goods could be detained, until an agreement was reached, and could easily deteriorate. Indeed, during Searle's trial the partner Paul Den, did 'little or no service' to the business as he did not know how to proceed.[117]

The frustration and stresses felt by the men in St Malo is hard to imagine. Communication was difficult and their agents were not fulfilling their obligations on the other side of the continent, potentially threatening the business and the reputation of the merchant house. In the commercial world, profitable careers were easily made, but equally easily undone. Unsurprisingly, for almost thirty years, nobody was enthusiastic about working with

[112] AY 37, f. 11, Business Correspondence. John Searle was the nephew of Mrs Wyse. He was from Dartmouth.
[113] AY 20, f. 3, Business Correspondence. Letter sent to John Aylward from Robert Butler in Malaga, 22 July 1687.
[114] AY 25 f. 11, Business Correspondence. Letter from John Aylward in London to Pablo Cloots in Amsterdam on 21 January 1688.
[115] AY 20, f. 6, Business Correspondence. Letter from Robert Butler in Malaga, 25 September 1687.
[116] AY 72, Business Correspondence. Letters to John Aylward from Peter Power and Richard Hill at London. May 1687– Aug. 1689. AY 16, f.1, Business Correspondence. Letter from Mr Bake and Thomas Hill about the trial with Mr Evans.
[117] AY 20, f. 33, Business Correspondence. Letter to John Aylward from Robert Butler on 20 June 1689.

the Aylwards' relatives, and any transaction that involved either Robert Butler or James Porter was first discussed directly with John Aylward. The nephew and brother-in-law were kept on merely as agents to follow orders. Henceforth family always played a minor role, mainly handling the merchandise or providing information so as to maintain family and community ties. Partners, on the other hand, were chosen only if reliable. Trust was a universal element among the mercantile communities, and became crucial to make the business work across so many countries. To work with able and well-behaved partners meant avoiding spilling so much ink and delaying transactions. Eventually, all the family partnerships fell apart. James Porter was accused of not following Aylward's orders from France, and in 1692 he left Spain. A year later, it would be Butler's time as he had built up enormous debts, owing 5,000 *reals* to Edward Creagh, 1,000 to Ryan, and 2,000 to Power. A further 8,000 was claimed for the keeping of Butler's house – a sum which Power took care of. Power complained that he had to stay away from his own house for 14 months in order to make amends for Butler's debts, writing that he would have needed a lot for all the coming and going and how 'fatal the journey must have been to him'. John Aylward was left to take care of the expenses and gave Power a further six crowns to buy shoes as perhaps his were 'consumed by too much travelling'.[118] He was willing to pay off his nephew's debts as Butler – alias Van Holstein – had proved at least to be a successful smuggler, living up to the family name and at last earning his uncle's trust.

Catholic Contacts

During the 1690s, the Catholics in St Malo looked to Cadiz. They constantly supervised the Anglo-Spanish trade which they supplied with French fabrics and provisions and also with Mediterranean, Irish, and Flemish goods. They needed to diversify their deals so as to minimise risks but also increase their supplies for the American fleets. The circle of partners grew constantly and many collaborations were retained throughout the years. Religion was not crucial in establishing partnerships but Catholic contacts and familial networks were not completely disregarded and could prove advantageous particularly in Spanish, Italian, or Flemish ports. By not disregarding religious contacts, traders also had the possibility to access many markets and retain links with the most important European ports. Indeed, when working with Spain, Italy, or Ostend, the correspondence features

---

[118] AY 109, Business Accounts. Bills and accounts for merchandise to Dec. 1697; AY 104, Business Accounts. Accounts, Bills for merchandise to Dec. 1690.

Catholic dynasties including the Lynchs, Brownes, Fitzgeralds, and Creaghs, whose expertise in the European Atlantic trade proved invaluable.

As previously mentioned, many of these families were of Anglo-Irish descent, having relocated to the continent during the Cromwellian conquest of the 1650s and during the Williamite War (1691).[119] Ireland's commercial relations with the continent had been developed since late medieval times. From Galway, Waterford, Dublin, and Wexford, supplies went to St Malo, to the Iberian ports of Cadiz, La Coruna, and Bilbao, and various other French ports such as Nantes, Bordeaux, and La Rochelle.[120] In the 1690s the Waterford community was the most active as a port where privateers had relocated after Cromwell took Wexford in 1649.[121] From there, the Comerford and the Lynch families featured often in the exchanges. The Lynchs were merchants of Anglo-Irish origin, operating in France, Spain, and the Indies and were well connected in the Catholic communities of expatriates in Europe. In the Indies they were also involved in politics – a valuable asset for the Aylwards' trade. The collaboration between the Aylwards and the Lynchs would be long, as the Lynchs were experienced, dependable, and extremely audacious, closing good deals in Algiers even when the city was besieged by 50,000 *moores* and 4,000 turks.[122] They became among the most prominent of the Aylwards' associates, financing various deals between England and Spain, and between Cadiz and the Italian ports. Alternatively, the Comerfords had strong ties in La Coruna and as merchants had specialised in the wine and fish trade. In Spain, they were members of the *consulado* and were extremely influential in the mercantile community.[123] From Waterford, the Comerfords supplied the St Malo partners with salted hides, however, the deals were often disappointing.

---

[119] Israel, *The Anglo-Dutch Moment*.

[120] *Irish and Scottish Mercantile Networks in Europe and Overseas in the Seventeenth and Eighteenth Centuries*, ed. David Dickson et al. (Gent: Academia Press, 2006).

[121] Jan Parmentier, 'The Sweets of Commerce: The Hennessys of Ostend and their Network in the Eighteenth Century' in *Irish and Scottish Mercantile Networks in Europe and Overseas in the Seventeenth and Eighteenth Centuries*, ed. David Dickson et al. (Gent: Academia Press, 2006), 70.

[122] AY 20, f. 1, Business Correspondence. Letter from Robert Butler in Malaga on 13 May 1687; AY 20, f. 29, Business Correspondence. Letter from Robert Butler in Cadiz on 25 April 1689; AY 20, f. 17, Business Correspondence. Letter from Robert Butler in Malaga on 8 June 1688; AY 20, f. 16, Business Correspondence. Letter from Robert Butler in Cadiz, 11 May 1688. Robert reports that thirty Spanish *marqueses* and *condes* were going to Oran, and a great many other officers and others were expected from Madrid; Thomas Truxes, *Irish–American Trade, 1660–1783* (Cambridge: Cambridge University Press, 1988).

[123] L. M. Cullen, *Economy, Trade and Irish Merchants at Home and Abroad, 1600–1988* (Dublin: Four Courts Press, 2012), 183.

Their trade was not always profitable and during the years of warfare it was thanks to the Aylwards that the Comerfords retrieved some losses, 'for till now no men could meet harder fortune'.[124] This business of hides was crucial for Comerford and everything was 'hanging like a sword of Damocles' on Aylward's bill of exchange as 'Aylward and God' gave him solace and hope. Other Catholics were involved in the hides exchange partnership, including the Brownes, and the prominent Irish bankers, the Arthurs.[125]

The Arthurs provided what was possibly the best partnership among the co-religionists. They were prominent bankers based in Paris and well acquainted with the Porters and Trublets.[126] The family were extremely well-connected and renowned money lenders, acting as exemplars of how religion was disregarded by governments when money was needed. As prominent French bankers of Irish origin, in times of international warfare they often lent money to the English government, as well as transferring funds to monarchs in Spain and France.[127] The Arthurs had been corresponding with Helena Aylward since the early 1680s and collaborated first with the Porters and then the Aylwards for almost two decades. They were based in Paris and had ties in both France and Spain. With the Aylwards they mainly invested in French linen and Irish goods; from Waterford the deals became highly profitable.[128] Being prominent financiers, they were constantly informed about the exchange rates enabling them to advise the Aylwards on the best markets and investments. During the summer of 1696, they advised them to remit money in London or Exeter in order to avoid losses in change. In London, they said, there could be losses if converting 'bank or goldsmiths notes in ready money' but paying the 'bills in gold or silver would be advantageous'.[129] Previously, Daniel Arthur had suggested that Aylward remit money to England or Holland as crowns were raising to '70 a piece' and he believed it would be profitable to have currency in other countries 'for to have return from them at the rise'.[130]

---

[124] AY 19, f. 2, Business Correspondence. Joseph Comerford was the brother-in-law of the Brownes.

[125] Ibid.

[126] AY 11, f. 61, Business Correspondence. Letters to John and Helena Aylward from Daniel Arthur and Daniel Arthur Jr, in Paris, Oct. 1691– Nov. 1696.

[127] Antoin E. Murphy, *Richard Cantillon: Entrepreneur and Economist* (Oxford: Clarendon Press, 1986), 26–27.

[128] AY 11, Business Correspondence. Letters to John and Helena Aylward from Daniel Arthur and Daniel Arthur Jr, in Paris, Oct. 1691–Nov. 1696.

[129] AY 11, f. 96, Business Correspondence. Letter from Daniel Arthur in Paris in August 1696.

[130] AY 11, f. 78, Business Correspondence. Letter from Daniel Arthur in Puerto Santa Maria in April 1696.

Being part of the most influential circles meant the Arthurs generally knew how political events would unfold and how the war would progress. Indeed, great hopes for peace with the Anglo-Dutch allies were raised when Namur Castle, in present-day Belgium, was besieged by the French in 1692. The 'Spaniards could not spend any more resources to face the French fleet approaching from Toulon,'[131] and so they carefully monitored the events, hoping for the end of the hostilities and turmoil which was hindering their trade of French linens. A peace treaty would re-open the market with Spain and indeed, a few weeks later, the family was informed of defeat of the Spanish in Catalonia, with Daniel Arthur briefing Aylward on how France was assured of a truce with Savoy which joined the Anglo-Dutch forces at the end of 1690.[132] Although related to James II, the Duke of Savoy, Vittorio Amedeo II, supported William III and the League of Augsburg, so as to diminish French encroachment in his territories. The League of Augsburg was possibly the most formidable coalition put in place against Louis XIV in the summer of 1690. The Duke of Savoy played a role in the military coalition and also in the English Succession. His wife, Anna Maria of Savoy was the granddaughter of Charles I of England, having a rightful claim to the throne, should William and Mary die childless. Anna Maria was also the sister of the Queen of Spain Maria Louise d'Orléans – who had died childless, of indigestion, on February 1689, giving the Duke of Savoy rights to succession to both thrones in Spain and England. Therefore, despite being a small dukedom, his position and role were strategic, giving the allies the opportunity to attack France from the south and potentially destabilising the European balance of power. Furthermore, William III hoped for a league of Catholic powers in the south of Europe and the support of Savoy looked timely. It weakened the position of France and would have perhaps pushed other states to follow suit.[133] After following the unfolding of these events, the Arthurs waited and hoped, writing 'we hear a great talk of a general peace' [...] 'the Prince of Orange will be acknowledged King of England.'[134] Unfortunately, they would have to wait a further few years for their wish.

---

[131] Ibid.

[132] AY 11, f. 86, Business Correspondence. Daniel Arthur recorded all the movements of the French fleet and King Louis XIV. His Majesty was in Calais on 21 March 1696, then a week later was in Boulogne, waiting for the fleet from Toulouse.

[133] Oresko, 'The Glorious Revolution of 1688–89 and the House of Savoy', 365–388: Ultimately, the Duke of Savoy's rights to succession (after the exclusion of both James II and his son, and the death of the Spanish queen) would play in his favour as he was made instead King of Sicily in 1713.

[134] AY 11, f. 103, Business Correspondence. Daniel Arthur from Paris, 14 November 1696.

However, although at times necessary, working with Catholic partners was not always particularly profitable for the associates. The Comerfords for instance, were constantly asking for loans and favours for a variety of purposes, from offering help for prisoners, to money to start new businesses during times of hardship. In 1696, John Aylward was asked to rescue one of the Comerfords, who had been wounded and taken prisoner in Waterford, most likely by privateers, and a certificate of French nativity was required for his release.[135] Around the same time, Butler was also imprisoned, although in the letter there was no request for release, just for maintenance; perhaps they reckoned it was better to keep him locked up.[136] In 1696, Joseph Comerford asked for 2,000 crowns to begin an exchange between Waterford and Holland. He could count on new relations and he wanted a fresh start, having lost all his money when his cargo was taken by a privateer in the Channel. The vessel which was meant to go to Dunkirk had been seized even though the Aylwards had procured French passes, and only Joseph and one crewman managed to escape and save the goods.[137] The Aylwards did not rule out working with co-religionists involved in the same exchanges in continental Europe and the West Indies, but deals with them were not so lucrative and the Aylwards seem to have mainly provided a network of support for them, rather than closing successful deals together.

From 1687 to 1698, the Catholic merchants in France showed their ability to resort to a diverse range of tactics and tap into a variety of different networks. Family members in Cadiz monitored the Spanish market, which was still of primary importance; Catholics in France helped supply the goods in demand, and Protestants proved crucial for coordinating smuggling operations in English waters. Religious contacts proved advantageous for procuring commodities but the ability to adapt and to deal with various partners ensured the survival of the business. As soon as the war erupted, the Aylwards and their Catholic associates sought the best strategies with their Protestant partners. As in the previous decade, their mercantile behaviour proved perfectly standard and it is possible that the Aylwards were forced into commerce because their status as members of a religious minority excluded them from public office. That said, their activities extended beyond their own community and from the 1690s onwards

---

[135] AY 11, f. 101, Business Correspondence. Letter from Patrick Comerford to John Aylward, from Waterford in 1696.

[136] AY 109, Business Accounts. The State of Robert Butler business on 6 March 1695.

[137] AY 9, f. 5, Business Correspondence. Letter from Joseph Comerford in Dunkirk, 30 April 1696.

and even more so later they proved that even Catholics could be successful entrepreneurs as influenced by the Spirit of Capitalism.[138]

In those years, the great alterations in trade inevitably affected the Aylwards; however, more than anything, they offered an opportunity to sever unreliable contacts: 'a knife that cuts not, *poco importa que se perda*', affirmed one agent in a letter.[139] Indeed, John Aylward greatly reduced the role of his family in the business, leaving them mainly to serve as wholesalers. He also decreased contacts with co-religionists, instead focusing on partnerships with skilled merchants chosen without regard for any religious or national affiliation. These associations sometimes lasted for more than a decade, clearly suggesting that Aylward relied on their reputation and abilities or that he simply just got along with them.[140] Before leaving St Malo, the Aylwards intensified their partnership with Paul Den, the agent blamed by Butler for living 'great and high' in Malaga. Den was possibly introduced by the Wyses, as the Brookings – the Wyses' in-laws – had known him since at least 1684.[141] Paul Den formed part of the merchant house of Power & Hill and was mainly based in Spain, unfortunately sharing accommodation with Butler and Porter. In fact, he was an answer to the unreliability of family members and would soon be chosen to supervise the Spanish deals instead of them. In 1688, Den found himself in partnership with the Butlers but, possibly after falling out over the bedding, would later correspond directly with the Aylwards. In the early 1690s, their correspondence was brief; however, what the Aylwards could not foresee was that in a few years this relationship would prove crucial to business. Paul Den was extremely skilled and during the War of the Spanish Succession, contributed to the survival of the Aylwards' business. The next chapter, by looking at Catholic merchants' undisturbed movements between Spain and Portugal and the British Isles, will shed light on their strategies during the War of the Spanish Succession when French and Spanish goods were smuggled to England through Portugal. Their cunning at this time would know no bounds and demonstrate their ability to regard religious and national contacts as assets to be used as opportunities in the marketplace.

---

[138] Gianfranco Poggi, *Calvinism and the Capitalist Spirit: Max Weber's Protestant Ethic* (London: Macmillan Press, 1983).

[139] AY 8, f. 13, Business Correspondence. Miscellaneous letters to John Aylward, Jan.– May 1693.

[140] Sheryllynne Haggerty, *The British-Atlantic Trading Community, 1760–1810, Men, Women, and the Distribution of Goods* (Leiden: Boydell Press, 2006), 135.

[141] AY 101, Business Accounts. Bills, accounts, receipts for merchandise to Dec. 1687; AY 3, f. 16, Business Correspondence. Miscellaneous letters to John Aylward, Jan– Oct. 1684.

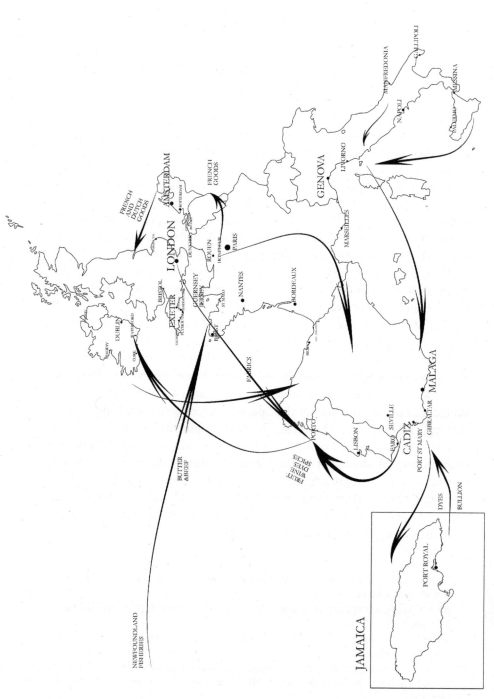

3: British Catholic Merchants' trading strategies before and during the first years of the War of the Spanish Succession, 1698–1705

Chapter 4

British Catholic Merchants in London and their Trading Strategies before and during the First Years of the War of the Spanish Succession, 1698–1705

The plan is layd by others, I know not why you may not do it as well.[1]

Early eighteenth-century London was the place to be for doing business. With its busy counting-houses, hectic docks, and bustling streets it had become one of the largest cities in Europe, where the majority of the British population lived and thrived.[2] The city and the opportunities it had to offer attracted people – especially tradesmen – from all over the world, and merchants were drawn to the lure of high profits and the chance to be a crucial part of the Atlantic trade. At this time, almost all commodities being traded around the world touched the city. From there they were either re-exported or distributed in the internal market meaning that on the streets of London it was possible to find all sorts of goods, from West Indian products to Persian silks. Moreover, the city was becoming the financial heart of Europe with its legal institutions offering the best trading opportunities. It was a thriving environment in which to develop commercial skills and professional training and, most of all, to tap into widely established networks.[3] In

---

[1] AY 30, f. 62, Business Correspondence. Letters to John Aylward from Paul Den at Malaga, 1703.

[2] E. A. Wrigley, 'British Population during the Long Eighteenth Century, 1680–1840' in *The Cambridge Economic History of Modern Britain: Industrialisation 1700–1860*, vol. I, ed. R. Floud and P. Johnson (Cambridge: Cambridge University Press, 2008), 57–95. In 1680, the population of Britain was of roughly 6.5 million people; Gauci, *Emporium of the World: The Merchants of London, 1660–1800* (London: Bloomsbury, 2007).

[3] David Hancock, *Citizens of the World: London Merchants and the Integration of the British Atlantic Community, 1735–1785* (Cambridge: Cambridge University Press, 1995), 85–88.

London at this time, and among the mercantile community especially, the Catholic presence was significant. The Aylward Papers have helped shed light on a varied group of Anglo-Irish merchants who were associated with merchant-houses operating in West Indian and European markets at this time. This was a community bound by ties of marriage and ethnicity, and whose trading networks connected them with the wider mercantile world.[4]

In this decade the British Catholics of London began working with many firms, not only those run by Catholics, having no religious discrimination in business. Indeed, the Aylwards' correspondence shows evidence of constant collaboration between these Catholic dynasties and prominent non-Catholics, including, among many others, the Londoner Charles Peers. Inter-faith relations were now common among the upper echelons of commerce and finance. For instance, as previously discussed, a man who financed many of the Aylwards' deals, Daniel Arthur, was a prominent banker and the first Catholic in the Directory of the London merchants in 1677. Daniel Arthur was from a family of famous money-lenders which signed loans to various European governments, including the British. The family's legacy was later received by Richard Cantillon, a Franco-Irish financier close to the French and British courts, and one of the minds behind the South Sea Bubble.[5] Other prominent names which featured many times in the Aylwards' accounts from the City are the Fitzgeralds, the Frenches, the Lynchs, the Blakes, and the Brownes – all Anglo-Irish and English families with extensive interests in the West Indies and in continental Europe and whose firms operated well into the 1750s.[6] Each of these families figured prominently in eighteenth-century mercantile literature. They were part of the network of Irish, Scottish, and English exiles who had settled in every port across Europe and retained important positions in both British commerce and Jacobite activism.

---

[4]   John Bergin, 'Irish Catholics and their Networks in Eighteenth-Century London', *Eighteenth-Century Life*, 39, 1 (2015): 66–102. Thomas Truxes, *Irish–American Trade, 1660–1783* (Cambridge: Cambridge University Press, 1988), 84; Craig Bailey, *Irish London: Middle-Class Migration in the Global Eighteenth Century* (Liverpool: Liverpool University Press, 2013). L. M. Cullen, 'The Two Fitzgeralds of London, 1718–1759' in *Irish and Scottish Mercantile Networks in Europe and Overseas in the Seventeenth and Eighteenth Centuries*, ed. David Dickson et al. (Gent: Academia Press, 2006), 251–270.

[5]   A. E. Murphy, *Richard Cantillon: Entrepreneur and Economist* (Oxford: Clarendon Press, 1986); Paul Monod, 'Dangerous Merchandise: Smuggling, Jacobitism, and Commercial Culture in Southeast England, 1690–1760', *The Journal of British Studies*, 30 (1991). Cantillon was a banker in London and a wine merchant in Paris.

[6]   Monod, 'Dangerous Merchandise'.

John and Helena Aylward moved to London in 1698, partly because the city was their family's home, but largely because of its commercial possibilities. Indeed, from London, it was possible to access England's fledgling imperial trade markets, and at the same time to supervise the exchanges from the continent. Spain, France, and Portugal allowed them to continue working with the Spanish Americas. Portugal in fact was Britain's ally in the War of the Spanish Succession, and the place from which Catholics could smuggle in French and Spanish colonial goods. During the war, Portugal secured the continuity and survival of the European trade, and involvement in its ports was crucial for any trader hoping to close profitable exchanges.[7] European merchants swarmed into Faro and Lisbon to buy English goods, while English merchants instead loaded their ships with French and Spanish products. From 1706 to 1710 English goods 'flooded' into Portugal[8] and British Catholics were able to secure partnerships in those hectic ports. Their aim was to keep their commerce going. During the 1680s and 1690s, in the business accounts of the Aylwards, Portugal played a marginal role. However, from the early 1700s, the London Catholics were mentioning partners in Faro and Lisbon, from where they exchanged their products for various European goods, in particular French and Spanish items. From Lisbon, the Catholics' wines, fruit, and dyes were all smuggled into England.

In the previous decades the Aylwards' associates had already been engaged in dubious activities but it was in these times that they would resort to the most diverse strategies in order to trade. For more than twenty years the London Catholics had moved between various European countries with

---

[7]   A. D. Francis, 'John Methuen and the Anglo-Portuguese Treaties of 1703', *The Historical Journal*, 3 (1960): 103–124: The Anglo-Portuguese treaty of Methuen was signed on 27 December 1703. It stated that English woollen cloths should be freely admitted to Portugal and that England would accept wine produced in the Portuguese dominions. On 16 May 1703, Portugal joined the Grand Alliance, supporting Austria, England, and the Netherlands. The alliance with Portugal proved important for fighting Spain, although the role of Portugal was mainly economic, assuring the survival of European trade in times of warfare. When the war erupted, Portuguese ports became hectic; H. E. S. Fisher, *The Portugal Trade: A Study of Anglo-Portuguese Commerce 1700– 1770* (London: Methuen & Co., 1971), 13–40. Export surplus rose from £155,000 in 1698–1702 to £413,000 in 1706–10. Export of Portuguese wines increased after 1689 and boomed during the War of the Spanish Succession when duties on Spanish and French wines were extremely high. In 1729, the value of exports from England was above any other European countries. Ibid., 128: in 1706, 10 per cent of all the exports of English long cloths were to Portugal.

[8]   AY 10, f. 18, Business Correspondence. Miscellaneous letters to John Aylward, Jan. 1700–Dec. 1703; Fisher, *The Portugal Trade*, 15, 128: shipments of *Perpetuanas* and *Serges* average £109,000 per annum. Between 1706 and 1710, the export of English cloths was worth around £58,000 per annum, about 27 per cent of the total exports.

the ultimate aim of supplying the transatlantic vessels in Cadiz. During the war at this time, they aimed to continue the same exchanges, investing even more resources into smuggling to meet their aim. Recent historiography has interpreted British Catholic smuggling as Jacobite activism, aimed at yet another Stuart Restoration.[9] Catholic merchants were reportedly introducing goods from the south-eastern English ports. With these were 'political agents and seditious information' from France, supported and protected by the Catholic gentry in land. On the other side of the Channel, this activity was supported by the vast network of Jacobite expatriates who believed in a return of James II and who always mixed politics with trade.[10] Although this link between religion and politics is undeniable, the Aylwards and their associates defied Catholic stereotypes. Indeed, although renowned Jacobite smugglers, such as the Brownes and the Fitzgeralds, appeared in their papers, neither the Aylwards nor their associates ever hinted at any political commitment. They were aware that politics could greatly affect commerce and, like all other merchants, simply discussed political issues as they needed up-to-date information before planning their exchanges.

When based in London, the Aylwards were suspected of Jacobitism due to their Catholicism; however, their friends at the time testified that during the Glorious Revolution from 1688 to 1689 the pair were in France and were never in the service of King James II.[11] It is clear from the Aylward Papers that the merchants constantly briefed each other about political events; particularly following James II's accession, the Monmouth Rebellion, and later the Spanish Succession. However, besides hoping for the defeat of the Protestant rivals and the success of the Catholic kings, there was never mention of support for the Jacobite cause and the unfolding of politics was followed only for the sake of trade. In actuality, in Britain, Catholic merchants were at times reluctant to join in the cause as a civil war would have created great instability, damaging internal trade and credit networks.[12] Furthermore, a new Stuart dynasty would have furthered French interests as a means of payback for the support received in France – another reason why merchants were never keen to support Jacobite sedition.[13] Between French and English ports, smuggling activities of the Catholic merchants

---

[9]   Monod, 'Dangerous Merchandise'.
[10] Ibid., 169.
[11] Julian Walton, *The Irish Genealogist*, 5 (1974): 216.
[12] Linda Colley, *Britons: Forging the Nation 1707–1837* (New Haven: Yale University Press, 1992), 79.
[13] Ibid.

increased during the war but this rise was primarily driven by profits, with religion remaining a very private matter.[14]

From London, the Aylwards corresponded with only the most reputable firms, such as Power & Hill, Woulfe & Trublet, Aldrington & Bowles, and Gardiner & Geraldin. In doing so through their associates in Spain and France, they were able to carefully select the best agents with whom they audaciously exchanged illegal goods, often resorting to fictitious identities and neutral vessels. Like any other smugglers they did not resist the temptation of disposing of in-demand goods (despite the prohibitions, although perhaps, with the turmoil of the Spanish conflict, their chances of being detected at this time were greatly reduced).[15] Moreover, British trade needed south European provisions that the internal market was not able to supply or produce at all. Britain was particularly fond of the Spanish market which they deemed 'solid and sure' and of the colonial goods accessed through Cadiz.[16] The traders' aim was to maximise exports by shipping off fabrics, tin, lead, skins of oxes, 'glue and bees wax', and to import raw materials, provisions, and silver.[17] Beyond profit and mercantilist policies, mere survival was at stake; halting trading would mean no source of income for entire families. This meant that during wartime, Catholics went to any length to work. Their ability to succeed in those times proved remarkable and shows the fundamental role played by the British Catholics in supporting their Protestant partners and furthering Britain's commercial interests.

Trade between Two European Wars

By 1698 the Catholic associates involved in the London trade had been in business for almost thirty years, always moving between various continental ports. They were established merchants with a great deal of experience, resources, and contacts. They knew how to trade and were well aware that their religious communities and outstanding skills had enabled them to thrive during the relative peaceful decade of the 1680s, as well as during the

---

[14] R. C. Nash, 'The English and Scottish Tobacco Trades in the Seventeenth and Eighteenth Centuries: Legal and Illegal Trade', *The Economic History Review*, 35 (1982): 361. This work challenges the theory that smuggling diminished in times of warfare.

[15] T. C. Barker, 'Smuggling in the Eighteenth Century: The Evidence of the Scottish Tobacco Trade', *The Virginia Magazine of History and Biography*, 62 (1954): 387–399.

[16] AY 31, f. 5, Business Correspondence. Letters to John Aylward from Robert Dermot at Brest and Rouen, July 1696–June 1699.

[17] AY 35, Business Correspondence. Letters to John Aylward from Benjamin England at Yarmouth, Sept.–Dec.1699.

Nine Years War. Indeed, for the Catholic traders, with experience came the ability to recognise the most reliable partners. In London, they were able to single out the best men from communities not just their own. They knew the best goods in which to invest and the best strategies to adopt. In fact, all the tactics previously learnt and tested were improved in these years. This time saw the culmination of the Aylwards' associates' careers and served to prove that the Catholics cannot be overlooked in the story of the expansion of British trade. It is true that in the previous decades religious contacts had been at times important in securing a foothold in the Anglo-Spanish trade, but in this period they became fundamental for international exchanges as Catholics were often allowed access to countries in which British merchants were not permitted.

The circle of associates working with the Aylwards were aware that such successful strategies resulted in not only profit and the continuity of their profession, but also their own survival, since the threat of political turmoil affected every aspect of the trading process. Any conflict would bring about immediate effects on their trade including delays in correspondence and shortages of supplies. Even if a merchant was able to acquire goods under such circumstances, his cargo could be seized or vessels wrecked leaving him to survive the perils of open sea. Even if he were lucky enough to escape such a fate and make a safe landing, the duties on imported merchandise could be extortionate. The first policy in warfare was always to raise import tariffs, so as to directly affect a political rival. The result, however, was that high duties tempted the merchants towards contraband where, although operating costs could be high, so could profits.[18] Greater costs came as a result of many things, in part because any illegal merchandise would be shipped on smaller vessels, reducing the net margins. Facing high risks, the crew would also demand higher wages pushing costs even higher, and illegal merchandise had to then be covertly moved from the landing port in any given country, to its main centres of distribution.[19] On top of the

---

[18]   Due to the nature of the business, it is challenging to provide exact figures. However, Hillman and Gathmann have calculated that the British Admiralty issued 25,000 letters of marque between 1689 and 1815 and British privateers and smugglers accounted for an average of 23 per cent of all ships during periods of war, in H. Hillman and C. Gathmann, 'Overseas Trade and the Decline of Privateering', *The Journal of Economic History*, 71, 3 (2011). During the war, Dunkirk only realised a gross sales value of at least £1,666,000 in privateering and smuggling, in David Starkey, *British Privateering Enterprise in the Eighteenth Century* (Exeter: Exeter University Press, 1990), 85–110.

[19]   Barker, 'Smuggling in the Eighteenth Century', 387–8; L. M. Cullen, 'The Smuggling Trade in Ireland in the Eighteenth Century', *Proceedings of the Royal Irish*

financial implications were the greatest risks of all as merchants dealing in contraband, could be imprisoned or killed. And while the commercial agents or seamen were more exposed to a variety of risks on the journey of goods, failure of an exchange could mean bankruptcy for the merchant and shame for his family. With a lot more than business at stake co-operation became vital and relying on trustworthy partners was what shaped such successful careers for the Aylwards' associates; a mixture of exceptional managerial skills, and fortunate circumstances.

As discussed in previous chapters, the Aylwards and their associates dealt with religious contacts to their advantage and the Protestant others worked with them, profiting from their ability to move undisturbed in the continental ports. During the Nine Years War, only French goods were illegal, but from 1701 Spanish products were also being banned by the English government. Therefore, the British Catholics needed to devise grand strategies to work around their limitations. In actuality, their tactics were simple. They knew Portugal was the only gateway to England and that all goods must be diverted there. To this end, they first moved French goods to Spain. Then, French commodities would join the Spanish and other south-Mediterranean provisions coming from Livorno and Genoa. Finally, all the merchandise would be moved to Portugal where non-Catholic partners would ship them to England. The process was basic, but a vast amount of capital, men, and resources were involved. The goods were shipped on vessels from Hamburg, Scandinavia or England; Hamburg's role in the Spanish war was always ambivalent. Although siding with the allies, the local authorities never enforced the prohibition on trade with the enemy. In actuality, Hamburg was constantly trading with France and Spain[20] and by using fictional names, the London Catholics and their partners fraudulently covered the shipments and signed the correspondence. Vast networks of co-religionists, relatives, and non-Catholic partners ensured the transactions, and inter-faith relations among merchants were essential. Only the best and tested contacts were selected from the various markets, but the Catholic community was the key, providing a competitive edge in accessing Catholic countries. The merchants involved, both Protestant and Catholic, were well aware of the advantage and the reasons for which they relied on each other.

Academy. Section C: Archaeology, Celtic Studies, History, Linguistics, Literature, 67 (1968/1969): 151.

[20] J. S. Bromley, 'The North Sea in Wartime' in *Corsairs and Navies, 1660–1760* (London: Hambledon Press, 1987), 53.

In the British Isles and in Spain, Catholics and Protestants partnered up frequently; it is only in France that the British Catholics seem to have exchanged letters mainly with their fellow co-religionists and kinsmen – notably those in Rouen, St Malo, Bordeaux, and Paris. What it is certain is that they selected and treasured only the best commercial ties. In fact, during these years correspondence was exchanged with a few partners including Paul Den, Julien Grant, and the firm Woulfe & Trublet. The Woulfe & Trublet house was created in Cadiz by the French Trublet de la Herse, first husband of Mrs Helena Aylward,[21] and carried on by their son Michael Trublet. It had ties with all the major European countries – contacts which proved crucial. During the war, by disregarding religion and nationality, and by 'acting merely for money', this vast network assured the endurance of British trade.[22]

Woulfe & Trublet specialised in manufacturing products such as buttons, linens, and rabbit wool, but at times also recorded in their accounts salted Irish beef and candles – both deemed a 'perfect drug' in the Spanish market.[23] The firm was based in Cadiz where it supervised the London Catholics' business. The partners associated with Power & Hill were also acquainted with Woulfe & Trublet and both houses supervised the exchanges of the same circle of merchants, in particular Paul Den, the Comerfords, the Creaghs, and the Arthurs. These associates had all worked together well since the 1680s, and despite relying largely on a few trusted partners, in Spain they resorted also to family, that could move freely in the Spanish and French ports. However, for the most part, this circle of 'honest though foulish' [sic] brothers-in-law, cousins, and nephews proved not fit for the job by causing troubles or squandering money, 'living high and spending a Louis d'Or a day'. It was often that such relatives were instead used as factors and in the warehouse.[24] The London merchants would discuss the exchanges with their firms or other partners, only notifying the family when the decision was taken. Over the years, the London associates certainly noticed poor commercial skills among their families and that dealing with them was not the best or most profitable strategy. More than once relatives showed their ineptitude, notably the time when

---

[21]   AY 54, f. 1, Business Correspondence. Letters to John Aylward from Nicholas Kehoe at Puerto de Santa Maria, Mar. 1701–Mar. 1702. Trublet was known to be a 'fine and modest man'.

[22]   Ibid.

[23]   CO 110–152, Brailsford Papers, Letters to John Aylward from Thomas Brailsford and the Halls, 1688–1690.

[24]   AY 31, f. 10, Business Correspondence. AY 10, f. 21, Business Correspondence. Miscellaneous letters to John Aylward, Jan. 1700–Dec. 1703.

Paul Aylward, cousin of John Aylward, mismanaged a business of iron chests because he could not 'readily recollect his memory' or remember the exchange. He pleaded for John to reflect on other agents' management, asking how 'many hands it [the iron] was to pass before [it] came to yours'. A privateer might have been responsible for the loss or a 'hundred other accidents' that made him blameless.[25] All Paul blamed was his bad luck, the state of life in which God 'hath been pleased to put him', but also John for extending his 'bounty [...] to strangers and all sorts of people' but for not supporting him, his cousin, his 'poor distressed relation'.[26] However, other associates complained about the management abilities of John Aylward's relatives and the way they sometimes left goods in the custom house 'without supervision'.[27] It is not surprising that the London associates more often relied on non-kinsmen or non-co-religionists to help them expand in the trading markets, extending their 'bounty to strangers and all sorts of people' rather than their untrustworthy families.

Indeed, it was with such 'strangers' that the British Catholics worked in the Atlantic and Mediterranean markets. Their interests touched ports in Spain, France, Italy, and the Netherlands and ultimately they always supplied the transatlantic vessels in Cadiz before returning the colonial goods to London. In the late 1690s, the London Catholics had many contacts with the French ports, where goods were bought and shipped off to Spain. In the summer of 1699, ships from St Malo unloaded textiles in Port St Mary and the most profitable sales were during the provisioning of the *flota*.[28] For the majority of traders in Cadiz spring was the time for buying when it was time to supply the fleets, and it was during the summer that goods were sold and the vessels would return from the Americas. French textiles were always highly requested, especially over the summer, but good *Sempiternas* cloth also came from Exeter. In the Spanish docks, the London associates could easily rely on firms of co-religionists such as Geraldin &

---

[25] AY 15, f. 1 Business Correspondence. Three letters to John Aylward from Paul Aylward at Cadiz, one with a note from Richard Hore, Apr. 1699–Mar. 1700.

[26] Ibid., AY 15, f. 3, f. 2. Business Correspondence. Aylward could not complain about the state of life in which 'God hath been pleased' to put Paul Aylward. Paul pleaded for his cousin to trust and understand him, because he continually struggled against the 'stream of poverty', having to provide for a weak father and '2 or 3 distressed sisters' whose fortune or ruin were linked to his. Paul was impatient for Aylward's resentment to have 'blown over' and he hoped for help, and a reconciliation.

[27] AY 93, f. 31, Business Correspondence. Letter from Patrick Woulfe in Puerto Santa Maria, on 19 January 1699. Goods, if mismanaged, could easily deteriorate. Indeed, lemons were a good commodity, but they had to be fresh.

[28] AY 93, f. 30, Business Correspondence. Letters to John Aylward from Woulfe and Trublet at Puerto de Santa Maria, on 8 June 1699.

Gardiner but also on other merchants settled in Malaga.[29] This circle of firms, which included in their network Woulfe & Trublet, was known for planning and securing the best deals. In 1699, they coordinated exchanges between France, Spain, and England on French *bottoms*, and consigned the merchandise to French partners so as to avoid the charges pressed upon 'strangers' (the English) by the French consul in Spain. During the spring, as the *flota* was about to sail, they sent pewter buttons, pins, and wines and used discretion in shipping over the English *kentins* they had in St Malo.[30] Always in French ports, particularly St Malo and Marseilles, the London associates relied on family and local merchants to supply fish coming from the French imperial possessions. These inter-imperial exchanges were facilitated by privateers in the Channel, including the White family, cousins of the Aylwards, who operated in those waters for years. Around this time North Atlantic cod would usually reach the south of Europe, finding the best market in Spain.

Trade exchanges between the British Isles and Spain were not smooth even in the years of relative peace between the two European conflicts. Privateers loomed just off the continental coasts and, in 1698, a shipment of Aylward's cargo sailing towards Cadiz was taken off San Sebastian. The Aylwards were informed that, the 'Lower court [of Admiralty] has set it [the vessel] free' but 'the Higher Court had not agreed yet', because of an appeal of the privateer that had seized it.[31] In Britain, the role of the High Court of Admiralty was to judge the vessels as fair prizes, checking whether the rights of legal and allied ships had been respected. If proven to in fact be legal prizes, the content could be distributed among the crew and owner of the privateer so it was highly possible all would be lost. In this instance, however, the Aylwards' linens were detained in Portugal, a country where they could sell better than in their intended destination because of the glut of linens in the Spanish ports. Moreover, the Aylwards were informed that it was safer not to work in Spain, although they had provided the right certificates and resorted to the help of French merchants.[32] Indeed, Spanish authorities required all merchants to prove the ownership of their goods,

---

[29]   AY 93, f. 32, Business Correspondence. Letter from Patrick Woulfe in Puerto Santa Maria on 2 February 1699.

[30]   AY 93, f. 34, Business Correspondence. Letter from Patrick Woulfe in Puerto Santa Maria on 2 March 1699; AY 35, f. 36, Business Correspondence. Letters to John Aylward from Benjamin England at Yarmouth, Sept.–Dec.1699.

[31]   H. Hillman and C. Gathmann, 'Overseas Trade and the Decline of Privateering', 734.

[32]   AY 83, f. 2, Business Correspondence. Letters to John Aylward from Willoughby Swift at Lisbon, Mar. 1697–Sept. 1698. In the same bundle of letters (April 1698), Willoughby complains about the high custom duties, and briefs Aylward about the

especially if there were more than two names on the packages, in order to prevent the English from trading in and out of their ports. But such prohibitionist policies or seizures by privateers did not stop Woulfe's firm and the Aylwards from carrying on their dealings. Indeed, from London, they shipped back manufactured goods, making sure the destination was concealed. From France they shipped lemons, oranges, and textiles provided by partners affiliated with Power & Hill. Fruit was also sent to London by using privateers across the Channel.

In all these exchanges, the Aylwards wanted to be sure that their British products would reach the transatlantic vessels, always expecting the departure of the galleons 'to put some life in trade' as the Spanish market could get extremely glutted in particular with fruit that came from France as well as from other South European countries.[33] In fact, it was not uncommon that packs of fruit would be kept all summer and by then they would not only 'be eaten'(by rats), but 'they were also full of dust' (covered in mould).[34] Some partners 'rubbed and sold them', although they could not manage to sell it all. Unlike fruit, the fabrics, in particular English *kentins* and 'Irish bays', were always successful, although, while they did not deteriorate, they were subject to changes in fashion.[35] Problems with the merchandise were frequent and not all exchanges proved profitable. Frequently the partners pledged that they had complied with their obligations towards 'both God and man', but 'accidents are what attend all men of commerce even the most cautious'.[36] In one of the accounts the associates Martin & Gardiner wrote about the disappointing sale of English *Jenkins* in Spain and noted quite sharply that it was easy for the Aylwards 'in prosperity, to condemn who is in adversity', but they warned them that when 'the tryalls comes on themselves they sing another song'.[37]

Of course, as was common in the commercial age, trade was not always a success. At times Catholics had to trade 'slow and leisurely' and would

---

goods that could sell well: mainly linens from Hamburg, which could yield well before the galleons arrived.

[33] AY 93, f. 38, Business Correspondence. Letter from Patrick Woulfe in Puerto Santa Maria on 8 April 1699. One of the partners, Benjamin England, wrote that in Yarmouth the market was extremely glutted and 'no money was stirring'.

[34] AY 93, f. 37, f. 36, Business Correspondence. Patrick Woulfe writing from Puerto Santa Maria on 16 and 30 March 1699.

[35] Ibid.

[36] AY 10, Business Correspondence. Miscellaneous Letters to John Aylward, Jan. 1700–Dec. 1703. The partners writing were Edward Gardiner and Thomas Martin.

[37] Ibid.

meet with 'cheap bargains'.[38] One answer was to diversify their business with investments in the stock market so as to mitigate potential losses. Knowing that the slightest negligence could have had tremendous consequences, they went a step further and secured their capital differently by also investing in government companies. In the early 1700s, British Catholics began subscribing bonds and prominent families including the Whites and the Aylwards invested bills of '500 pieces of eight' on the 'governor and committee of the East India Company'.[39] Many Jacobites in exile also speculated in various companies such as the Mississippi or the Ostend East India Trade.[40] Investing was as much of a gamble as trading but gains had potential to be high and some of the associates subscribed also to the South Sea Company during the last year of the war in 1713.[41] Nearing the end of the conflict the bond prices were relatively low and profits could be high once peace was established. Investing in the stock market became common practice among merchants of the time which further strengthens the argument that Catholics had a role in the British economy. Theirs was the time of the financial revolution, a time that saw the establishment of the Bank of England and the flourishing of private banking, insurance companies, and brokerage firms. Buying up shares in companies became fairly common among traders,[42] and as Catholics were not banned from government companies, they supported the new fiscal-military state. The fledgling British government needed funds and was not precious about the identity of its moneylenders.

Perhaps it was because of these extensive interests that British Catholics became acute observers of the political landscape. In correspondence between Spain and London in 1700 it was often reported that since the King of Spain was sick, 'the Hollanders, the emperor and the crowne may quarrel with the kingdom', fearing that a war might soon erupt.[43] They decided to carry on with their exchanges, but the uncertain political situation concerned them, particularly when it was time to unload the West

---

[38]   AY 87, Business Correspondence. Letters to John Aylward from Francis White at St Malo, July 1698– Jan. 1701.

[39]   AY 54, f. 6, Business Correspondence. Letter from Charles Horde. One of the agents involved in these financial transactions was the Irishman Nicholas Kehoe.

[40]   Monod, 'Dangerous Merchandise', 172–173.

[41]   P. G. M. Dickson, *The Financial Revolution in England: A Study in the Development of Public Credit, 1688–1756* (London: Macmillan, 1967).

[42]   Perry Gauci, *The Politics of Trade: The Overseas Merchant in State and Society, 1660–1720* (Oxford: Oxford University Press, 2010).

[43]   Ibid.; AY 28, Business Correspondence. Letters to John Aylward from David and Widow Creagh at Amsterdam, Jan. 1696– Dec. 1703.

Indian flotilla and sell the goods in Cadiz. Everyone was in great distress fearing imminent conflict, which would bring the direct consequences of disruptions in communications and the new commercial policies. On 23 November 1700, one of these letters reported that the death of the King of Spain had caused 'no alteration in public affairs', and they hoped everything would remain peaceful. Merchants could not have predicted how soon a decade of warfare would erupt. In that year, Louis XIV and William III attempted to come to a compromise with an agreement on the crucial issue of succession. Although the new King Philip V was 'greeted warmly' by the Spanish,[44] dynastic claims were raised by the French Bourbons and the Austrian Habsburgs, leaving England and France to find a balance between natural rights and economic interests.[45]

Political upheaval could well have been detrimental for the social and economic life of an early modern merchant, as well as for his own personal safety. In fact, in 1700, the Aylwards' nephew, Francis White, was forced to move from his home in Malaga to St Malo from fear of persecution against British traders.[46] The same worry concerned Nicholas Kehoe, an Irishman of the house of Woulfe & Trublet who, on March 1701, briefed the Aylwards about the expatriates' situation in the south of Spain. War was imminent, and all the foreigners feared expulsion. They hoped the new King of Spain would be as lenient as his predecessors in extending the same privileges to Catholics, especially because they could count on the support of 'the Archbishop of Seville, some cardinals and the French ambassadors'. Fortunately, the new King Philip V showed leniency and granted foreign Catholic merchants all privileges 'they could wish, to work and live in Cadiz without any restriction'. In one of the letters, Nicholas Aylward commented that everyone was extremely happy: 'nothing shall hinder from making up all the new and old accounts'.[47] As Catholics, they were confident of the old liberties being assured and being able to continue to work. It was believed, however, that since the war would soon break out, foreigners, especially

---

[44] AY 93, f. 75, Business Correspondence. Woulfe briefed Aylward that the Duke of Anjou was proclaimed king in Madrid, on 6 December 1700. Then on 20 December Philip V was greeted in Cadiz.

[45] Black, *European International Relations, 1648–1815* (New York: Palgrave), 2002, pp. 100–101.

[46] AY 87, Business Correspondence. Letters to John Aylward from Francis White at St Malo, July 1698– Jan. 1701.

[47] AY 94, Business Correspondence. Letters to John Aylward from Woulfe and Trublet, written mainly from Puerto de Santa Maria but a few from Cadiz and Xeres. From July 1702, letters were signed mainly from Symon Michel and from May 1703 by Peter Willson. When Patrick Woulfe received the letter he replied that for the time being he would keep his books hidden.

the British, would be at risk of retaliation. A succession of associates began to go to Madrid to receive naturalisation to help them feel secure. As a safety measure, all of the British merchant houses had hidden their account books, fearing possible raids by the Spanish authorities.[48] During the first months of escalations there was confusion on how best to act, but the Cadiz community showed solidarity and British traders continued to operate there seemingly undisturbed.

Trade during the War of the Spanish Succession

> there is so much rigour even though war has not been declared, can you imagine what will happen when it is declared?[49]

In the summer of 1701, after the death of the childless Carlos II in Spain, rumours of the hostilities between the Spanish Crown and England began to spread. In 1701, Catholic merchants were certain that a new conflict would erupt on a huge scale after hearing of the alliance between 'England, Holland and Brandenburg'. The scene facing them was dire and their advice to the Catholics in London was to be 'speedy in the answer'.[50] In Spain, the merchants were aware that there were concerns over the European balance of power among the English and the Dutch, who would have never accepted a powerful French dynasty ruling over the vast Spanish empire. The tone of their correspondence changed. The London Catholic traders worried not only for their businesses but their safety. They became extremely cautious, wondering at times if 'it was better [to] wait for another occasion'.[51] However, it was clear that British trade could not stop and their resolution was instead to deploy more targeted strategies and to use their communal contacts to their advantage. During these years the London associates mainly worked with non-Catholic partners in Portugal, and with family and co-religionists in Spain and France. The agents based in

---

[48] AY 54, f. 1, Business Correspondence. In March 1701, from Cadiz, Nicholas Kehoe briefed Aylward in London.

[49] AY 30, f. 38, Business Correspondence. Paul Den from Cadiz, on 13 May 1702.

[50] AY 28, f. 64, Business Correspondence. Letters to John Aylward from David and Widow Creagh at Amsterdam, Jan. 1696–Dec. 1703, John Aylward's first partner was Edward Creagh, but after his death in 1697, the partnership was maintained by David Creagh and Edward's widow.

[51] AY 30, f. 15, Business Correspondence. The new King came to Spain, and on 8 February 1701 he would have been at court, therefore the relations with the French ambassadors became more frequent.

Portugal proved fundamental in suggesting strategies and choosing factors. From Portuguese ports they could monitor the arrival of the English ships while Catholic relations and family in the north of France and in the south of Spain supplied the commodities. In those years, the hundreds of tonnes of goods mentioned in the letters which returned to London from Portugal suggest that British trade was not disrupted and continued successfully. British fabrics, beef, butter, and fish continued to be exchanged for French wines, Spanish fruit, and south Mediterranean olive oil, wheat, and silks. The main concern at this time was instead how to import the goods to the English ports, avoiding all the privateers off the Atlantic–European coasts. British tradesmen needed south European provisions in order to balance their books, and thanks to the strength of the British Catholics it seemed as if they had a way to provide them. To carry out such operations the traders resorted to a host of tactics, including signing letters with pseudonyms, sending them under cover of trusted friends via France, Portugal, or the Netherlands, and shipping off the goods on neutral fishing vessels. The aim was simple: to keep profiting from the Spanish–American trade through the harbour of Cadiz, where British fabrics, beef, butter, and various wares would all ultimately be shipped. Judging from long accounts from the time the gains were significant, even at a time in which everyone complained 'no money was stirring'.[52]

In these first years of turmoil, the Catholics in London resorted to various partners in Portugal and to men who never professed their Catholicism. The most prominent of these were Julien Grant and Paul Den, associates of the firms Woulfe & Trublet and Aldrington & Bowles. The pair constantly moved around the Iberian commercial cities of Antequera, Port St Mary, Malaga, Cadiz, Faro, and Lisbon, as well as Livorno, Genoa, and Marseilles, always looking for the best deals and the best goods. They frequently mentioned wines, which could be easily procured from France through Catholic contacts. Then, thanks to the partners' organisational skills, the goods would arrive in Portugal before landing in England. In the first two years of the war, the vessels used mainly came from Hamburg which was a neutral port whose vessels could move freely between England, Portugal, and Livorno.[53] On their return journey, after regular stops in the Spanish ports, the vessels would then stop in the south of England. The British Catholics used these Hamburg vessels often at least until 1703

---

[52] AY 93, f. 38, Business Correspondence. Letter from Patrick Woulfe in Puerto Santa Maria, on 8 April 1699.

[53] J. S. Bromley, 'The North Sea in Wartime' in *Corsairs and Navies, 1660–1760* (London: Hambledon Press, 1987), 53.

when Hamburg 'declared for the Emperor', losing its neutrality.[54] From then onwards, traders decided it would be safer to deploy Scandinavian or Italian ships, in particular from Genoa, which cherished not only its neutrality during the conflict, but its commercial relations with Flanders and England. During the early modern period, Genoa maintained a special relationship with Spain, both in the financial and commercial senses. In the seventeenth century, the role of the city was less prominent on the financial scene, but her mercantile community in Cadiz was still dominant. That port was part of trading maritime routes from 'Barbary' to the north of Europe, and during the conflict, Genoese merchants continued working there, importing silk, satin, and taffeta.[55] It was no surprise that the associates of the London Catholics went to Livorno and Genoa to organise shipments bound for England.

Catholic merchants were aware of the political situation and that prospects could be dire in such circumstances, and that in order to succeed, they needed specific trading strategies. Seeking ways besides the Italian ports to access England, they focused their attention on the Channel Islands, particularly Guernsey. Guernsey was often mentioned in the correspondence as its fishermen were always involved in exchanges between England and the continent, eager to continue a trade that the war had disrupted.[56] However, the area was rife with privateers as these armed vessels were mainly the ones used for the shipments in the Channel at that time and so the risk of seizure was constant. Indeed, some associates lamented an English vessel taken thirty leagues off Lisbon by a French privateer, loaded with iron and other goods bound for Guernsey.[57] As a consequence, Catholics thought it was time to adopt even more secure measures for assuring trade.

In 1702, the Catholic associates turned to protecting their identities using aliases. The Catholics' associates in the Iberian ports had begun to sign letters with fictive names, calling themselves Parento Maquing, Lorenzo Baptista, or Peter Jackson, and ensuring that even had the Spanish authorities sifted through the mail, neither they nor their partners back in

---

[54]   AY 30, f. 50, Business Correspondence. Letter from Paul Den in Cartagena on 13 February 1703.

[55]   Catia Brilli, 'Genoese Migration to Cadiz, A Persisting Alliance' in *Genoese Trade and Migration in the Spanish Atlantic* (Cambridge: Cambridge University Press, 2016), 21—55.

[56]   'The Fisherman, Friend of all Nations?' in R. Morieux, *The Channel: England, France and the Construction of a Maritime Border in the Eighteenth Century* (Cambridge: Cambridge University Press, 2016), 211–247.

[57]   AY 30, f. 54, Business Correspondence. Letter from Paul Den in Antequera on 27 February 1703.

London could be caught. Later in the year, writing as Anthony Mosset, a trade partner informed the Aylwards that their goods were ready in Cadiz, possibly loaded on transatlantic vessels. The tactic of resorting to pseudonyms had already been tested by British Catholics in the previous decade during the Nine Years War and now letters were exchanged under cover of other merchants and sent via France where they would then be brought to England by the Channel privateers.

This ability to devise many strategies, to invest in various markets, and to tap into many trading networks offered the London Catholics an opportunity to support British exchanges as some of the partners with whom they worked had been part of their circles since the 1680s. As already mentioned, in the previous decade, Catholics moved within a group of family and wider commercial relations; however, during the conflict they worked mainly with non-Catholic partners such as the Londoner Charles Peers. The religious community and various relatives remained involved in the deals but with a lesser role. British Catholics and Protestants associated to retain their businesses, basing their partnerships on trust. They were involved in smuggling as the only option offered to merchants at the time and by cooperating, ensured the survival of British trade.

Catholics' constant focus was the bay of Cadiz as the transatlantic vessels were a blessing for the European merchants, providing an outlet to the colonial markets. In order to ensure that their goods reached Cadiz, every aspect of the transactions had to be accurate and strategic. First and foremost, it was vital to work with loyal and skilled agents and the London Catholics carefully chose their men on the ground. These associates would provide up-to-date information and inform the London merchants when it was time to buy and sell and what was worth investing in, according to the season and fashion. Their constant monitoring of the market was essential, as according to the movements of the American vessels prices could rise or fall in a matter of days or a commodity could become over-supplied or scarce. Therefore, for the ones able to trade timely, profits were potentially huge. The Catholics and their associates in London bought on credit what was produced in their own country to ship to the Americas. In return, they trusted their agents to advise them on what was available elsewhere. The Spanish market and its ocean vessels mainly demanded *Colchester* fabrics, pewter buttons, and buckles. The English ports wanted in return *lexia* fruit, in particular oranges and lemons from Malaga, or Italian olive oil.[58]

---

[58] AY 30, f. 23, Business Correspondence. *Benamargosa* and *Comares* refer to the area surrounding Malaga. Apparently, the agent kept the fruit for twelve months.

In these difficult times, caution was imperative in all stages of the trading process. Agents needed to buy the goods at the right time, and the factors needed to handle them with care. False packing could be detrimental, as could holding the merchandise for too long since freshness was fundamental.[59] Incorrect packing could result in a great loss and a few times the Aylwards complained about the poor quality of fruit shipped to England. It was in response to this complaint that the factor in Spain insisted that when he had the product, 'it was no bad [sic] and had no trash', but if the other agent had kept it for more than a year it was not his fault and no surprise that it turned 'candit' [candied fruit].[60] Besides the goods, another crucial aspect of the exchanges was the correspondence. Commodities were always accompanied by letters, accounts which could be a liability if intercepted. Indeed, in a few exchanges, although merchandise was shipped to England, letters were sent via other European countries and many letters of the Catholic associates were miscarried, causing distress and problems in receiving orders and information. A missed account caused delays and a loss of money. One account tells how one of the associates inquired about the shipment of '30 butts of wine', but the agent in Spain replied that he had no idea whatsoever where this account was. He had not received the order, missing the opportunity of a good deal.[61]

During the last months of 1702, the Creaghs were increasingly concerned about Port St Mary in the bay of Cadiz where the Spanish fleet had sailed to fight off the Anglo-Dutch fleet that in September landed 15,000 men 'who did not encounter any kind of opposition and took Port St Mary'. From Cadiz, Paul Den also wrote to the Aylwards; 'you can imagine the consternation of the poor merchants and inhabitants, no manner of sale for any sort of goods'.[62] Meanwhile, he commented about the Italian campaigns where the French fought the Grand Alliance for the control of the peninsula. Den had heard news of the French King's victory over the Germans 'where 6,000 of yours [French] were killed and 1,000 taken prisoners'; and though saddened by the loss of so many lives, he was confident that business in Spain was safe as 'the German will not appear here [Spain]'.

Obviously, it turned 'candit'; AY 109, f. 111, Business Correspondence. Bills and accounts for merchandise to Dec. 1697.

[59] Nuala Zahedieh in her *The Capital and the Colonies: London and the Atlantic Economy, 1660–1700* (Cambridge: Cambridge University Press, 2010) analyses the various issues faced by merchants in their daily routines.

[60] AY 30, f. 23, Business Correspondence. Letter from Paul Den.

[61] AY 30, f. 30, Business Correspondence. Letter from Paul Den on 3 January 1702.

[62] AY 30, f. 41, Business Correspondence. Letters to John Aylward from Paul Den at Malaga, on 5 September 1702.

Nevertheless, he had decided to remove and secure all the French and British goods out of his house, although he still hoped for protection 'from his [Spanish] King, for himself and his friends'. He worried about the hostilities and remained uncertain whether to sell or keep the goods.[63]

The Aylwards and their associates were extremely concerned for their friends after hearing that some families had been rescued by their privateers; and indeed, the hostilities had left 2,000 casualties, among which were many merchants. At that juncture, trading was deemed almost impossible as goods were being confiscated.[64] Indeed, in the summer months of 1702 an embargo was placed on all English and Dutch ships and associates heard news of captains whose ships had been seized and taken away by French *brigantins*.[65] British merchant houses in Spain were also plundered by the authorities hindering any goods departing at the ports.[66] During this time, commercial transactions were more difficult and the usual running costs of trade soared. Letters of the Aylwards were delayed, goods were seized, cargo was wrecked, and crew members were imprisoned.[67] Moreover, trading policies became more rigorous and sharing the enemy's nationality could prove disastrous. Nevertheless, 'the wheels of commerce could not stop spinning' with the fleets towards the Americas remaining loaded and British traders devising ever safer strategies.

The correlation between the beginning of the hostilities and the increase of correspondence between partners in London and the Dutch and Flemish territories is quite revealing. Many Catholics worked in Ostend, Amsterdam, and Rotterdam; and Ostend, in particular, hosted a vast Catholic community. From the second half of the seventeenth century, this city saw a multifaceted group of merchants, attracted by the social, religious, and

---

[63] AY 30, Business Correspondence. Letters to John Aylward from Paul Den at Malaga, one from Cadiz and one from St Malo, June 1685–Nov. 1703; mainly 1693 and 1701–1703.

[64] AY 28, f. 26, f. 64, Business Correspondence. Letters to John Aylward from David and Widow Creagh at Amsterdam, Jan. 1696–Dec. 1703.

[65] AY 30, Business Correspondence. Letters from Paul Den.

[66] AY 93, Business Correspondence. Letters to John Aylward from Woulfe and Trublet at Puerto de Santa Maria, Jan. 1698–Dec. 1700; AY 94, Business Correspondence. Letters to John Aylward from Woulfe and Trublet, written mainly from Puerto de Santa Maria but a few from Cadiz. From July 1702 letter were signed mainly from Symon Michel and from May 1703 by Peter Willson. Symon Michel, of the firm Woulfe & Trublet, said his house was safe in Port St Mary, because he had left a servant and one of the Aylwards there.

[67] AY 30, Business Correspondence. Letters to John Aylward from Paul Den at Malaga, one from Cadiz and one from St Malo, June 1685–Nov. 1703; mainly 1693 and 1701–1703.

economic peculiarities of the region. Ostend then became a crossroads of English, Dutch, and French economies, a gateway into the European routes of communication, and the only outlet for Brabant or Flemish merchants. The city offered splendid opportunities for merchants to involve themselves in both legal and illegal trade and opened the possibility to tap into various European commercial routes including through England to engage in transatlantic trade. Furthermore, until 1713 the city was under Spanish rule, thus fostering links between merchant communities in Spain mainly in Cadiz and Seville. With a continuation of conflict and the proximity to the French shores of Dunkirk, the hub of contraband, the port became a place in which privateers and smugglers thrived.[68] Many families in the area regularly worked with the Catholics in London, mainly the Brownes and the Creaghs in Ostend and Bruges, and the Cloots in Amsterdam.[69] The Brownes were a family of English origin who clung on to their Catholic faith for centuries.[70] They financed contraband in the Channel and did not hide their Jacobite sympathies. They were also related to the Aylwards. The Creagh family had fled Ireland after the Cromwellian War and became prominent in the economic and political life of the region.[71] They were part of the Catholic diaspora but not necessarily Jacobite exiles. The Aylwards had worked comfortably with both families from the 1680s onwards, but it would be in these times of political turmoil that the contacts intensified as all their exchanges between the Netherlands and the Spanish ports were mainly carried out through privateers.[72] Privateering was a constant

---

[68] Jan Parmentier, 'The Sweets of Commerce: The Hennessys of Ostend and their Networks in the Eighteenth Century' in *Irish and Scottish Mercantile Networks in Europe and Overseas in the Seventeenth and Eighteenth Centuries*, ed. David Dickson et al. (Gent: Academia Press, 2006), 70; Jan Parmentier, 'The Irish Connection: The Irish Merchant Community in Ostend and Bruges during the Late Seventeenth and Eighteenth Centuries', *Eighteenth Century Ireland*, 20 (2005): 31–54.

[69] AY 93, f. 40, Business Correspondence. Letter from Patrick Woulfe in Puerto Santa Maria, on 27 April 1699.

[70] Michael Questier, *Catholicism and Community in Early Modern England: Politics, Aristocratic Patronage and Religion, c. 1550–1640* (Cambridge: Cambridge University Press, 2006).

[71] Ibid., In August 1691, Andrew Browne commented about Don Francisco de Castillo, who was removed from the government of the town about a year before and was then general of the artillery, chief manager of the revenue of the Spanish Netherlands, a duty that kept him mainly in Brussels; Monod, 'Dangerous Merchandise', 156, 171, 173.

[72] AY 10, f. 22, Business Correspondence. Miscellaneous letters to John Aylward, Jan. 1700–Dec. 1703; AY 48, Business Correspondence, Letters to John Aylward from Harris and Pyne at Exeter, Aug–Sept. 1704. In 1704, Mr Harris and Mr Pyne from Exeter talked about the *Phoenix*, which had the misfortune of being taken, and £30

feature in times of war. Run by private entrepreneurs it was certainly less costly than an organised fleet. France especially supported the corsairs' war against England, and simultaneously the same tactics were being adopted by the English against French or Spanish vessels.[73] The Brownes and the Creaghs were at this time renowned smugglers and, from their base in the Dutch territories always tried to protect the interest of the London merchants and to secure their partners' interests on the first entrance of the French troops into that country.[74] In particular, the most prominent of the associates was the Londoner Charles Peers who became involved in many of these Dutch exchanges. Dutch commerce complemented British trade by providing manufactured goods and Baltic grains to be re-exchanged for south European provisions; from the Dutch territories, the Catholic agents looked with apprehension at the fleets in the south of Spain.

As the hostilities continued, in 1703 the associates became more diligent in preparing their shipments. It was imperative to ensure secrecy and that as few people as possible were aware of their work. The Aylwards were advised by partners to keep their plans to themselves 'and made [sic] no body privy to it'.[75] The associates in Portugal supervised all incoming shipments to make sure there were no 'English leads'. They also began either de-anglicising the vessels' names by adopting more Catholic connotations or using only neutral fishing vessels.[76] It was common practice for ships to be given either female names, perhaps in honour of a beloved back at home, or even far loftier titles such as *the Apparition of St Peter* or *James the Second*.[77] Furthermore, at this time it was common for fishing vessels to be used in clandestine traffic due to their small size – usually being no more than 20 or 30 tonnes – and so easy to manoeuvre into busy ports. They were also cheaper to run than standard commercial ships which meant fewer losses in cases of seizure.[78] As in the previous decades, and particu-

---

had to be drawn by them to pay for the hostage. They wanted the security that the hostage would be freed and they would pay the debt of £500.

[73] David Starkey, *British Privateering Enterprise in the Eighteenth Century* (Exeter: University of Exeter Press, 1990); W. R. Meyer, 'English Privateering in the War of the Spanish Succession 1702–1713', *Mariner's Mirror*, 69 (1983): 435–446.

[74] AY 19, f. 6, Business Correspondence. Letters to John Aylward from Andrew Browne at Ostend and Bruges, Aug. 1691–July 1692, Jan.–Mar. 1701.

[75] AY 30, f. 48, Business Correspondence. Letter from Paul Den in Malaga on 16 January 1703.

[76] AY 30, f. 62, Business Correspondence. Letter of the 19 July 1703 from Paul Den.

[77] AY, Business Correspondence. Record of new names can be found in almost all the papers.

[78] Cullen, 'The Smuggling Trade in Ireland in the Eighteenth Century', 151; Morieux, 'The Fisherman, Friend of All Nations?' 211–47.

larly when transporting goods across the Channel, smuggled goods were often moved by fishing boats as traders took advantage of the availability of compliant fishermen.

During 1702 and 1703, the situation escalated and the Aylwards' accounts report many vessels seized with many sea captains assaulted and taken prisoner. In one instance, a vessel coming from Livorno containing 23 bales of silk, wine, and rice was seized. The goods were taken by the enemies' privateers and two Englishmen were killed. The captain was maltreated by the soldiers who 'left him no more than what he had on his back'.[79] Things were not much better inland and in fact in the Spanish ports, authorities visited all known merchant houses to control their accounts, leaving guards to prevent illicit dealings. Two agents, Skerret and Den, were made prisoners in their homes in Malaga for three days after being suspected of trading with British goods. The pair had taken some precautions having been previously warned of the situation, and since the authorities did not find anything, they were freed on bail.[80]

As Anglo-Spanish transactions were being prohibited by the British government and hindered by the Spanish authorities, Catholic merchants became even more creative in their tactics. Letters from Spain were diverted either to Portugal or the Netherlands, using nicknames and either hiding or redrawing the marks on the transport barrels. In 1702, the Aylwards received new letters from Peter Jackson (alias Paul Den) under cover of a merchant in Rotterdam.[81] They were waiting for dispatches from Madrid but in the meantime sold British pewter buttons and barrels of buckles in the south of Spain. From London they needed more fabrics. Later that year, 'Anthony Mosset' sent letters under cover via Lisbon, assuring the Aylwards

[79]   AY 30, f. 40, Business Correspondence. Some merchants left for fear of persecution including Consul Hollway. AY 30, f. 39, Business Correspondence. Den mentions the *cedula* granted by the King of Spain, on which he had to register. Some of their friends found shelter in the churches.

[80]   AY 30, f. 38, Business Correspondence. On 13 May 1702, English and Dutch merchants and goods were embargoed in Spain. Two English seamen were killed. The English ship taken was *The Expectation*. 'There is so much rigour even though war has not been declared, can you imagine what will happen when it is declared'; AY 30, f. 34, Business Correspondence. The Spanish market was greatly affected and there were no prospects for the sale of oil. Den also tried his best for disposing of the textile *bays*. It is probable that ships bound for the Levant would have taken them. In the meantime, they waited for the incoming of the *flota*. Aylward was impatient about the arrival of the American vessels, because he had invested in some commodities shipped to Jamaica and he needed to enquire about wine and 'vellon'.

[81]   AY 30, f. 42, Business Correspondence. Parento Maquing (Paul Den) writes from Livorno on 10 October 1702. In f. 40, Peter Jackson writes from Malaga.

that in Cadiz, 'all things [are] packd [sic] up in order to send them into the country in case they should bomb'. The traders needed to be extremely cautious as Dutch and English ships were off Cadiz, hindering Spanish exchanges.[82] Goods from Malaga and Cadiz were ready to be shipped on Portuguese or neutral vessels and in order to supply the English market, the Mediterranean was crucial. In the winter months of 1702 and 1703, agents moved between Genoa and Livorno taking advantage of the neutrality of these ports. In Livorno, commodities were not always available, sales could be 'extremely dull', and English ships were not always 'in sight'.[83] Nevertheless, when the Hamburg convoys approached that port, exchanges of wines and fruit restarted. In Livorno, Portuguese boats from Faro and Lisbon were anchored, and together with Genoese ships were loaded with fruit for England and Cadiz, after English manufactures coming from Lisbon had been unloaded. It was not easy to find neutral ships, but the Italian ports of Genoa and Livorno secured cargoes that could safely get to London. There were plenty of sweet wines and fruit to be shipped, and the vessels could sail safely through Faro and Lisbon, or any other way they 'shall judge best'.[84]

British partners moved quickly between Livorno, Genoa, and Marseilles, where Genoese and Spanish merchants loaded French goods on to vessels from Hamburg. In Marseilles, good deals were closed on fruit and many of the associated traders loaded there. The operations were coordinated by the firm of Doliffe & Radbourne. Commodities would be shipped to Lisbon and also to Holland; from Portugal, French goods found their way to England, 'if there can be a way'.[85] However, many of the partners were against these dealings; perhaps being overly cautious, and deemed them too hazardous. But 'since a man cannot say what it is the best to do', they tried nevertheless, trusting that vessels from Genoa or Hamburg would be secure enough. Portugal was the 'place all people aims [sic] to go' and they knew that their vessels had to make contact there.[86]

The Aylwards and their associates knew their schemes were dangerous and before organising such cargoes required assurances from their partners

---

[82] AY 30, f. 41, Business Correspondence. Letter from Paul Den in Malaga on 5 September 1702.

[83] AY 30, f. 44, Business Correspondence. Letter from Paul Den in Livorno on 7 November 1702. They could not even sell one pair of *bayes* nor other sorts of goods.

[84] AY 30, f. 42, Business Correspondence. The partners involved were Mr Carter, Mr Persival, and March, advised by Mr Willmot. They covered the letters and were based in Lisbon.

[85] AY 30, f. 43, Business Correspondence. From Marseilles, Den is writing as Parentius Baptista, on 21 October 1702.

[86] Ibid.

in Faro. Their deals involved not only importing French and Spanish goods into London, but also sending out British goods and provisions – none of which was legitimate and all of which came with heavy consequences. They were constantly considering what options they had to profit or at least to minimise their losses. Whether it was from Italy or from Spain, the vessels used were of many nationalities, and anything from Portuguese to Swedish. When writing from Livorno, some agents suggested resorting to Swedish cargoes which loaded there, and on their way back always stopped in the English 'Downs'. Meanwhile, Portuguese ships in Gibraltar exchanged English fabrics for Livorno's pipes of oil. In the south of Spain these ships loaded fruit 'as there was no war'.[87] Good deals were closed by shipping to Portugal and from there on to London and Holland; the accounts give information about successful sales of wine and other merchandise. Despite the new institutional arrangements, the London Catholics still also resorted to Hamburg vessels, even when Hamburg had entered the hostilities, as their vessels continued to access English ports. The strategies were sophisticated and the agents involved were not only British associates but also local traders. Indeed, more than once, the British Catholics in London relied on 'trusty Spanish gentlemen'[88] who they instructed to carry English textiles on a Portuguese or French *imbarcation* and not to stop until they reached the port of Fuengirola, in the province of Malaga. It was here that a man would come ashore and the transaction would be facilitated by someone whose name was never mentioned in the correspondence. However, it is known that he was a good friend introduced by a British agent that 'could inform very well of him'.[89] The English *long ells* were in high demand on the Spanish market and London traders were regularly encouraged to send them. The goods for which these fabrics were exchanged were mainly procured in the province of Malaga.[90] The traders were forced to deal with what was available as many commodities were scarce or forbidden, such as Spanish and French wines on which an embargo was placed. Indeed, many merchants who had supplies of wines in the Spanish warehouses were ready to petition the king, for the ones commissioned before 'the prohibition was heard'.[91]

---

[87] AY 30, f. 46, Business Correspondence. Letter from Paul Den in Cartagena on 18 December 1702.

[88] AY 30, f. 62, Business Correspondence. Den is writing as Nicholas Baptista di Sandonat.

[89] AY 30, f. 62, Business Correspondence. Letter from Paul Den on 19 July 1703.

[90] AY 30, f. 62, Business Correspondence. Letter from Paul Den on 19 July 1703.

[91] Ibid.

Nevertheless, although wines were forbidden, Spanish fruit was not, and this offered the perfect opportunity for contraband goods to be moved. In fact, the accounts listed shipments of hundreds of barrels of 'very good fruit', among which the London Catholics hid barrels of wine.[92] Always through Lisbon, they returned barrels of buckles, pewter buttons, and the usual fabrics. Introducing the goods through Portugal was easy as long as the traders gave the right instructions to 'the right men'.[93] One of the most common strategies during the conflict was to import English fabrics under Swedish marks. 'The plan is layd by others, I know not why you may not do it as well' commented Paul Den in Faro. The plan so carefully laid out was to send the English fabric to Sweden. After leaving a Scandinavian port with new marks on the barrels technically they were no longer English goods and they could enter Iberian ports 'with no hazard'. The secret was to hide the country's marks and this practice 'will turn to your advantage'.[94] Many new merchants emerged for forwarding the letters such as James Rice and John Goold of Lisbon, Joseph Percivalls, or the Creaghs in Amsterdam.[95]

The collaboration with British traders in Portugal further suggests how crucial a role Catholics played in British trade. Being able to survive commercially during these years of warfare proved an outstanding advantage and stemmed from years of experience, an instrumental use of Catholicism and strategic use of various partners. The British Catholics in London deftly used familial networks, religious ties, and national identity. Partnerships were based only on mutual trust and common interests, never with any mention of religion. Inter-faith co-operation was crucial in envisioning the smuggling scheme, whereas Catholicism ensured a competitive edge. British Catholics survived in trade thanks to their abilities and religious identity. They moved beyond their religious community, trading with anyone they deemed reliable and trustworthy. The non-Catholics in London needed partners able to inform about what the south European markets wanted and to provide the merchandise. In times of warfare, being able to supply the most requested goods, despite the difficulties, was crucial for surviving in business. Smuggling was possibly the only option offered to merchants during the conflict, and the Aylwards and their associates resorted to these tactics, like any other traders willing to survive the War of the Spanish Succession. Ultimately, what their accounts suggest is how

---

[92] Ibid.
[93] Ibid.
[94] AY 30, f. 62, Business Correspondence. Letter from Paul Den on 19 July 1703.
[95] Monod, 'Dangerous Merchandise', 170. The Goold family were renowned smugglers and Jacobites.

the Catholic contacts proved fundamental at this stage. Without their input British exchanges would have certainly been more problematic.

In all of these exchanges, British Catholics played a crucial role and were aware of it. They showed a clear business knowledge and shrewdness in organising their cargoes. They tapped into Catholic networks to secure the goods needed and to import the merchandise into Portuguese docks. They then resorted to nationality and the London mercantile community to ship the products towards England – though not necessarily London. Frequently, the cargoes landed in Sussex, Kent, Portsmouth, Bristol, or the ports of Yarmouth and Falmouth.[96] Not surprisingly, these were the ports mostly affected by contraband, being both in position to control the movements in the Channel and close enough to London.

During the conflict, the London Catholics continued dealing with the same ports used so successfully in peacetime and depending on the situation, they tapped into different networks, always acting to their own advantage. They continued procuring French commodities thanks to the contacts – a vast circle of Catholic merchants and family relations – established in France during their residence in St Malo. Letters were constantly exchanged between London, St Malo, Rouen, Nantes, and Paris; French imperial goods were moved from Marseilles to Spain and Portugal, whereas from St Malo, Brest, and Dunkirk they would reach England or Spain. In the Iberian ports, a circle of partners was constantly juggling businesses between Malaga, Cadiz, Bilbao, Madrid, and Cartagena, and kept the London merchants informed of all political developments as well as of what the market needed. From Italy, British merchants relied on contacts in Livorno and Genoa and also in Naples and Sicily from where they accessed the Levantine markets of currants, silk, and pepper. From the Netherlands, a network of co-religionists in Ostend, Rotterdam, and Amsterdam secured the supplies of manufactured goods. The aim was to somehow send the goods to Cadiz and to return them to London, and the only option was through Portugal.

During the conflict, religion, the use of skilled partners, and shrewd tactics allowed British Catholics to close various lucrative transactions. They established partnerships through trust and common values; once an associate proved reliable, they counted on him constantly, disregarding faith or nationality. Through these tactics the Catholic community allowed British traders in London to survive and prosper, because they led to safer trading

---

[96] AY 30, f. 32, Business Correspondence. Letters to John Aylward from Paul Den at Malaga, on 21 February 1702; Monod, 'Dangerous Merchandise', 154.

strategies, and ultimately allowed non-Catholic partners to continue working and profiting in the Spanish colonial market.

In the years leading up to the War of the Spanish Succession, Catholic merchants mentioned in the Aylward Papers had been in the trade for almost
thirty years and were aware of how commerce worked. They had proved
themselves to be not only skilled traders but also able financiers, investing in government companies. The London Catholics' strength lay in their
ability to manage different transactions at the same time, and to be able to
access the enemies' markets. Experience, strategies, and the right contacts
assured them the possibility of dealing with both contenders during the
War of the Spanish Succession, and this opportunity meant that they could
negotiate from a privileged position. There were at this time a variety of
strategically available trade circuits for securing successful deals. When-
ever the conflict threatened to stop exchanges in one route, another would
be found immediately, and interests diverted into other trades. In particular, dealing with so many merchant houses guaranteed the survival of the
Catholics' enterprise. In these years, they worked with the firms of Power
& Hill and Woulfe & Trublet, which could provide information, new contacts, and credit.[97] Indeed, they would introduce partners in the Portuguese
market, such as Paul Den, who would prove crucial for British exchanges.
These partners would never profess their Catholicism, and the decision to
work with them was probably based only on their excellent trading skills
and contacts.

The record of Catholics in trade certainly suggests economic and religious integration, at a time when the British Isles were undergoing profound
changes. The new commercial and financial economy had introduced a
more pragmatic society, and new values and social classes were undermin-
ing the traditional tenets of land and faith as means to political power and
wealth. Possibly it was this uncertainty that allowed the Catholics to defy
hostile rules. The London Catholics were close to all of the institutions and
people that counted in commerce and they traded from a privileged position. By the beginning of the century, they had accumulated vast capital and,
to their Protestant associates, they offered the advantage of dealing with
the Catholic enemies overseas. Certainly, in the British Isles, Catholicism
was not facing rehabilitation; however, the London Catholics experienced
tolerance in the mercantile community. They were supported by family
and co-religionists who allowed them to access illegal markets. However,

---

[97] MS, Eng. Lett. c.192, Bodleian Library. Julien Grant writing. John Aylward's son-in-
law was the cousin of Julien Grant, and worked for the firm Woulfe & Trubet.

without the support of non-Catholics they could never have closed their deals in England. They smuggled because this was one of the few options for traders at the time. However, their dealings had no other aim than profit. As in the previous decades, even the London phase of the Aylward story suggests a tale of social and economic integration. The Atlantic and Mediterranean world was too vast to be controlled and it was impossible to supervise the agents involved or to know their personal circumstances and beliefs. All the partners in the Aylwards' trading networks trusted only mercantile values. Catholics worked with non-Catholic merchants as this was in both parties' interests. The merchants in London looked at the galleons in Spain, coveting their precious cargoes. It was essential for British manufactures to be sold in the colonial markets and it was important to access provisions that the north of Europe needed but could not produce. Collaboration among merchants of different denominations was in both groups' interests, and Catholicism did not disbar or inhibit traders. This practice secured inclusion, but ultimately shows how Catholics fundamentally sustained British trade both in times of war and of peace.

Chapter 5
Catholic Merchants and their Inter-Imperial Networks

From the late sixteenth century onwards, expatriates from the British Isles settled in various European–Atlantic ports. These included Catholics who had escaped persecution or displacement, particularly in Ireland during the Elizabethan and Cromwellian regimes.[1] Once abroad, British Catholics worked alongside Protestants, who had been lured by the potential profits that the continental ports could offer, in particular Cadiz and St Malo, the ports of the Spanish and French imperial fleets. Trading with continental Europe was indeed necessary for balancing British trade. England, in particular, traded with Spain, Portugal, and the Netherlands on a consistent basis whereas Scotland and Ireland traded with France and the Flemish territories. The continent demanded English colonial goods, and Dutch and English manufactures, whereas the British Isles absorbed Mediterranean fruit, wine, oil, South American dyes, Indian spices, and Asian pepper. The wealth of names, firms, and ports mentioned in the Aylwards' papers allow investigation into networks that not only crossed faiths, but also moved beyond national and imperial borders, seeing Spanish goods being exchanged for French and British commodities. With the ultimate aim to satisfy the needs of the British markets, Catholic merchants ensured a constant relation with the continent. Therefore, their role in British commerce cannot be disregarded.

The Catholic merchants working with the Aylwards were ordinary transatlantic traders and their careers do not stray from the path pursued by many merchants of the time. Initially, they developed their careers with co-religionists and family. Religion in fact allowed them to settle in Spain and to tap into other Catholic networks already established in various European ports.[2] However, in order to operate in those vast waters, wider

---

[1]   C. Brady and R. Gillespie, eds, *Natives and Newcomers: The Making of Irish Colonial Society, 1534–1641* (Dublin: Irish Academic Press, 1986).

[2]   *Irish and Scottish Mercantile Networks in Europe and Overseas in the Seventeenth and Eighteenth Centuries*, ed. David Dickson, Jan Parmentier, and Jane Ohlmeyer

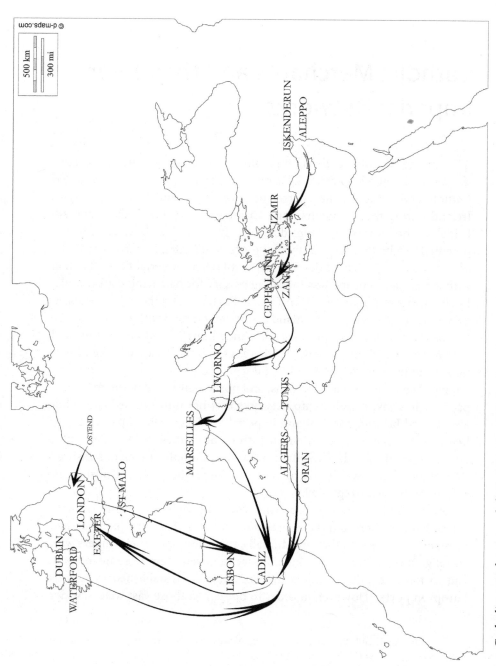

4: Catholic merchants and their inter-imperial networks

networks were needed, and the Aylwards and their associates worked with anyone deemed trustworthy, Catholic or not, meaning that deals were closed with Protestants as much as with co-religionists. Catholics adapted to the demands of the new markets, moving beyond their religious community, although they did not disregard religious ties. The Aylward family operated in those markets for forty years. This commercial longevity allowed them to work with hundreds of different partners and firms. Their papers allow for a reconstruction of their commercial and financial activities and therefore an increased understanding of their role in commerce. Likewise, their papers allow for investigation into the role played by Catholics within the British mercantile community. Some associates featured in their papers for only one transaction, but many partners were part of merchant dynasties that operated in European–Atlantic trade for over two centuries, from the mid-seventeenth century to the early nineteenth century.[3] Catholic merchants fit into a widely studied narrative, showing how their religious community worked according to universal patterns and codes of behaviour.[4] However, their strength was in the possibility of moving between imperial markets to provide a constant flow of commodities to the British Isles. They contributed to the support of the first British commercial

---

(Gent: Academia Press, 2006).

[3]   L. M. Cullen, 'Galway Merchants in the Outside World, c.1650– 1800' in *Economy, Trade and Irish Merchants at Home and Abroad*, ed. L. M. Cullen, 165–192 (Dublin: Four Courts Press, 2012); L. M. Cullen, 'The Two George Fitzgeralds of London, 1718–1759' in *Irish and Scottish Mercantile Networks*, 251–270; C. Bailey, 'The Nesbitts of London and their Networks' in *Irish and Scottish Mercantile Networks*, 231–250; C. Bailey, *Irish London: Middle-Class Migration in the Global Eighteenth Century* (Liverpool: Liverpool University Press, 2013); John Bergin, 'Irish Catholics and their Networks in Eighteenth-Century London', *Eighteenth-Century Life*, 39, 1 (2015): 66–102.

[4]   Nuala Zahedieh, 'Making Mercantilism Work: London Merchants and Atlantic Trade in the Seventeenth Century', *Transactions of the Royal Historical Society*, 6th series (1999): 143–160. Nuala Zahedieh, 'Overseas Expansion and Trade in the Seventeenth Century' in *The Oxford History of the British Empire: The Origins of Empire*, ed. Nicholas Canny, Alaine Low, and W. Roger Louis, vol. I (Oxford: Oxford University Press, 2011), 398–421; Nuala Zahedieh, *The Capital and the Colonies: London and the Atlantic Economy, 1660–1700* (Cambridge: Cambridge University Press, 2010); Sheryllynne Haggerty, *'Merely for money'? Business Culture in the British Atlantic, 1750–1815* (Liverpool: Liverpool University Press, 2012); David Hancock, *Citizens of the World: London Merchants and the Integration of the British Atlantic Community, 1735–1785* (Cambridge: Cambridge University Press, 1995), 85–88; Richard Grassby, *Kinship and Capitalism: Marriage, Family and Business in the English-Speaking World, 1580–1740* (Cambridge: Cambridge University Press, 2001); Perry Gauci, *Emporium of the World: The Merchants of London, 1660–1800* (London: Bloomsbury, 2007).

expansion whereby Catholic and Protestant traders worked together to further common interests. With regard to the associates, nationalities varied. Though mainly British, there were also French, Spanish, Italian, and Dutch traders. In each port, the associates numbered more than twenty at a time, who introduced them to other contacts moving between the main ports and the provincial areas.[5] The networks which the Aylwards tapped into were becoming ever more global, reaching from the West Indies to the Ottoman Levant (see Figure 5).[6] However, despite operating on an international scale and between European ports, they ultimately furthered the commercial interests of the British Isles. Their ability to move between various imperial waters allowed the wheels of British commerce to turn.[7]

Trade with Spain

From the 1570s, Spain saw an influx of British immigrants, particularly Catholic.[8] Scottish, Anglo-Irish, and English merchants were driven by the economic opportunities that the Iberian ports offered. In the British Isles,

[5]   See Appendix for names, ports, and nationalities.
[6]   *Global Goods and the Spanish Empire, 1492–1824: Circulation, Resistance and Diversity*, ed. B. Aram and B. Yun-Casalilla (Basingstoke: Palgrave Macmillan 2014); *The Rise of Merchant Empires, Long Distance Trade in the Early Modern World, 1350–1750*, ed. J. D. Tracy (Cambridge: Cambridge University Press, 1990); Maxine Berg, *Luxury and Pleasure in Eighteenth Century Britain* (Oxford: Oxford University Press, 2005); R. Findlay and K. O'Rourke, 'World Trade, 1650–1780: The Age of Mercantilism' in *Power and Plenty: Trade, War, and the World Economy in the Second Millennium*, ed. R. Findlay and K. O'Rourke (Princeton: Princeton University Press, 2007), 227–310; G. V. Scammell, *The First Imperial Age: European Overseas Expansion, c.1400–1715* (London: Routledge, 1992); *The Oxford Handbook of The Atlantic World c.1450–c.1850*, ed. N. Canny and P. Morgan (Oxford: Oxford University Press, 2011), 324–340; Perry Gauci, *The Politics of Trade: The Overseas Merchant in State and Society, 1660–1720* (Oxford: Oxford University Press, 2003); Carla Gardina Pestana, *The English Atlantic in the Age of Revolution 1640–1661* (London: Harvard University Press, 2004); Sheryllynne Haggerty, *The British Atlantic Trading Community, 1760–1810: Men, Women and the Distribution of Goods* (Leiden: Brill, 2006). David Hancock, *Citizens of the World: London Merchants and the Integration of the British Atlantic Community, 1735–1785* (Cambridge: Cambridge University Press, 1995); W. E. Minchinton, *The Growth of the English Overseas Trade in the Seventeenth and Eighteenth Centuries* (London: Methuen, 1969).
[7]   Fernand Braudel, *The Wheels of Commerce: Civilization and Capitalism 15th–18th Century*, vol. II (London: Collins, 1982).
[8]   Oscar Recio Morales, 'Identity and Loyalty: Irish Traders in Seventeenth Century Iberia' in *Irish and Scottish Mercantile Networks*; O' Flanagan, *Port Cities of Atlantic Iberia, c.1500–1900* (Burlington: Ashgate, 2008); Croft, 'Trading with the Enemy', *The Historical Journal*, 32, 2 (1989): 281–302.

their position was precarious. Despite the fact that in the 1660s the Stuart Restoration had brought back order and relative toleration, the position of the Catholic community was still tenuous, and their liberties restricted.[9] In Ireland, after the Cromwellian conquest, the Catholic nation had been 'vanquished' and Catholics had been forced to leave their properties. Those who had the opportunity fled to Europe, and many traders from the Irish and English south-east coasts settled in Iberian ports.[10] In Spain, foreign Catholics could access trade and claim naturalisation, an opportunity that offered them the possibility to circumvent the Spanish monopoly and to trade 'on commission' for other foreign merchants.[11] This policy meant that Catholics could secure the constant involvement of the British in Spanish ports. The Irish took advantage of the privileges their Catholicism afforded as well as a traditional claim to Iberian heritage. The Spanish authorities were, however, suspicious of them, as the Irish constantly traded with other nations belonging to the British archipelago, making it difficult for the authorities to differentiate between the Irish, the Scottish, and the English. Very often, the English used Irish merchants as intermediaries, especially during the eighteenth century when Irish traders worked with the Spanish possessions in America, meanwhile tapping into the trading networks of the British colonial empire. The Anglo-Irish community in particular drew suspicions for having multiple identities, as some of them remained Catholic but politically felt loyal to England; placing them in a more difficult position. The Protestant Irish were altogether another matter, a group whose identity was always subject for debate.[12] Nevertheless, the Spanish authorities were pragmatic and accepted traders from the British Isles; as long as they professed Catholicism they were free to work and live in Spain. Informers, *Comisarios*, usually of Spanish origin but sometimes British, would watch them, assessing who professed and who did not – a task that

[9] M. Kishlansky, *A Monarchy Transformed: Britain 1603–1714* (Penguin: London, 1996); J. Miller, *Popery and Politics in England, 1660–1688* (Cambridge: Cambridge University Press, 1973); Tony Claydon and Ian McBride, *Protestantism and National Identity: Britain and Ireland, c. 1650–1850* (Cambridge: Cambridge University Press, 1998).

[10] Recio Morales, 'Identity and Loyalty'; Brady and Gillespie, eds., *Natives and New-comers*.

[11] P. O'Flanagan, *Port Cities of Atlantic Iberia, c.1500–1900* (Burlington: Ashgate, 2008), 85.

[12] J. Smyth, 'Like Amphibious Animals: Irish Protestants, Ancient Britons 1691–1707', *Historical Journal* (1993); J. Smyth, 'The Communities of Ireland and the British State, 1660–1707' in *The British Problem c. 1534–1707: State Formation in the Atlantic Archipelago, ed.* B. Bradshaw and J. Morrill (London: Palgrave,1996).

became ever more challenging when the number of traders increased.[13] In 1698 and 1701, and again in 1718, foreign Catholics in Spain were granted the same rights as all native religious communities. In 1701, Nicholas Aylward commented that the new King Philip V showed leniency and granted foreign Catholic merchants all the privileges 'they could wish: to work and live' in Cadiz without any restriction. He added that everyone was extremely happy: 'nothing shall hinder from making up all the new and old accounts'. He did, however, travel to Madrid to gain naturalisation, 'so as to be safe' – a right that, as previously mentioned, implied free access to trade.[14] Indeed, in terms of trading opportunities, many accounts were to be made from Cadiz, the *tacita de plata* (the silver cup of Europe), where the American fleets, and their cargo of bullion, anchored twice a year.[15]

Initially, the fleets had been stopping at Seville which by the late fifteenth century was already a flourishing trading centre. Its geographical position up the river Guadalquivir ensured protection, and its political independence from the powerful Andalusian family of Medina Sidonia, which controlled most of the south of Spain, made sure the port would be controlled directly by the Crown. From 1503, the House of Trade in Seville, *consulado*, supervised the exchanges and collected taxes. The *consulado* was formed by the consuls, representatives elected annually by the merchants. This institution managed the merchants' civil suits and it issued financial and commercial policies. Within the seventeenth century, the *consulado* became a corporation involving a small number of merchant houses. Its commercial power soon allowed this institution to monopolise transatlantic trade.[16] However, this situation of monopoly benefited only a few. Merchants having to pay taxes and share the costs of the convoy soon opted for smuggling, which could explain why between the 1620s and 1680s trade from the Indies declined. Seville dominated this monopoly

---

[13]   Pauline Croft, 'Englishmen and the Spanish Inquisition, 1558–1625, *The English Historical Review*, 87, 343 (1972): 249–268.

[14]   AY 94, Business Correspondence. Letters to John Aylward from Woulfe and Trublet, written mainly from Puerto de Santa Maria but a few from Cadiz and Xeres. From July 1702 signed mainly from Symon Michel and from May 1703 by Peter Willson; AY 54, f. 1, Business Correspondence.

[15]   M. Del Carmen Lario de Onate, 'The Irish Traders of Eighteenth Century Cadiz' in *Irish and Scottish Mercantile Networks*, 227; O'Flanagan, *Port Cities of Atlantic Iberia*.

[16]   C. H. Haring, *The Spanish Empire in America* (New York: Harcourt, Brace & World, 1952), 306–307; 'The Growth and Composition of Trade in the Iberian Empires, 1450–1750' in *The Rise of Merchant Empires: Long Distance Trade in the Early Modern World, 1350–1750*, ed. J. D. Tracy (Cambridge: Cambridge University Press, 1990), 34–101; O'Flanagan, *Port Cities of Atlantic Iberia*, 42–43.

until the early eighteenth century, but due to its sheltered geographical position, which offered protection but not easy access, the fleets gradually moved to Cadiz. In 1679, a royal decree accepted Cadiz as the destination of the fleet, acknowledging a situation already accomplished.[17] Throughout the seventeenth century, Cadiz increased in importance and attained a virtual monopoly on the American trade, although this was only officially acknowledged between 1717 and 1778. From the British Isles, a constant relationship with Cadiz was crucial and in Spain, Catholics were fundamental for strengthening the relations with the British ports. Mercantilist English foreign policy valued this Iberian relationship as England could maximise its exports and reduce the imports only to raw materials and bullion. The aim was to increase its own national wealth, disregarding its trading partner's Catholic identity.[18] The south Iberian ports offered the greatest opportunity for European trade, as the transatlantic vessels, *flotas*, would sail from Cadiz twice a year, laden with European manufactures, iron, fabrics, wine, and beef. Since the 1540s, one fleet each year sailed for the Indies, dividing into two parts in the Caribbean. One half would sail to New Spain, the other to Tierra Firme, in present-day Colombia. Later, the two fleets set off separately: the New Spain fleet would leave Cadiz on 1 July, arriving in Veracruz in September, then leaving for Havana and returning to Spain in May or June of the following year. The fleet bound for Tierra Firme would leave Spain earlier, in May, reaching Cartagena in June before travelling on to the Isthmus of Panama, where in Nombre de Dios the merchandise and treasures from the South American colonies would be sold at fairs. The Tierra Firme fleet would then return the following summer. Escorted by galleons,[19] they came back with exotic dyes, a wide range of aromatic and medicinal plants, gold, pearls, and silver.[20] Overall, a round

---

[17] Ward Barrett, 'World Bullion Flows, 1450–1800' in J. D. Tracy, ed., *The Rise of Merchant Empires*, 224–254; C. Phillips Rahn, 'The Growth and Composition of Trade'; O'Flanagan, *Port Cities of Atlantic Iberia*.

[18] J. O. McLachlan, *Trade and Peace with Old Spain, 1667–1750: A Study of the Influence of Commerce on Anglo-Spanish Diplomacy in the First Half of the Eighteenth Century* (Cambridge: Cambridge University Press, 1940), 6; S. Pincus, 'Rethinking Mercantilism: Political Economy, the British Empire, and the Atlantic World in the Seventeenth and Eighteenth Centuries', *The William and Mary Quarterly*, 69 (2012): 10.

[19] Phillips Rahn, 'The Growth and Composition of Trade in the Iberian Empires, 1450–1750', 34–101.

[20] AY 37, f. 6, Business Correspondence. Letter from Power & Hill on 26 May 1687. In one letter the associates Power & Hill hoped for pearls coming from Buenos Ayres, but they were disappointed as none had come and they needed a necklace for 'a special person of so great essence'.

trip could take between one and three years. In the late seventeenth century, returning ships stopped in Cadiz, or in times of war were diverted to Lisbon or other Atlantic–Iberian ports.

The Aylwards worked with some of the most prominent Catholic merchant families, whose work in Iberian ports has been extensively documented for generations. These included: the Grants and the Comerfords, operating in La Coruna and Lisbon; the Walshes and the Carews, based in the Canaries; and the Whites, Butlers & Matthews, the Lynchs, Frenches, and the Porters, operating in Cadiz.[21] Those firms worked primarily with family members but also with 'strangers'.[22] With the ability to buy and sell properties and engage in commerce, this vast community of foreign Catholics operated in various Iberian ports, such as Port St Mary, Sanlucar, Cartagena, Malaga, Porto, Faro, and Lisbon. In the seventeenth century, Iberia was England's most important partner as it provided access to the vast colonial empire. When diplomatic relations with Spain were strained, the Americas were accessed through the Portuguese ports of Lisbon or Porto, which redistributed goods from Brazil, China, Japan, West Africa, and the South Mediterranean. Indeed, during the last decade of the seventeenth century, when England was at war with Spain, relations between London, Lisbon, and Porto strengthened.[23] By moving outside their community, Catholic merchants helped secure those contacts in various Iberian ports, so that the economic relation between Britain and Iberia would be maintained.

From Cadiz, British merchants worked mainly with English ports, particularly Exeter, London, Bristol, and Plymouth. Among the various firms operating in these ports, many Catholics featured in the accounts, such as Warren & Caunter, Porters & Matthews, and Woulfe & Trublet, firms with branches both in London and Cadiz. The possibility of liaising with English ports potentially allowed for the steady supply of fish, fabrics, and other commodities to the Spanish market. England furnished up to thirty-three

---

[21] *Irish and Scottish Mercantile Networks in Europe and Overseas in the Seventeenth and Eighteenth Centuries*, ed. David Dickson et al. (Gent: Academia Press, 2006); L. M. Cullen, 'Galway Merchants in the Outside World, c.1650–1800' in *Economy, Trade and Irish Merchants at Home and Abroad*, ed. L. M. Cullen (Dublin: Four Courts Press, 2012), 165–192.

[22] Francesca Trivellato, *The Familiarity of Strangers: The Sephardic Diaspora, Livorno, and Cross-Cultural Trade in the Early Modern Period* (London: Yale University Press, 2009).

[23] O'Flanagan, *Port Cities of the Atlantic*, 193–195. Lisbon and Porto re-exported, among many goods: fish, salt, dyes, bullion, spices, pepper, textiles, aromatic shrubs, sugar, salt, and diamonds.

different types of textiles, the most popular being the *Creas Rescones*, a so-called quality of English fabrics in Cadiz.[24]

In Spain, Catholic associates followed the dynamics of British trade. They moved between Cadiz and the province of Malaga, provisioning in the towns of Antequera, Benamargosa, Comares, Fuenguirola, Cichlana, Jerez de la Frontera, and Velez-Malaga. From this hinterland, the goods would then reach the Bay of Cadiz and were shipped off to the colonies through the minor ports of Sanlucar de Barrameda and Port St Mary. In the *Bahia* of Cadiz merchants waited patiently for the *flotas* and their rich imports. Tons of goods were loaded and unloaded in this bay, among the most important including dyes, such as indigo, cochineal, pimento, brazilwood, and silver pesos. Of these, the silver peso was perhaps the most crucial. It 'put life in trade',[25] as it was the standard currency of the Spanish empire and circulated all over Europe and beyond. In terms of dyes, cochineal, and indigo were the main ones imported by the Aylwards and in general from the colonies. At the time in fact, cochineal was the second most important export from Mexico, after silver. Indigo was more important in terms of volume, but cochineal was the most lucrative. It had a low weight and high value, so it was ideal for mercantile transactions. From Veracruz and Havana, it found its way to Seville, Cadiz, and Livorno, and from there to England and Holland, in order to support their emerging manufacturing industry. By the early seventeenth century, imports of cochineal ranged from 10,000 to 12,000 *arrobas*, with each *arroba* valued at 25 pounds. One pound would cost between 1 and 6 silver pesos.[26] Cochineal came from insects, and produced a deep scarlet dye, used to colour woollens and silks. With its crimson colour, cochineal soon became the most expensive luxury dye in the western world, becoming the primary choice of the upper classes of Europe. The Aylwards, perhaps because of their Catholicism, even sold textiles to the Inquisition in Spain for a time. However, they soon stopped, as their partner Patrick Woulfe, hearing

---

[24] O'Flanagan, *Port Cities of Atlantic Iberia*, 90; AY 93, Business Correspondence. Letter from Patrick Woulfe in Puerto Santa Maria.

[25] AY 93, f. 38, Business Correspondence. Letter from Patrick Woulfe in Puerto Santa Maria on 9 April 1698. About the silver peso see C. Marichal, 'The Spanish-America Silver Peso: Export Commodity and Global Money of the Ancien Regime, 1550–1800' in *From Silver to Cocaine: Latin America Commodity Chaines and the Building of the World Economy, 1500–2000*, ed. S. Topik, C. Marichal, and Z. Frank (London: Duke University Press, 2006), 25–52. The silver peso was 272 *maravedis*, equal to 8 silver *reals*. *Real* of eight was an ounce of silver.

[26] C. Marichal, 'Mexican Cochineal and the European Demand for America Dyes, 1550–1850' in *From Silver to Cocaine*, 76–92. About measurement see Phillips Rahn, 'The Growth and Composition of Trade'.

about their persecution of the Jews, decided to disassociate himself from such a dreadful institution.[27] As well as cochineal, there is also evidence in their accounts of indigo, coming from South America and both the English and the French West Indies, specifically Jamaica and present-day Haiti (Saint-Domingue). Indigo replaced woad from France and Germany as a blue dye; England's manufacturers needed it and Catholics helped import. From South America, particularly Guatemala and San Salavador, indigo would travel to Spain and from there to England and Holland. From Haiti, it would find its way to France, especially St Malo and even from there to England. Britain in the mid-eighteenth century consumed some 60,000 pounds annually.[28] From Cadiz and St Malo, Catholics contributed to the movement of tonnes of the dye, creating inter-imperial transactions that satisfied the demands of the home markets. From France, indigo was constantly shipped, even during the twenty years of warfare between the two countries (1688–1713). The strategies varied as necessary, from exchanging the dye for prisoners, to faking a privateer's seizure. Usually the London market was accessed through Plymouth or the ports in the Channel such as Falmouth or Exeter. For instance, in 1692, Jamaica, the main indigo-producing colony, experienced a devastating earthquake that 'shook down all the houses' and the 'town of Port Royal was swallowed up in the sea, with 2,000 of the inhabitants'.[29] Production therefore stopped and merchants, whose suppliers were based solely in Port Royal, grew anxious as they could not procure a commodity that was still in demand in England. An added complication also meant that the price of indigo rose as a consequence of the shortage. However, thanks to their French partners, the Aylwards were able to supply the English market via the French colonies, ensuring a constant flow of the blue dye. The only precaution was to carefully check the quality of the dye as supplies from Antigua, Montserrat, and the Leeward Islands could be falsely packed – or so they reported.[30]

---

[27]   AY 93, f. 12, Business Correspondence. Letter from Patrick Woulfe and Nicholas Aylward on 7 July 1698.

[28]   D. McCreery, 'Indigo Commodity Chains in the Spanish and British Empires, 1560–1860' in *From Silver to Cocaine*, 53–75; R. S. Smith, 'Indigo Production and Trade in Colonial Guatemala', *The Hispanic American Historical Review*, 39, 2 (1959): 181–211; G. A. Nadri, 'The Indigo Trade: Local and Global Demand' in *The Political Economy of Indigo in India, 1580–1930: A Global Perspective* (Leiden: Brill, 2016), 85–123.

[29]   AY 51, f. 14, Business Correspondence. Letter from Charles Horde on 12 August 1692.

[30]   AY 54, f. 2, Business Correspondence. Letter from Nicholas Kehoe in Puerto Santa Maria on 12 September 1701; AY 51, f. 6, Business Correspondence. Letter from Charles Horde in London on February 1693.

In order to sustain the growing English demand for dyes, Catholics tapped into various imperial networks to import brazilwood, boxwood, and Japan wood (dye-producing trees). From the British and French colonial markets they imported indigo and cochineal, and through Portugal they introduced hardwoods of different types such as red and Braziletto wood from Brazil. Until the wood was cut, it was difficult to assess its quality; however, a standard measurement based on 'its goodness and straightness of stick' meant that it was worth trading as it bore prices of £18 per tonne when sold. Portugal tried to regulate this trade as it was potentially lucrative but also subject to all sorts of fraud and contraband. From Lisbon, brazilwood was re-exported to various European ports and beyond. The Aylwards planned to ship it to Smyrna, Livorno, Marseilles, or Amsterdam, where they would find good markets.[31] Amsterdam took the 'lion's share of dyewoods' from Brazil.[32] However, ultimately the merchandise was directed to London.

Other than dyestuff, Catholic merchants shipped Mediterranean fruit and wines northwards, through Spain and Portugal. From the late middle ages, fruit had featured heavily as an item of trade within English imports. This was so much the case that in 1585, the political thinker Thomas Hariot had hoped to find these items in North America so as to stop trade with the Catholic enemies.[33] Trade with continental Europe never ceased and in the late seventeenth century it flourished. As late as the 1770s, Europe provided 47 per cent of total British imports and received 62 per cent of her exports.[34] The Catholic merchants participated in this trade and secured constant supplies. Fruit came from Spain and the Greek Islands. If Spain supplied fresh fruit, Zante and Cephalonia supplied dried fruit, currants, *raisins solis*, and *lexia fruit*, for which England developed an 'insatiable' palate.[35] One transaction could consist of 130,000 oranges and 3,000 lemons,[36] shipped in 429 boxes from Spain. The costs incurred included

[31]   AY 51, f. 21, Business Correspondence, Letter from Charles Horde on 18 October 1692. O'Flanagan, *Port Cities of the Atlantic*, 139.

[32]   O'Flanagan, *Port Cities of the Atlantic*, 139

[33]   *A Brief and True Report of the New Found Land of Virginia* by Thomas Hariot (1585), Documenting the American South, University of North Carolina, 2003, accessed through the University of Warwick website.

[34]   J. Brewer, *The Sinews of Power: War, Money and the English State, 1688–1783* (London: Unwin Hyman, 1989), 185.

[35]   Maria Fusaro, *Political Economies of Empire in the Early Modern Mediterranean: The Decline of Venice and the Rise of England, 1450–1700* (Cambridge: Cambridge University Press, 2015), 300.

[36]   AY 101, Business Accounts. Bills, accounts, receipts, etc., for merchandise to Dec. 1687.

horse-hire, to procure the fruit, the broker who provided the empty boxes, reams of paper for packing, and nails for the boxes. They also had to pay for the meals of the 'fifteen men during the twenty three days that the fruit was making up' (ripening) and the man 'tasting' the product – especially if it was wine; all of these expenses needed to be added to existing wages and after high duties of *consulado* and *portage*.[37] Transactions were expensive but, if successful, they could be extremely profitable as Europeans desired sweet goods. During the late seventeenth century, chocolate started to take hold. It was a semi-luxury product that had been introduced in the 1590s in Iberia and in the 1620s in the north of Europe. It mainly came from Mexico and Venezuela, but from the 1650s the English started importing it from Jamaica where cacao plantations had already been established. That island soon became the main source for the English market. Chocolate, with its dose of caffeine, became a drink fit for a busy and dynamic mercantile culture, together with tea and coffee. Catholics started to participate in this trade as well. In 1689, Butler briefed Aylward that a small quantity of cocoa had arrived from the Indies. In Spain, the shops sold it at 22 *reales* per *millar* – about a sailor's monthly wage – and since there was none in town, it was worth buying.[38] Aside from fruit and cacao, England also had an insatiable taste for south European wines. Wine was a lucrative commodity in England, although deemed an unproductive import in the sense that it was for consumption alone. Nevertheless, since wine was in high demand, the English government thought it better to export it from Spain and Portugal, rather than France.[39] Spanish wines dominated the market as port and sherry were cheaper than the Italian wines and better suited to the English climate as they could last longer in colder temperatures. However, the Spanish constantly competed with wines from the Canary Islands, Madeira, or Porto and the name 'sherry' was adopted to distinguish the original Spanish product.[40] The bitter sherry was mainly imported from

[37] Ibid.; AY 93, f.74, Business Correspondence. Letter from Patrick Woulfe in Puerto Santa Maria on 6 December 1700.

[38] AY 20, f. 34, Business Correspondence. Letter from Robert Butler in Cadiz in 1689; M. Norton, 'Tasting Empire: Chocolate and the European Internalisation of Mesoamerican Aesthetics', *The American Historical Review*, 211, 3 (2006); I. Fattacciu, 'The Resilience and Boomerang Effect of Chocolate: A Product's Globalisation and Commodification' in *Global Goods*, 255–273; S. D. Coe and M. D. Coe, *The True History of Chocolate* (London: Thames and Hudson, 1996), 165–175.

[39] McLachlan, *Trade and Peace with Old Spain*, 17; David Hancock, *Oceans of Wine: Madeira and the Emergence of American Trade and Taste* (New Haven: Yale University Press, 2009).

[40] AY 5, f. 35, Business Correspondence. AY 4, Business Correspondence. Miscellaneous letters to John Aylward, Jan.–Dec. 1685; McLachlan, *Trade and Peace with Old*

Port St Mary, Seville, and Cadiz. In the 1680s, the Aylwards, in partnership with George Sitwell, shipped sherry wine to London and Exeter. When sending the wine to Exeter in exchange for draperies, a partner recommended the Aylwards to save the money on the freight, and encouraged them to charge the master to ensure that the wines would not be 'drawn out by the *Liccorishness* of any of his crews, filled again with salt water and so spoiled'.[41] The wines had been sold in Plymouth but at great loss. Therefore, it would have been better to exchange *raisins solis* or perhaps dispatch the wines from the Canary Islands.

The ability to work in Iberian ports, whilst cooperating with Protestant merchants in English ones, formed the basis of Catholic strength in British trade. The Catholics secured constant supplies and they worked in all the major port cities of the time; Exeter was where many associates of the Aylwards were based. It was a port bustling with European traders and specialising in Spanish exchanges.[42] In Exeter, prominent merchants introduced a new circle of merchants operating in Devon and Cornish ports such as Weymouth, Topsham, Dartmouth, and Plymouth. From these south English ports, Catholics exported black Colchester bays, *hondura black*, especially popular when it was time 'to put yourself in mourning' in Spain at the time of a monarch's death.[43] Indeed, on the 4 August 1699, the Queen of Portugal, Maria Sophia Elisabeth of Neuburg, died. Her death 'occasions that most people here goes into mourning' and gave rise to the need to obtain dark clothes. Again, for two weeks in October 1700, Woulfe & Trublet monitored the health of the ailing Spanish King Carlos II with close attention, stating that 'he has been violently taken ill of a bloody flux' but 'he was much better, though not entirely', causing uncertainty in terms of how to proceed with the black textile.[44]

Textiles and fabrics were one of the most prominent English imports to Spain, as Spanish manufacturers were unable to produce cheap clothing, which was in high demand in the colonies. The only competition was

---

Spain, 17.

[41]   AY 5, f. 4, Business Correspondence. Letter from Thomas Jefford.

[42]   W. B. Stephens, *Seventeenth Century Exeter: A Study of Industrial and Commercial Development, 1625–1688* (Exeter: University of Exeter Press, 1958).

[43]   AY 20, f. 28, Business Correspondence. Letter from Robert Butler in Cadiz; AY 10, Business Correspondence, Letter from Andrew Hackett from Cadiz in 1701; AY 6 f.11, Business Correspondence. Among the most prominent merchant families in Exeter, the Aylwards worked with the Wyses and the Brookings.

[44]   AY 93, f. 70, f. 71, Business Correspondence, Letter from Patrick Woulfe in Puerto Santa Maria on 11 and 25 October 1700; MS, Lett. c. 192, Bodleian Library, Letter from Julien Grant, cousin of the Aylwards' son-in-law and agent of Woulfe & Trublet.

from the cheap cloth produced by the Genoese, and the imitations of white *Colchester bays* produced in Antequera; here *bays* could be produced cheaper, 'all tho not with that perfection, yet sufficient to spoile the seale of these others'.[45] Counterfeiting affected the sales of English fabrics; though, grey and brown *sarges, long ell*, white *Colchester* and drapery, stockings, brooches, pockets, and knives continued to arrive from Exeter, London, and Bristol. All sorts of fabrics were registered including *presillias* and *bramanta cruda, cambricks*, and *slesia*. The fabrics were one of the main imports which were then loaded onto the fleets together with pointed knives, thread, and *surgers*, plus goods from the East such as mainly blue calicoes, cinnamon, cloves, and pepper. Catholic merchants contributed to this trade. In 1683, through London, the Aylwards and Floyer & Ryan shipped convoys of bales of cloth and men's silks. The money needed for purchasing commodities was least concerning, since all the transactions involved taxes and the expenses of whitening, folding, and dyeing. In 1686, they imported 400 pairs of men's silk stockings to Spain, complaining about the £14 spent on dyeing, packing, and custom fees. The colours chosen were yellow, black, green, and red, with the most popular being black, 'muske greens', and yellows.[46] In the same year, a shipment of seven bales from London cost 14,868 *reals* and 22 *maravedis* in freighting, custom, and national duties. The bales contained 60 pieces of *Colchester bayes*, 75 pieces of *Perpetuana* cloth, and 2 cases with 240 dyed calicoes, recorded by the firm Power & Hill on account of the two traders John Aylward and Walter Watkins. Again in the late 1680s, they imported 3,000 pairs of *kentins*, sold at 2 *reals* and 28 *maravedis* per pair, a value they sustained throughout the years.[47] In the summer of 1689, they mainly looked for coloured textiles, as the whites were not popular in the Indies and they were bearing no profit.[48] Another £67 was spent for 'watching them' and money was given to assure freight and to pay 'coopers' and 'porters' to ensure the security of freight. Fabrics came not only from England but also from Ireland and France. In order to meet the demand of the Spanish colonial market, they bought textiles in France and Ireland by using Catholic networks. By doing so they secured a constant supply. Many firms based in Port St Mary invested in French fabrics, working with many merchants in France. In French centres

[45] AY 30 f. 62, Business Correspondence. Letter from Paul Den in Cadiz in 1703.

[46] AY 20, f. 30, Business Correspondence. Letter from Robert Butler in Cadiz on 9 May 1689.

[47] AY 20, f. 31, f. 30, Business Correspondence. Even a few years later the value was at 2 *reals* and 26 *maravedis*.

[48] AY 20, f. 33, Business Correspondence. Letter from Robert Butler in Cadiz on 20 June 1689.

of production, Catholic contacts procured the fabric. One such place was Rouen, where Robert Dermott was in charge of buying the fabrics at fairs. They agreed on buying ecru-coloured fabrics, as they were cheaper, and then bleaching them white, to make them similar to the most popular white *flouretts*. Generally, the 'oxing' and the golden colour were hard to sell. However, fashion varied with the seasons and in the autumn of 1700, the winter narrow *calamencoes* were 'what they run now, good quality and with lively stripes'. In the winter months of 1701 and 1702, there was a shipment of 100 pieces of coloured bayes and 50 pieces of whites, from Ireland. It was specifically recommended to carefully avoid *abuccardos* or *tangayas* and to send red, blue, yellow, or green colours fit for 'footmen and soldiers', and which were much in demand in the war-ridden Mediterranean.[49]

These manufactured goods were exchanged for Mediterranean provisions which also reached Bristol, as well as Exeter. During the sixteenth and seventeenth centuries, the commercial role of Bristol grew, but it was in the eighteenth century that the city would reach its zenith as an Atlantic port.[50] Its trade rivalled London and it fostered a wealthy mercantile community. From the 1670s, for at least ten years, the Aylwards and their Catholic associates' interests included Bristol, from where manufactured goods were shipped. Transactions in Bristol involved non-Catholic partners. In the Bristol market, Spanish fruit and Spanish wine were quite popular, although at the time the Aylwards also shipped wheat and butter. The exchanges with Bristol were less frequent than those with London or Exeter; nevertheless at the end of the seventeenth century, it was impossible to overlook the rising importance of this port within the Atlantic trade. Since early modern times, Bristol had played an active role in the Atlantic, mainly in the commercial routes from Newfoundland, Chesapeake Bay, and the Caribbean. Bristol developed as a result of the growth of Atlantic commerce, exporting manufactures, and importing American commodities.[51] In 1685, Bristol was part of the Aylwards' networks that touched various European ports. The journeys could have been from three to seven months, and the costs of hiring the freight were 400 pieces of eight double plate[52] – a charge that seemed very expensive given that 61 *reals* would

---

[49] AY 31, f. 8, Business Correspondence; AY 93, f. 70, Business Correspondence. Letter from Patrick Woulfe in Puerto Santa Maria on 11 October 1700. One of the most valuable associates was Robert Dermott, brother-in-law of James Porter.

[50] K. Morgan, *Bristol and the Atlantic Trade in the Eighteenth Century* (Cambridge: Cambridge University Press, 1993), 1–6.

[51] Ibid.

[52] AY 2, Business Correspondence. Miscellaneous letters to John Aylward, 1683. A piece of eight was worth eight *reals* and it was a Spanish dollar. AY 101, Business

have been enough for twenty-three days' worth of wages for fifteen sailors. In the late seventeenth century, Bristol was not yet a prominent Atlantic hub, and from there the accounts of Catholic merchants were scant, with the main partners residing in London. With its bustling counting-houses, hectic docks, and hustling streets, London was the place to be for conducting business. It was one of the largest cities in Europe, where the majority of the British population lived and thrived. People from all over the world, especially tradesmen, were attracted by the opportunities it had to offer. Merchants were drawn to the city by the prospects of high profits and by the crucial role it played in Atlantic and Mediterranean trade. Almost all of the commodities from around the world touched the city and were then either re-exported or distributed to the internal markets. In London, it was possible to find all sorts of goods, from American products to oriental silks. Moreover, the city became the financial heart of Europe, and its legal institutions offered the best trading opportunities. It was a thriving environment in which to develop the best commercial skills, to receive excellent professional training and most of all to tap into wide and already established networks.[53]

At the end of the seventeenth century, London was the most important European port after Cadiz for Catholic merchants. Here, they established inter-faith collaborations and through their contacts in Spain, fuelled the Anglo-Spanish trade. Catholic merchant houses operated in London from the second half of the seventeenth century until the nineteenth. They participated in trade with North America, the West Indies, and continental Europe. Sources mention the Fitzgeralds, the Butlers, and the Walshes as among the many names and dynasties that operated in London until the 1750s or 1790s, moving between the commercial and financial worlds.[54] Among these families there were ties of kinship and financial interests, encompassing the West Indies, France, and Spain. They passed on capital and experiences through generations and their engagement had a global reach. The Fitzgeralds shared interests in the wine trade and, besides London, branches of the family worked and settled in Nantes and Ostend. In London, within the Catholic community the name 'Arthur' stands out.

Accounts. Bills, accounts, receipts, etc., for merchandise to Dec. 1687.

[53]   D. Hancock, *Citizens of the World: London Merchants and the Integration of the British Atlantic Community, 1735–1785* (Cambridge: Cambridge University Press, 1995), 85–88; Gauci, *Emporium of the World*; Zahedieh, *The Capital and the Colonies*.

[54]   Cullen, 'The Two George Fitzgeralds of London'; Bailey, 'The Nesbitts of London and their Networks'; Bailey, *Irish London*; Bergin, 'Irish Catholics and their Networks in Eighteenth-Century London'.

The Arthurs were merchant–financiers from Limerick and were active in London from the 1670s. After the Popish Plot of 1679, where Catholics allegedly plotted against the monarch Charles II, Daniel Arthur moved to Paris, keeping financial links with London.[55] In the 1690s, the Arthurs, senior and junior, although based in Paris, moved constantly between England, France, and Spain, lending money to the governments, and cherishing their high-profile contacts; indeed in January 1693, Daniel Arthur Junior ordered from St Malo a 'little barrel of pickled oysters' for the Queen of England, provided of course they were the 'best' [quality].[56] However, they also had interests in the French linen trade, involvement in the Flemish grain trade, and they were prominent bankers, keeping a watchful eye on the market and often looking for silver, for '2 or 300 marks of silver plate' and 'silver lace well cleaned'.[57] Ultimately, their financial network would be inherited by the Cantillons, speculators of the South Sea Company.[58] The Arthurs were particularly successful, but nonetheless they exemplify how Catholic families merged into the London mercantile world, and by forging inter-faith collaborations, played a prominent role as protagonists in the economic and financial revolutions of the late seventeenth century.

Through the Channel, from the North to the South of Europe

During the seventeenth century, trade between England and Spain was the most lucrative and the most valued by policy makers. However, England was not able to supply all of the provisions, grains, and manufactured products demanded by the vast Spanish empire, therefore, merchandise also came from Ireland, the Netherlands, or France. Cooperation among many mercantile communities complemented trade and Catholics sustained these vast networks by working with Protestant merchants. Major Catholic networks were established in Ireland, France, and the Flemish territories, from where English, Dutch, and Baltic merchandise was diverted to Spain. The colonial and continental links remained active until the end of the eighteenth century, withering only after the Napoleonic Wars.[59]

---

[55] For a brief history of Britain see Kishlansky, *A Monarchy Transformed*.

[56] AY 11, f. 30, Business Correspondence. 21 January 1693, Daniel Arthur writing from Paris to John Aylward in St Malo.

[57] AY 11, f. 100. Business Correspondence. Letter from Daniel Arthur.

[58] Antoin E. Murphy, *Richard Cantillon: Entrepreneur and Economist* (Oxford: Clarendon Press, 1986), 59.

[59] Ibid.

Irish ports did not play such a prominent role in comparison to the English; nevertheless, the Aylwards and their associates did work with Ireland. Irish–Iberian exchanges had developed in the fourteenth century and flourished throughout the early modern centuries. On the continent, Ireland mainly traded with Spain and Portugal, exporting hides, butter, beef, herring, and salmon, and importing wine.[60] The ports involved in these exchanges were mainly Anglo-Irish towns of the south east, whose geographical position facilitated contacts with the Atlantic–Iberian ports. From the south east, Irish exports were directed to France also, which was a growing market for Irish butter especially in the 1670s and 1680s. Between 1689 and 1697, due to the Nine Years War, trade with France was banned, and while it declined, it did not stop completely.

Catholics in London and Cadiz worked with Ireland to find provisions or introduce continental goods into the colonial market that were not easily available in England. In these international exchanges, the main Irish port was likely to have been Waterford, whose geographical position in the south east of the island enabled exchanges not only within the British Isles, but also in the Channel and Spain. In the seventeenth century, Dublin rose in importance as a port to serve a growing hinterland. It exported mainly grain that allegedly in 1683 was generally not 'so fit for transport as the English'; its wheat, however, was the best in the country and its barley and butter were sought after in Cadiz.[61] On the east coast, merchants also operated from Drogheda, Wexford, and Dungarvan, although to a lesser extent. In the south, Kinsale was renowned for pilchards, and Cork and Youghall specialised in butter, although Youghall butter was apparently always too salty, and not so successful.[62] On the west coast, Galway and Limerick held some significance and engaged in the Iberian and Dutch trade, primarily with the port of Rotterdam. In Ulster, the only port with continental ties was Londonderry, which specialised in salmon. Overall, Irish ports exported tallow, salted ox hides, butter, *yellow beeswax*, glue, *fustel*, and tin.[63] These goods were mainly directed to Iberia and France. On the Spanish coast, Irish networks mainly traded in the Bay of Biscay, the port of Bilbao or San Sebastian, where commodities would be exchanged

---

[60] Karin Schuller, 'Irish–Iberian Trade from the Mid-Sixteenth to the Mid-Seventeenth Centuries' in *Irish and Scottish Mercantile Networks*.

[61] AY 2, f. 4, Business Correspondence. Letter from Dublin in 1683.

[62] AY 93, f. 74, Business Correspondence. Letter from Patrick Woulfe in Puerto Santa Maria, on 6 December 1700. He complains that the Power & Agnes' Youghall butter has too much salt.

[63] AY 31, f. 5, Business Correspondence. Letters to John Aylward from Robert Dermot at Brest and Rouen, July 1696–June 1699.

for iron.[64] Iron was one of the main exports of the Basque ports and in the early eighteenth century Basque iron represented 10 per cent of English imports.[65] In the south of Spain, they mainly dealt with Cadiz and Port St Mary. Frequent exchanges were also conducted with Lisbon. The Irish–Iberian trade was run by merchant families that had been active in this trade for generations, including the Blakes from Galway, the Lynchs, or the Comerfords from Waterford, who had branches of the family in La Coruna, the Netherlands, and London. On their southward bound journey, Irish vessels frequently stopped in French ports. The exchanges between Spain, France, Ireland, and England never completely ceased, despite warfare. In the second half of the seventeenth century, France still supplied 40 per cent of the colonial products, especially 'linnins'.[66] In the 1740s, Irish linen trade with England increased and it is not clear how much of it was produced in Ireland, or came from France. Within these exchanges, Catholic merchants always played an integral role, particularly during the Anglo-Spanish wars, when they could obtain licences and move freely as Catholics in Iberian and French ports, despite being subjects of the English crown.

Indeed, the strength of British Catholics resided in their ability to work with Spain but also with other Catholic 'enemies' such as France. French trade was the main competitor for England. When England signed the commercial treaty with Spain in 1667, it aimed to impact on French commerce. The Spanish treaty allowed English merchants to export bullion and assured lenient policies. Ships were not inspected, factors were not questioned, and goods were not detained.[67] A cargo could carry 3 million *reales of plate*.[68] However, despite this advantageous and preferential treatment in the 1690s, French products were still in high demand. France was the most populated European country and its trade was flourishing. In the ports where the Aylwards operated, such as St Malo, Nantes, Dunkirk, and Bordeaux, Catholic communities had settled since the 1660s, after the Cromwellian wars. Merchants from Galway in particular had extensive ties with France and families such as the Lynchs as well as the Blakes, Skerrets, Brown(e)s, and Langtons were considered among the most prominent merchant families in 1740s London, operating in minor ports such

---

[64] AY 15, f. 1, Business Correspondence. Paul Aylward in Cadiz in the early months of 1700. From Bilbao, the Aylwards shipped iron chests to London through Faro.

[65] O'Flanagan, *Port Cities of Atlantic Iberia*, 261.

[66] AY 13, f. 7, Business Correspondence. Letters to John Aylward from Aaron Atkins at Amsterdam and Port Royal, Apr. 1684–Jul. 1688.

[67] McLachlan, *Trade and Peace with Old Spain*, 14.

[68] AY 37, f. 6, Business Correspondence. Letters from Richard Enys, Eustace Power, and Mr Bowles in Cadiz on 26 May 1687.

as Brest, Lorient, La Rochelle, and also the hinterland's towns of Rouen or Morlaix. Working with local French merchants allowed them to provide the merchandise needed in the British Isles.[69] Meanwhile, these families valued contact with relatives in London, Dublin, Lisbon, or Malaga; families like the Kirwans worked in London for 140 years. Their networks were attested in France in cities such as Nantes, Lorient, Bordeaux, and Marseilles, working well into the eighteenth century. Even in the last decades of the eighteenth century they were still active in European–Atlantic ports and transatlantic shipping. They had offices in Spain and London and in the late eighteenth century the house of Lynch & Bellew, operating in Cadiz, intermarried with the Blakes. The Lynchs, however, had ties in Bruges, North America, and Bilbao. Other prominent houses were the Frenches and the Burkes. Men from Galway were also active in the West Indies as planters and politicians, involving members of the Blake or the Lynch families. These various ports were close to the international trading routes, whilst allowing access to continental trade as well. St Malo in particular was a centre of privateering in the Channel. From there, French privateers exchanged prizes between Dunkirk and Brest, and ventured to South America, the Caribbean, and Newfoundland, but also to West Africa, China, and Arabia. From England, the Malouins imported tin, lead, Irish provisions, and cod. They re-exported French linen and indigo. The main ports of call were Bristol and London, after stopping at Guernsey and Jersey.[70] The Catholic network allowed ease of access to trade on both sides of the Channel in order to sustain the flow of goods in and out of the British Isles and French ports.

France provided England with the most popular commodities, and access to her markets was vital for the colonial trade. The Aylwards lived in St Malo for ten years and from there they worked with a vast Catholic community of expatriates settled in various French ports and involved themselves in smuggling and privateering. From the French ports, Catholic merchants accessed the flourishing colonial and continental trade. They supplied the English vessels with French linen, sent indigo to English manufacturers, and tapped into the Channel exchanges of Newfoundland fish. Their strength was in their ability to tap into inter-imperial networks and to easily cross the national borders in the Channel waters. The British Isles demanded indigo, fabrics, and wine, whereas the south of Europe

---

[69] Cullen, 'Galway Merchants in the Outside World, c.1650–1800'.

[70] Bromley, 'The Trade and Privateering of St Malo during the War of the Spanish Succession' in *Corsairs and Navies, 1660–1760* (London: Hambledon Press, 1987), 339–388.

demanded north Atlantic fish that came from London or from St Malo. Indeed, Newfoundland fish soon became the main staple food source of the French empire, in the same way it was for the English colonial markets. From the Channel, this commodity reached the south Mediterranean ports from St Malo and Marseilles, or directly from England. In the seventeenth and eighteenth centuries, cod from New England and Newfoundland increased in success within the Spanish market, responding to the needs of a Catholic population, fasting and abstaining from eating meat each Friday and during Lent. At the end of the eighteenth century, the consumption was calculated at 64,000 tons, roughly three kilograms per person, accounting for more than 5 per cent of Spanish imports. It was one of the first transatlantic staple trades, and it slowly displaced the existing trade in dried and salted fish. Cod could spoil less easily than herring or pilchards. In Spain, the main port that specialised in cod was Bilbao, which in the late sixteenth century witnessed multilateral trade, whereby Castilian wool was shipped to England and exchanged for colonial cod. Wool, especially fine merino, reached England either directly or through the Netherlands or Portugal. The main destinations for Spanish wool were Bristol, London, and Exeter. In return, England offered North American cod, for which Spain had an insatiable appetite. Cod was popular because, besides meeting Catholics' fasting needs, it was also a cheap source of protein. Between the 1650s and 1670s, cod became profitable in its own right and Bilbao became the cod capital of Spain, also trading directly with Terranova. In 1699, this Basque port funnelled 75 per cent of the cod exported from Boston.[71] However, pilchard fish was not abandoned by European merchants and in 1686, the Aylwards financed exchanges of pilchard fish, usually from Plymouth, where one transaction could consist of 5,000 hogsheads, each sold at 22 dollars per plate.[72]

Partners would move from Portsmouth to Marseilles where they would trade with associates in mullet fish, as well as the white wool of Castile, Levant rice, and almonds.[73] Investing in fish was common for merchants of the time, as Spain constantly demanded this commodity. It had been

---

[71] R. Grafe, *Distant Tyranny, Markets, Power and Backwardness in Spain, 1650–1800* (Princeton: Princeton University Press, 2012), 52–79; O'Flanagan, *Port Cities of Atlantic Iberia*, 173–187, 259.

[72] AY 5, f. 1, Business Correspondence. Miscellaneous letters to John Aylward from Jan.–Dec. 1686. The partner was Martyn, who in that particular deal did not sell the merchandise from Spain, as the Aylwards hoped to barter and this practice would have not yielded good profits.

[73] AY 5, f. 20, Business Correspondence. Miscellaneous letters to John Aylward from Jan.–Dec. 1686.

profitable since the mid-1680s when pilchards sold at 55 pieces of eight or Spanish dollars per hogshead; a good profit, given the initial cost of 22 or 16 pieces of eight. From Plymouth, English merchants shipped hogsheads of 'very good well cured pilchards' to be quickly dispatched and exchanged for butts of wine and molasses. Fish was shipped to Marseilles, Genoa, Livorno, and even to the Barbary coast.[74] Many firms were efficient in dealing with the shipments, 'with clear orders and discretion' knowing how fish could easily deteriorate, resulting in a loss of profit.

With 'discretion' and often under cover of Protestant partners, Catholics also traded with the Netherlands, where they would complement the English trade with manufactured goods and grains from the Baltic. From the Baltic region, the English imported wheat, rye, flax, tallow, wax, leather, furs, skins, and irons; all basic commodities unavailable elsewhere and soon monopolised by the English.[75] Masts, crucial for the Spanish imperial fleets, also came from Holland. Commodities from the Dutch, Swedish territories, or the Baltic would be exchanged for south European provisions and bullion. The Netherlands needed European, and in particular British manufactured goods to sustain their re-export trade based in Amsterdam; therefore, it was always a profitable market for British merchants. Their goods were directed south, usually to Cadiz where merchants often complained about duty customs, fee entries, freight, and *weighter*.[76] Bad weather often hindered the successful outcome of their transactions and they paid men to look for lost cargoes on more than one occasion. However, the trader William Gramar deemed praying a good tactic and when writing to Aylward about wine, butter, and melons travelling from Malaga to Amsterdam, he quipped 'God will help'.[77]

To access Dutch ports, Catholic merchants utilised the collaboration with non-Catholics or local networks established through the Flemish territories. Particularly in the port of Ostend, the community of Catholic expatriates was prominent. This port, due to its geographical position, provided a link between British and continental trades, connecting London with the Baltic and, as it was part of the Spanish Netherlands, with the Mediterranean. Its proximity with Dunkirk soon turned it into a centre

[74] AY 5, f. 1, Business Correspondence; AY 21, f. 3, Business Correspondence. Letters from Caunter & Howe in Alicante in 1684.

[75] Barrett, 'World Bullion Flows, 1450–1800' in *The Rise of Merchant Empires*, 224–254.

[76] AY 98, Business Accounts. Accounts, receipts, bills of Exchange for merchandise to Dec. 1684; AY 100, Bills, receipts for merchandise to December 1686. William Gramar writing to the Aylwards.

[77] Ibid.

for privateering and smugglers as well.[78] During the seventeenth century an extensive network of Catholic merchants from Cork, Wexford, and Waterford moved to this city. Among the most prominent families were the Carews, the Lynchs, and the Blakes who had networks within Spain and the West Indies. Other affluent families from Waterford were the Fitzgeralds and the Porters. Marriages with other merchant families, such as the Goolds or the Comerfords, strengthened wider networks, spanning from Spain to Bruges, Nantes, and Bordeaux. The staple items exported were Irish butter and hides, and tea and other Indian goods were imported to the south coast of Ireland and England. From the Iberian ports, wine was imported, especially Malaga and the Canaries: In Malaga, two firms, the Brownes and the Blakes, had interest in the grain trade, exporting wheat from the Flemish territories, and re-exporting salt and English dried cod. Through London, they also had interests in West Indian and North American exports. In the Flemish ports and the Dutch territories, these families operated at least until the end of the eighteenth century.[79] Catholic networks extended from Ireland to England, France, the Netherlands, and Spain and their strength was determined by the market's need, tapping at times into Protestant networks and, on occasion, into Catholic ones. Their main focus was the continent but their goods came from as far as India or the Caribbean, contributing to the establishment of international and far-reaching global networks.

From West to East

Although the operations focused on European ports, British merchants looked at the West Indies and the Levant for the most lucrative commodities. In return for their manufacturing products, they wanted exotic goods, fuelling a trade that was becoming ever more global. The accounts registered all sorts of fabrics, mainly blue *presillas*, cinnamon, cloves, and pepper; goods that came from the Middle East or the north of Europe were exchanged for merchandise from Spanish America or from Brazil, where the Portuguese confirmed the presence of 'Indian' spices.[80] Some Catholic families had settlements in the Caribbean dating back to the 1630s, work-

---

[78] Jan Parmentier, 'The Sweets of Commerce: The Hennessys of Ostend and their Networks in the Eighteenth Century' in *Irish and Scottish Mercantile Networks.*

[79] Jan Parmentier, 'A Touch of Ireland: Migrants and Migrations in and to Ostend, Bruges and Dunkirk in the Seventeenth and Eighteenth Centuries', *The International Journal of Maritime History*, 27, 4 (2015): 662–679.

[80] O'Flanagan, *Port Cities of Atlantic Iberia*, 141.

ing as planters and merchants, which continued into the seventeenth and the eighteenth century. In the West Indies they settled in both British and French territories, such as Jamaica, Barbados, Saint Domingue, Martinique, or Montserrat.[81] The Caribbean was an area where strategic planning meant that European powers had the potential to outmanoeuvre one other. The English soon became the key players in this area; settlements of any importance started in the 1620s but it was only in the 1650s, after the conquest of Jamaica (1655), that they posed a serious threat for the Spaniards. From their colonies, the English monitored the movement of the Spanish fleet, while smuggling goods from the Spanish empire in exchanges that involved European as much as North American provisions. The Caribbean was the focal point for inter-imperial exchanges, 'rich for competition, conflict, and intrigue.'[82] Jamaica was a hub for smugglers and privateers that soon became a gem in the British colonial possessions.[83] In Jamaica, Catholics had contacts in Port Royal. These agents were introduced by the Protestant English traders and together they shipped dyes, indigo, pimento, cochineal, and sugar, importing European provisions and manufactured goods. In 1689, for instance, Brailsford asked John Aylward to organise a cargo of 1,000 or 1,200 barrels of beef and 200 or 300 half barrels of pork. They also loaded candles, butter, but refused to stop at Madeira on their voyage in order to load wine.[84] When shipping beef and pork, Aylward was warned to be watchful of his agents because it was quite common to mix pickles with old beef and pork so as to hide the stench. In the West Indies, Irish products, especially beef, were the most marketable, whereas French textiles did not sell well, deemed 'too good' – perhaps expensive – by the Spaniards.[85] Catholic merchants relied on ties of religion, family, and the mercantile community to secure commissions from the area. Colonial goods were in fact becoming essential in the balance of European exchanges. Partners,

---

[81]   K. Block and J. Shaw, 'Subjects without an Empire: The Irish in the Early Modern Caribbean', *Past and Present*, 210 (2011): 33–60.

[82]   F. Quinn, *The French Overseas Empire* (Westport, CT: Praeger, 2002); CO 110–152, Brailsford Papers, National Archives.

[83]   Zahedieh,'The Merchants of Port Royal, Jamaica, and the Spanish Contraband Trade, 1655–1692', *The William and Mary Quarterly*, 43 (1986); A. McFarlane, *The British in the Americas, 1480–1815* (London: Longman, 1994).

[84]   AY 18, f. 13, f. 9, Business Correspondence. Letters from Thomas Brailsford in London on 1 August 1689 and on 27 June 1689.

[85]   L. M. Cullen, *An Economic History of Ireland since 1660* (London: B. T. Batsford, 1972), 26–49. Irish shipping and seamen were treated as English and could engage in England's trade. Ireland could ship linens but limit imports. Since 1663, England allowed Irish exports of beef to be sent directly to the Americas, instead of passing through English ports.

like William Gramar or Aaron Atkins, travelled back and forth between Jamaica and the Netherlands, and in 1686 advised the Aylwards that 'if the trade now we have with the Spaniards will continue, all the sorts of linnins will be demanded, fine flannel, woollen goods *Norwich stuff* goes quick off at good ratios, also all sort of liqueurs and Irish product sell generally well, this being the best in all the West Indies'.[86] From there, the goods would be unloaded in Spain, where they would be redirected to the north of Europe, together with Mediterranean goods, Levantine spices, and peppers accessed through North Africa and the Italian ports.

The North African coast was dangerous, rife with pirates and disease. However, this area also offered splendid opportunities to tap into the East India trade, where spices, silks, pepper, and slaves could be purchased. Europe, in particular, craved pepper, consuming up to seven million pounds per year;[87] therefore, despite the difficult trading conditions and potential problems, European merchants were attracted to the area.[88] Catholic merchants invested in the area throughout their whole career, but according to their records it was where they experienced the most problems. Transactions were difficult as cargoes could be detained; in 1685, the ship of the Captain John Macharell (Mackerel) was kept for forty days in quarantine because of the plague from Algeria. His cargo of wheat, in which the Aylwards had a share, was severely delayed. The quality of the North African wheat was extremely good and the captain should have obtained it at the most moderate price possible, 'not exceeding 13 *reals* per *fanega*'.[89] Then, after unloading the cargo at Marseilles, he would go back to Oran and load for Malaga, where the cargo was expected by the Aylwards and Charles Peers. Mackerell was also supposed to go in search of corn as well; perhaps in Cape Negro, Tunisia, after inquiring as to whether or not the war had ended.[90]

In North Africa, Catholics worked mainly with Protestant merchants as the English, in particular, had established communities of expatriates

---

[86] AY 13, f. 7, Business Correspondence. Letters to John Aylward from Aaron Atkins at Amsterdam and Port Royal, Apr. 1684–Jul. 1688.

[87] H. Furber, *Rival Empires of Trade in the Orient, 1600–1800: Europe and the World in the Age of Expansion*, vol. II (London: Oxford University Press, 1976), 236; C. M. Cipolla, *Allegro ma non troppo* (Bologna: Il Mulino, 1988); O'Flanagan, *Port Cities of Atlantic Iberia*, 141. Pepper came from Africa or India and it was soon monopolised by Lisbon.

[88] Fusaro, *Political Economies.*

[89] AY 4, f. 36, Business Correspondence. Miscellaneous letters to John Aylward, Jan.–Dec. 1685.

[90] Ibid. Among Peers' network featured the merchant Patrick Lynch and Charles Price. Another partner involved was Goodwin.

since the sixteenth century. This collaboration exemplifies how Catholics and Protestants worked together to further exchanges within the Mediterranean. Wheat also came from North Africa and could perhaps be found in Cape Negro, Tunisia. In spite of the instruction, merchants at times failed to inform their captains about possible epidemics and the insalubrious conditions of the African ports. As a result, the exchanges would not be profitable. On contracting the plague, Mackarell was forced to rest for thirty days on arrival in Marseilles, coming from the 'cost of Barbarie'. After importuning the 'intendants of the health' and at the relentless demand of some friends, they let him go before the quarantine was over.[91] In Europe, by the end of the seventeenth century, measures to prevent the spread of epidemics worked quite effectively; the belief was that plague came solely from North Africa and the Levant areas. Mediterranean ports elected health representatives who would forbid travellers from suspected plague areas to come into their cities and also built houses for the sick outside the city wall. The ships were kept just outside the port and their cargo was cleaned through fumigation. In the Lazzaretto, the crew and the passengers had to be kept in isolation and the goods purified. After these procedures, they could access the port. All the Mediterranean countries had a similar sanitary policy and, through patents, officials monitored the 'health' of the ports where the ships had originated and stopped. If the port was at high risk, then the captains and the goods could be detained for as long as sixty days. Ultimately, the corn and wheat were never procured. From North Africa they once imported elephants' 'teeth', a commodity quite popular in France, requiring them to be without 'cracks or roughness'.[92]

In the 'Barbary Coast', British merchants were concerned about trading with the port of Alessandria, Egypt, because of the competition from the Jewish community and the French merchants, who apparently 'enjoyed more privileges in custom'.[93] In Egypt, the Aylwards' ships could be detained for three or four months due to embargo. From there, they were ready to go to Zante, Smyrna, looking for corn, currants, and silks. The first stop would have been Zante, where the English bought currants and tapped into

---

[91]   AY 4, Business Correspondence. Miscellaneous letters to John Aylward. Jan.–Dec. 1685; D. Panzac, 'Plague and Seafaring in the Ottoman Mediterranean in the Eighteenth Century' in *Trade and Cultural Exchange in the Early Modern Mediterranean: Braudel's Maritime Legacy*, ed. Maria Fusaro, Colin Heywood, and M.-S. Omri (London: Tauris, 2010), 45–68.

[92]   AY 18, f. 13, Business Correspondence. Letter from Brailsford in London on 1 August 1689.

[93]   AY 49, f. 1, Business Correspondence. Letters to John Aylward from Edward Hill at Livorno on 8 December 1683; AY 4, f. 31, Business Correspondence.

the Greek mercantile networks in the Ottoman Morea. Subsequently, they would move slightly farther east towards Smyrna and Alexandretta, where they could buy spices and silks. Smyrna emerged in the early seventeenth century as an outlet for Iranian silks. It was the distribution centre for silk travelling to Europe, managed by the Armenians. There, merchants took advantage of low custom fees and excellent port facilities.[94] From the Turkish dominion, other imports included wine, oil, and alum; however, the most valuable commodity was raw cotton, which sustained the growing English manufacturing industry. Luxury fabrics also came from Aleppo, another major port in the eastern Mediterranean, linked to Smyrna.[95] Many English merchants were in fact established in present-day Syria, from where they accessed the silk routes. The Iranian silks would reach Livorno, Marseilles, Amsterdam, and Venice. Silks came from Persia, through Turkey, and from Sicily, Piedmont, and Calabria. In fact, Italy had been one of the main producers of silks in the West since the Middle Ages, and fuelled the emerging English silk weaving industry that developed thanks to the contribution of the Huguenot immigrants from France in the 1680s. Italian silk was of finer quality than silk from the Levant and, in England, *Filofino* silk was used to produce Italian style 'organzines'.[96] The trade was lucrative, as in 1700 Sicily was flooded with silk. At the time, Indian silk was prohibited on the island and local silk was in high demand. The Aylwards were informed that the warehouses in Calabria were well supplied, so they thought the product would be a good investment, a cheap commodity and easy to use in barter. But being a highly sought-after product also meant that it was subject to fraud and indeed a firm in Messina was sorry to hear the Aylwards' 'lament' that the silk previously consigned was of poor quality. They had probably been cheated by the 'silk-men', but they hoped Aylward had managed to

[94] G. Ambrose, 'English Traders at Aleppo (1658–1758)', *The Economic History Review*, 3, 2 (1931): 246–267; I. B. McCabe, 'Small Town Merchants, Global Ventures: The Maritime Trade of the New Julfa Armenians in the Seventeenth and Eighteenth Centuries' in *Maritime History as Global History?* ed. M. Fusaro and A. Polonia (Newfoundland: International Maritime Economic History Association, 2010).

[95] Steensgaard, *The Asian Trade Revolution of the Seventeenth Century: The East India Companies and the Decline of the Caravan Trade* (Chicago: University of Chicago Press, 1973); Furber, *Rival Empires of Trade in the Orient, 1600–1800*; *Goods from the East: Trading Eurasia*, ed. Maxine Berg with F. Gottmann, H. Hodacs, and C. Nierstrasz (Basingstoke: Palgrave Macmillan:, 2015); D. Goffman, *Izmir and the Levantine World, 1550–1650* (Seattle: University of Washington Press, 1990).

[96] G. Symcox, 'Savoy Britain and Victor Amadeus II: Or, the Use and Abuse of Allies in England's Rise to Greatness, 1660–1763 in *Britain's Rise to Greatness, 1660–1763*, ed. Stephen B. Baxter (Berkeley: University of California Press, 1983), 151–184.

sell it at the height of its value.[97] Among the accounts it is documented that the Aylwards sometimes imported calicoes;[98] however, this fabric was not in popular demand and the associates preferred cheap textiles or the finer silks.[99] Ultimately, in the Italian peninsula, silks would be joined with oil and wine and shipped to Spain or to the British Isles.

The Mediterranean made global exchanges possible and explains why the northern powers 'swarmed' there 'like many heavy insects'.[100] The Catholics were among those 'insects', investing in the area, braving political turmoil, pirates, maladies, and competing with other nations. More than once, the Aylwards and associates commissioned ships to search for lost vessels. In 1685, the cargo of Captain Thomas Rover went missing after setting off from Cadiz. The ship was supposed to have landed in Cape Negro, in Tunisia, but had gotten lost. Despite the troubles, Catholics were aware that the area could be potentially lucrative. Especially during the years in Malaga, they took advantage of the strategic position of this port, which offered easy entrance into the wider south-eastern Mediterranean routes. From Malaga and Cadiz they often worked with Italian ports as well. From the peninsula, it was possible to access the Levantine trade indirectly, by accessing the networks already established by the Venetians. The first English ship to re-enter the Mediterranean was the *Swallow* in 1573, embarking from London.[101] After that, the English aimed to disrupt Venice's monopoly and never traded with her. Indeed, the Aylwards' trade with Venice was almost non-existent; only in 1683 did Edward Hill brief them about shipments from the Gulf of Venice.

Italy itself did not offer much: mainly olive oil, wine, corn, and wheat. Transactions involving Italian goods alone were scant. Among the transactions listed, only a few mentioned solely Italian staples; in 1684, corn came from Sardinia, but it was extremely expensive and the arrangement ended, considered to be 'shut up'.[102] In 1685, corn would come from Manfredonia,

---

[97]   AY 22, Business Correspondence, Letters to John Aylward from Chamberlin, Slocombe and Lee at Messina, Oct. 1698–Dec. 1700. The Italian traders that advised on the barter were Carlo V, Vincenzo Marletta, and Francesco Cardia. The correspondents were Mr Enys and Mr Aldington of Cales.

[98]   Berg, *Luxury and Pleasure*, 49.

[99]   AY 93, Business Correspondence. Letters from Patrick Woulfe in Puerto Santa Maria.

[100] Fusaro, *Trade and Cultural Exchange in the Early Modern Mediterranean*, 10.

[101] Fusaro, *Political Economies*, 44; G. Pagano de Divitiis, *Mercanti Inglesi Nell'Italia del Seicento: Navi, Traffic, Egemonie* (Venezia: Marsilio Editori, 1990), 19.

[102] AY 3, f. 16, Business Correspondence. Miscellaneous letters to John Aylward, Jan.–Oct. 1684.

Apulia. From Genoa and Livorno, they exported 'white lemons' and wheat.[103] Nevertheless, the firms that operated in Italian ports, such as Brooking & Parker, Harper & Cross, Warren, Caunter & Howe, the Pincettis, Cucco, Costa & Sanguineti, Chamberlain, Slocombe & Lee, were numerous; from Spain or Britain, contacts with all of them were prized. In fact, Italy was the Mediterranean dock from which the surrounding waters could be controlled. Foreign Catholics had easy access to Italian ports and helped secure the control of the region. In particular, the Aylwards had correspondence with Livorno, which, thanks to its status as a free port and its welcoming religious policies, had quickly developed into the redistribution centre of the Mediterranean. Many religious groups, in particular Armenians and Jews, worked there, bringing with them knowledge and connections from the east.[104] The 'northerners' chose it also because of the lenient commercial policies that allowed them to dispose of merchandise of dubious origin. It soon became a destination for merchants who did not want to be constrained by government regulation, including the Levant Company, and it became an entry port for colonial goods from Cadiz. It became an operational base in the centre of the Mediterranean and the British soon turned it into their 'nest', from which they could disrupt the Venetian monopoly with the Levant.[105] By the late 1660s, almost all English imports from the Italian peninsula came from there. English merchants would import dry fish, *piggs lead*, tin, iron, and textiles, and they would re-export grain, alum from the papal state, pepper, currants, saffron, pepper, silks from the Levant, and wool, leather, and wax from North Africa.[106] Livorno redistributed goods coming from the Levant, Spain, and France, and also from the south Italian ports of Naples, Palermo, and Gallipoli. By taking advantage of the Messinese War (1674–1679), English merchants monopolised the south Italian

---

[103] AY 49, f. 1, Business Correspondence. Letters to John Aylward: two from Edward Hill at Livorno (1683), five from Thomas Hill at Exeter, one from old Mr Edward Hill, at Priory (a personal letter), Dec. 1683, July 1685– Nov. 1688; AY 4, f. 31, Business Correspondence. Brooking was the brother-in-law of John Wyse. All those firms were introduced through Power & Hill.

[104] I. B. McCabe, 'Small Town Merchants, Global Ventures: The Maritime Trade of the New Julfa Armenians in the Seventeenth and Eighteenth Centuries' in *Maritime History as Global History?* ed. M. Fusaro and A. Polonia (Newfoundland: International Maritime Economic History Association, 2010); Trivellato, *The Familiarity of Strangers.*

[105] M. D'Angelo, *Mercanti Inglesi a Livorno, 1573–1737* (Messina: Istituto di Studi Storici Gaetano Salvemini, 2004); Trivellato, *The Familiarity of Strangers.*

[106] AY 51, f. 2, Business Correspondence. Letter from Charles Horde in London on 18 December 1691.

trade, even the internal exchanges from Apulia to Naples.[107] These south Italian ports were not necessarily important in economic terms, but their geopolitical role was crucial, as the area allowed the control of the Spanish imperial exchanges within Mediterranean ports. In Livorno, Catholic merchants disposed of plenty of goods, such as rice, cochineal, pepper, and Barbadian and Jamaican sugar. They also received Gallipoli oil, from Apulia, thanks to several ships coming from Scandarone (Alexandretta), in Turkey, that would stop along the Adriatic coast.[108]

Mediterranean goods were in high demand in the British Isles, but equally British exports were highly sought after as they fed and clothed the continent and its colonies cheaply, as well as helping to arm the war-ridden Mediterranean. At the beginning of the seventeenth century, in a few decades, English ships were in service in Algiers, Alexandretta, Constantinople, and Alexandria. The English soon settled in Minorca, Malta, Tangier, and Gibraltar and for almost two centuries witnessed French attempts to control the area and fight the Spanish. From the south of Spain and the south of France, the interests in the Mediterranean were extensive. Ultimately, the goods were directed to the British Isles, the Netherlands, and the Flemish territories. Indeed, despite the rising importance of the Atlantic in the imperial age, the Mediterranean was not forgotten as it played a crucial role as *trait d'union* between the old and the new world, making global exchanges truly possible. In fact, the importance of this sea perhaps increased and Catholics participated in this process by helping secure networks in Spanish, French, and Italian ports where American goods could be exchanged for Levantine spices. This process had its origins in the seventeenth century when northern Europeans re-entered the Mediterranean, and Catholics were instrumental in this development.

The goods and the networks examined here explain how British traders worked in both the Atlantic and the Mediterranean. Global markets were emerging, but the relationship between the British Isles and continental Europe remained vital. Despite the desire to refrain from trading with Catholic enemies, Britain, and England in particular, increased its relations with Spain, France and the Italian ports. The south of Europe offered a

---

[107] H. Koenigsberger, 'English Merchants in Naples and Sicily in the Seventeenth Century, *The English Historical Review*, 62, 244 (1947): 304–326.

[108] AY 49, Business Correspondence. Letters to John Aylward: two from Edward Hill at Livorno (1683), five from Thomas Hill at Exeter, one from old Mr Edward Hill, at Priory (a personal letter), Dec. 1683, July 1685– Nov. 1688; AY 4, f. 31, Business Correspondence. Brooking was the brother-in-law of John Wyse. All those firms were introduced through Power & Hill.

market for the colonial re-exports, whereas the provisions produced in the Mediterranean were necessary for the British balance of trade. The goods traded ranged from fabrics to Virginia tobacco, brandy, wine, and cacao. Alum, pepper, hats, and woollen drapery of English manufacture; rice, raisins, nutmeg, salmon, and bee's wax were moved from one continent to another within transactions that always involved many participants. Calicoes, button, gold threads, and socks flowed across the Atlantic and the Mediterranean. From Cadiz, London, and St Malo, letters were exchanged with many partners in England, Spain, Ireland, Italy, and Jamaica. From London, one account listed 1,200 needles, padlocks, boxes of musk, women's thimbles, and fifty pounds of *sempiternas* fabrics. From Jamaica the order might be for *Norwich stuff*, mixt *sarges*, and fine flannel. In 1691, on *flotas* they shipped musk, *ellbroads*, and *scarletts* fabrics, chests of *mercurios* and thimbles. In return, they expected cochineal and cinnamon.[109] British Catholics participated in those inter-imperial markets. Their religion facilitated acceptance in continental ports, allowing British firms to operate undisturbed. The importance of the merchants examined here clarifies not only the importance of Catholics in enforcing global networks, but also the opportunity they had to establish inter-imperial exchanges that ultimately benefited British commerce. Catholic networks were already established in the early seventeenth century, initially participating in the English colonial trade. They showed the necessity of working alongside Protestants and the latter's acceptance, in order to benefit the national economy.

There is nothing exceptional in Catholics' dynamics in trade. They were ordinary merchants who participated in the emerging markets, but the endurance of their networks depicts a new role for the Catholic community of the British Isles. They fit perfectly into the image sketched by Perry Gauci of the London merchant, the notion that success was achieved through steady accumulation rather than spectacular profits, and 'through no remedy but patience'.[110] Undoubtedly, within the mercantile community, ties of friendship and solidarity helped in achieving the unexpected. In April 1686, Champneys & Pitts, in Seville, thanked John Aylward for warning them that French men were off the coast of Cadiz, and of their

---

[109] AY 109, f. 111, Business Correspondence. Bills and accounts for merchandise to Dec. 1697; AY 13, f. 7, Business Correspondence. Letters to John Aylward from Aaron Atkins at Amsterdam and Port Royal, Apr. 1684–Jul. 1688; AY 6, f. 22, Business Correspondence. Miscellaneous letters to John Aylward, Jan. 1687–Dec. 1691.

[110] AY 93, Business Correspondence. Letter from Patrick Woulfe in Puerto Santa Maria; Gauci, *Emporium of the World*.

concern about the Galleons.[111] At about the same time, Atkins, writing from Amsterdam, informed Aylward, who was in Malaga, about a present sent on a freight that had departed the week before. 'I have sent you a small barrel of the best Rein wine which I pray you accept [...] I am glad the wine proved so good and at the first opportunity I will send some of the same [...] I will be satisfied with whatever you do. I am totally careful having suffered sufficiently.[112] In 1685, Sardner wrote about his disappointment in the 'affreightment' of the *Gionetta* and her loading of corn in Naples. He begged patience as the trade was subject to such accidents and reconciled with the fact that the corn from Palermo had at least arrived. Indeed, as Gauci and Patrick Woulfe suggest, patience was possibly the most important quality for a merchant in the 'competitive world of international trade'.[113] However, beside a trustworthy partner, a merchant could also find 'more a brother than a friend' who, despite the disappointments, would write a letter primarily sending wishes for a Merry Christmas and joyful holidays, 'wishing health and happiness, I kiss your hands. Buenas Fiestas'.[114]

[111] AY 23, f. 8, Business Correspondence. Letters to John Aylward from Messrs Champneys and Pitts at Seville, July 1684–Apr. 1686.

[112] AY 13, f. 4, Business Correspondence. Letters to John Aylward from Aaron Atkins at Amsterdam and Port Royal, Apr. 1684–July 1688.

[113] Gauci, *Emporium of the World.*

[114] AY 93, f. 20, Business Correspondence. Patrick Woulfe describes Mr Arthur as a brother; AY 4, f. 26, Business Correspondence. Miscellaneous letters to John Aylward, Jan.–Dec. 1685. The holiday wishes were from Mr Sardner.

Chapter 6
Catholic Women in the Mercantile Community: A Female Epilogue?

The Aylward Papers are predominantly made up of correspondence between male merchants, but sometimes letters do emerge from women, offering glimpses into their lives and work. I felt it would further understanding of the community as a whole to explore how both men and women operated in Atlantic–Mediterranean trade. My research into the history of women in business thus came about almost by chance, as my focus had up until that point been on their apparently dominant male counterparts. Yet I soon realised the importance for my study of looking into the lives of women, or of those few who had left behind valuable traces of their work and thoughts. Unlike their husbands, fathers, or brothers, women in their business correspondence would also often discuss their health and families, worries and emotions, offering the opportunity, I felt, to humanise the work and explore what merchants experienced when operating in those ports. This chapter is not an exhaustive analysis of female traders in a religious minority, but opens a new line of enquiry that might benefit from further investigation.

Trying to understand if the women represented in the Aylward Papers were anomalous or not, I started to investigate the literature, which is extremely rich on the topic. All over Europe – in Germany, the Netherlands, and Britain – women worked alongside their husbands and fathers in the most diverse businesses, ranging from trade to retail, and from shipbuilding to the textile industry.[1] When necessary, they refocused the family

---

[1] D. Rabuzzi, 'Women as Merchants in Eighteenth-Century Northern Germany: The Case of Stralsund, 1750–1830', *Central European History*, 28, 4 (1995): 435–456; Danielle Van Den Heuvel and Elise Van Nederveen Meerkerk, 'Partners in Business? Spousal Cooperation in Trades in Early Modern England and the Dutch Republic', *Continuity & Change* 23/2 (2008); H. Doe, 'Waiting for her Ship to Come in? The Female Investor in Nineteenth-century Sailing Vessels', *Economic History Review*, 63, 1 (2010): 85–106; Amy Froide, *Silent Partners: Women as Public Investors during Britain's Financial Revolution* (Oxford: Oxford University Press, 2017); Pamela Sharpe 'Gender in the Economy: Female Merchants and Family Businesses in the

business and certainly showed more entrepreneurship than male family members did in similar situations. For men's business craft, the contribution of their wives seems to have been indispensable, and judging by the relative ease with which these women were able to continue their husband's trade following bereavement, scholars disagree that married women were restricted in their labour by their reproductive and domestic duties. Marriage could be vital to provide access to the business world, and no one denies that many women failed in business due to lack of expertise and contacts. Female business owners always ranged between five and nine per cent of the total number of owners. There were barriers against women in the political and legal systems but economic practice diverged –women knew business and when working they outperformed men. Businesses varied, and in trading, European women were involved in continental and Atlantic deals, shipping wine to Britain or coordinating smuggling and privateering in the Caribbean. In Jamaica for instance, British women were involved in trans-Atlantic and trans-imperial negotiations; they traded with the Spanish territories in a clear violation of Britain's commercial policies, especially in times of war, and they financed assaults on enemy vessels and slavery.[2] Overall, in the marketplace women and men pursued similar interests. They worked with the same ports and commodities, and mastered the same knowledge as they pursued connections and financial success. Women were not outliers or anomalous and contributed to building business empires alongside their spouses or parents. But more than just trade, they were also involved in finance, with the literature showing records of them owning stocks worth more than £1,000 in the South Sea Company, East India Company, and the Bank of England – fuelling the slave and cotton trades while enriching themselves and furthering the interests of the mother country.[3] Among these narratives I found the exact same story that I was observing in the Aylward Papers, and thought I could not miss the opportunity to include Catholic women.

When looking at female Catholics I did not find any substantial difference between the way men and women wrote about or dealt in trade. As previously mentioned, these women knew their business and at times outperformed their male partners. Perhaps men did not necessarily think of them as equals and were not always enthusiastic about working alongside

---

British Isles, 1600–1850', *Social History/Histoire Sociale* 34 (2001); Christine Walker, 'Pursuing her Profits: Women in Jamaica, Atlantic Slavery and a Globalising Market, 1700–60', 26, 3 (2014): 478–501.

2   Walker, 'Pursuing Her Profits'.

3   Ibid.; Anne Laurence, 'Lady Betty Hastings (1682–1739): Godly Patron', *Women's History Review*, 19, 2 (2010): 201–213.

female counterparts. Indeed, a certain Benjamin Bake in August 1689 wrote to John Aylward that 'if a creature is not used according to the intent of the creator [...] looks to me but little less than dreadful.'[4] The woman referred to is Mary Wyse and the advice he sought from his friend was how to persuade her to marry him. Mary Wyse (formerly Mary Brooking) was born in Exeter to a family of merchants. Years later, in the late 1680s, she went on to take over the family business after the death of her husband John Wyse and would go on to invest in the exchanges between English ports and the Spanish empire with her accounts recording transactions between London, Exeter, and Cadiz. Mr Bake had known Mary for many years, yet felt that after the loss of her husband she should accept somebody else and refuse this new 'unnatural' role within the business. Bake thought that as a widow, refusing to remarry would mean she would 'be deprived of the pleasures of a new world [...] and would 'sit down under the unhappy thought of the calamities of the old ones, which [would] interrupt all those pleasant moments which otherwise she might be capable to enjoy [with a new husband].'[5] Mrs Wyse, however, like many other women at the time, refused to remarry and instead became heavily involved in Atlantic–Mediterranean trade. Like hers, many other families including the Creaghs, the Comerfords, the Aylwards, and the Brookings – who operated along international networks – allowed for a redefinition of the role of Catholic women within Atlantic–Mediterranean trade in the late seventeenth and early eighteenth centuries. Mr Bake, after being refused, snapped back that women in business were 'unnatural'; nevertheless, my documents suggest otherwise: showing how they participated in the economy and contributed to support the British commercial expansion.

Early Modern Women and the Economy

In the most recent works on the early modern economy, the contribution of women has been reconsidered.[6] Whether widows, spouses, spinsters,

---

[4] AY 16, f. 6, Business Correspondence. Letter to John Aylward from Benjamin Bake in Exeter.

[5] Ibid.

[6] Pamela Sharpe, 'Gender in the Economy': 283–306; Susan A. Amussen and Allyson M. Poska, 'Shifting the Frame: Trans-imperial Approaches to Gender in the Atlantic World', *Early Modern Women: An Interdisciplinary Journal*, 9 (2014): 3–24; Hannah Barker, *The Business of Women, Female Enterprise and Urban Development in Northern England 1760–1830* (Oxford: Oxford University Press, 2006), 105–133; Sheryllynne Haggerty, *The British Atlantic Trading Community, 1760–1810*; Sara

and both in business or in finance, women played an active role in the economy.[7] 'Older' women, and in particular middle-class widows, would not necessarily remarry or retire to a reclusive life, but would instead take charge of the family business and work; for them leaving the command to adult children or male relatives was not the only option.[8] In addition, even married women would not necessarily leave their profession and so work did not always stop at marriage and resume at widowhood. Amy Erickson and Alexandra Shephard argue that marital identity was not more important than the occupational one and in early modern Europe, married women worked, defying legal constraints and social conventions. They worked with their husbands or in separate businesses, contributing to the family income even without an urgent need, and possessed skills that would allow them to take over trade when, or if, their husbands suddenly passed away.[9]

In commerce, Margaret Hunt argues that women contributed to the capitalisation of the family business with their dowry, and provided assistance when their husbands were alive. She concurs with Grassby that women had a personal stake in the survival of the family business as they had spent their own money on it.[10] Equally, Anne Laurence has revalued the female role in business, accounting, and finance where the narrative is predominantly male. Women were resourceful and they participated in the economy, particularly as in the late seventeenth century the financial revolution offered opportunities to anyone with capital to invest.[11] This

Mendelson and Patricia Crawford, *Women in Early Modern England, 1550–1720* (Oxford: Clarendon Press, 1998).

[7]   B. Moring and R. Wall, *Widows in European Economy and Society, 1600–1920* (Woodbridge: Boydell Press, 2017).

[8]   Sara Mendelson and Patricia Crawford, *Women in Early Modern England, 1550–1720*, 174–183; Barbara J. Todd, 'The Remarrying Widow: A Stereotype Reconsidered' in *Women in English Society, 1500–1800, ed.* Mary Prior (London and New York: Routledge, 1985), 54–85; Jeremy Boulton, 'London Widowhood Revisited: The Decline of Female Remarriage in the Seventeenth and Early Eighteenth Century', *Continuity and Change,* 5, 3 (1990): 323–355.

[9]   Amy L. Erickson, 'Married Women's Occupations in Eighteenth-Century London', *Continuity and Change,* 23, 2 (2008): 267–307; Alexandra Shephard, 'Minding their own Business: Married Women and Credit in Early Eighteenth-Century London', *Transactions of the RHS,* 25 (2015): 53–74.

[10]   Margaret Hunt, *Women in Eighteenth-Century Europe* (London: Routledge, 2014), 168–208; Richard Grassby, *Kinship and Capitalism: Marriage, Family and Business in the English-Speaking World, 1580–1740* (Cambridge: Cambridge University Press, 2001), 117–150.

[11]   *Women and their Money 1700–1950: Essays on Women and Finance,* ed. Anne Laurence, Josephine Maltby, and Janette Rutterford (London: Routledge, 2009).

work concurs with the recent studies on women in the early modern commercial world. Within the mercantile community, women worked alongside their husbands and male relatives, and were acquainted with accounting, writing, reading, and speaking more than one language. If not directly involved with the family firm, they were commonly involved in trade-related activities such as retailing or inn keeping, taking charge of the business when their fathers or husbands died. Regarding religious minorities, historians who have looked at various religious groups agree on this point; whether Quakers, Presbyterians, or Jews, women in widowhood would take control of the family activity and continue it.[12] Although at times resorting to a guardian, they would still have a say in it and only occasionally would they sell up or perhaps remarry. Therefore, recent historiography seems to agree that it is time to rewrite the histories of religion, of women, and of the economy.

On British Catholic women, literature has so far offered traditional figures, women as nuns or matrons. But their work has not been denied;[13] in fact, as matrons or as nuns, women worked for the community running charities or sponsoring female schools. However, regarding the Catholic mercantile community, literature is scant, evaluating only groups of religious *conversos* that worked between France and Spain, moving along

---

[12] Frederick B. Tolles, *Meeting House and Counting House: The Quaker Merchants of Colonial Philadelphia, 1682–1763* (New York: Norton & Co., 1963); Sheryllynne Haggerty, *The British-Atlantic Trading Community, 1760–1810, Men, Women, and the Distribution of Goods* (Leiden: Boydell Press, 2006), 79, 222; Sharpe, 'Gender in the Economy', 291; A. Froide, 'The Religious Lives of Single Women in the Anglo-Atlantic World: Quaker Missionaries, Protestant Nuns, and Covert Catholics' in *Women, Religion and the Atlantic World (1600–1800)*, ed. D. Kostroun and L. Vollendorf (Toronto: University of Toronto Press, 2009), 60–78.

[13] On women and religion see J. Lay, 'An English Nun's Authority: Early Modern Spiritual Controversy and the Manuscripts of Barbara Constable' in *Gender, Catholicism and Spirituality: Women and the Roman Catholic Church in Britain and Europe, 1200–1900*, ed. Laurence Lux-Sterritt and Carmen Mangion (New York: Palgrave , 2011), 99–114; C. Walker, '"When God Shall Restore them to their Kingdoms": Nuns, Exiled Stuarts and English Catholic Identity, 1688–1745' in *Religion and Women in Britain, c. 1660–1760*, ed. S. Apetri and H. Smith (Burlington: Ashgate, 2014), 79–98; C. Bowden, 'The English Convents in Exile and Questions of National Identity, 1600–1688' in *British and Irish Emigrants and Exiles in Europe 1603–1688, ed.* David Worthington (Leiden: Brill, 2010), 297–314; J. Goodrich, 'Ensigne-Bearers of St Claire: Elizabeth Evelinge's Early Translations and the Restoration of English Franciscanism', 83–101 and S. Brietz-Monta, 'Anne Dacre Howard, Countess of Arundel and Catholic Patronage', 59–82 in *English Women: Religion and Textual Production 1500–1625*, ed. M. White (Burlington: Ashgate, 2011).

family ties but within a Catholic world.[14] Instead, the Aylwards' partners hereby examined allowed a depiction of a new figure of Catholic women who also worked as merchants, either alongside their fathers and husbands or independently, within a Protestant commercial world. Between 1670 and 1714, the British Catholic community established networks extending from the West Indies to the Levant and Catholic merchants moved between imperial waters, blurring the boundaries of Spanish, French, and British colonial routes and possessions. Business was run by men, but the women in their families contributed to the effort. Their role cannot be disregarded; if nothing else, simply for strengthening connections in long distance trade and in ensuring the survival of the family business from one generation to the next. Catholic firms are attested in Atlantic–Mediterranean trade for centuries and women contributed to the capitalisation and to the survival of the family firms. They worked for their families and they fostered British exchanges that were becoming ever more global.

Mrs Helena Aylward offers one of the most prominent examples of Catholic women's involvement in trade.[15] She was an entrepreneur who, when widowed for the second time, took over the family business and ran it as her husband did. The case of Mrs Aylward –beyond its individual interest – suggests that Catholic women played an active role in the early British economy, participating in business and sustaining the commercial and financial revolution led by Protestant men. Although Helena had a son, Michael Trublet, she acted independently and never in partnership with him. They exchanged correspondence in which they discussed their well-being, but rarely business. Trublet seemed to have stayed in France, working at times with his mother's associates; and although he had taken over the business of his father, Helena's first husband, the pair did not work together.

Mrs Aylward is perhaps just one case. However, her family moved within a mercantile group in which many other women worked. Comparing their life and work to those of others allows us to rethink the relation of Catholic women and the economy. It cannot be denied that even when part of merchant families, female Catholics followed traditional paths of marriage,

---

[14]   G. Brunelle, 'The Price of Assimilation: Spanish and Portuguese Women in French Cities, 1500–1650' in *Women in Port: Gendering Communities, Economies, and Social Networks in Atlantic Port Cities, 1500–1850*, ed. Douglas Catterall and Jodi Campbell (Leiden: Brill, 2012), 155–182.

[15]   On Mrs Aylward, see my own article 'Mrs Helena Aylward: A British Catholic Mother, Spouse and Businesswoman in the Commercial Age (1705–1714)', *British Catholic History*, 33, 4 (2017): 603–621.

motherhood, or of entering a convent. However, alongside these roles, they also worked. They mastered knowledge of the dynamics of trade, and showed great business acumen. They proved able to run businesses when their husbands were absent, suggesting that they had been trained for the job ready to take over at fairly short notice. They are addressed by the other partners as merchants, suggesting that they played on the same level. In trade, they worked like any other merchant, securing transatlantic deals, diversifying interests and working with Catholic associates and others outside the community when needed. Ultimately, they secured the continuity of the family trades from one generation to the other, and ensured their survival in Atlantic–Mediterranean commerce for centuries.

In various European ports, Mrs Wyse, Mrs Creagh, Mrs Brooking, and Mrs Comerford each worked, mourned, cleared debts, and carried on with their lives, working as proactively as their late husbands did; investing in the same markets and adopting the same commercial strategies. Ultimately, they contributed to sustaining the emerging British commercial expansion.[16] Their dealings show that Catholic traders, both male and female, together sustained the British economy, playing an active role during the late seventeenth and early eighteenth centuries. Women worked with their male counterparts and did not disregard partners based on religion. Catholic women worked with other Catholics, both male and female, but also with Protestants when the need arose. These women did not access business independently, but as daughters or wives, and being born into merchant families and marrying into others allowed them to master the literary and numerical skills needed to keep account books in order. They were aware of the markets, gathered information, and took business decisions. Catholic women tended to marry within the community and there was no attempt to defy female stereotypes and social conventions of the time. As Catholics, for the most part they married and bore children, or became nuns. Nevertheless, when they had the opportunity, they worked, they traded in their own right and operated both within and outside the community. Mainly based in English and Dutch ports, they fuelled the exchanges with the south of Europe. They kept the business going, even at times of warfare. Given the width of their networks and the business longevity of their families, they exemplify the important role of Catholic women in the first British commercial expansion.

[16]   AY 7, Business Correspondence. Miscellaneous letters to John Aylward, Jan.–Dec. 1692; AY 128, Personal Correspondence. Letters from Helena Aylward to various relatives on the death of her husband, June and August 1705.
AY 101, Business Accounts. Bills, accounts, receipts for merchandise to Dec. 1687.

Traditional Roles

Within the Catholic community, women filled different roles, certainly as traders but also as more conventional figures such as nuns, lodgers, or simply daughters to be married off.[17] In 1701, one of the Aylwards' partners in Spain, Nicholas Kehoe, wrote about his niece Mary Bray in Cadiz. She had been advised by John Aylward to spend two years in a convent as becoming a nun was thought the best solution for her happiness. She was willing to comply, and was free to choose as she wished, however her uncle strongly believed that she was more inclined to be a nun than to marry, so as to be secure for her lifetime, 'because marriage is uncertain if not well'.[18] Kehoe also thought that a nunnery was safer when there were rumours of yet another conflict. He was confident that the religious and political authorities such as the 'Archbishop of Seville, some cardinals and the French ambassador' were on their side, but the situation was volatile and seen as difficult for a young girl. At 3pm on 29 March 1701, Mary Bray entered the Conception convent 'for a trial', to see if she could bear life in a nunnery, a necessary step given that she did not understand the language,[19] yet she wanted to keep the promise made to her friends in Spain and in Ireland. It was not easy for Irish women to integrate in foreign convents. The problem was not only the language, but also identity, as on the continent anyone from the British Isles was presumed to be English – something which could cause conflict when the two nations were at war.

Irish nuns in Spain did not lead a reclusive life, but had the opportunity to be involved in work. They kept ties with their families and communities. Mary Bray was thankful that Mr Trublet, the son of Mrs Aylward, and his business partner Woulfe sometimes visited her, *'de quando en quando'*.[20] Indeed, these visits allowed nuns to remain close to their community and to strengthen local networks. Despite being in nunneries, women, especially from wealthy backgrounds, sponsored pastoral as well as educational

---

[17]   Lay, 'An English Nun's Authority', 99–114; Walker, 'When God Shall Restore them to their Kingdoms', 79–98; Bowden, 'The English Convents in Exile and Questions of National Identity', 297–314; Goodrich, 'Ensigne-Bearers of St Claire: Elizabeth Evelinge's Early Translations and the Restoration of English Franciscanism', 83–101 and Brietz Monta, 'Anne Dacre Howard, Countess of Arundel and Catholic Patronage', 59–82.

[18]   AY 54, f. 1, Business Correspondence. Letter from Nicholas Kehoe in Puerto Santa Maria, on 29 March 1701.

[19]   Ibid.

[20]   AY 54, f. 2, Business Correspondence. Letter from Nicholas Kehoe in Puerto Santa Maria, on 12 September 1701.

activities. They offered patronage that entailed funding schools or hospitals, and maintained business and financial relations with the surrounding community. They offered employment to the local people, and bought and sold surrounding land. As nuns, female members of merchant families worked for their communities, their charitable work usually directed towards female learning. In their wills, they could choose for their wealth to be either used to sponsor such projects, or left to their family. If anything, they show how nuns were proactive in society and although their role did not defy female stereotypes, their work and their influence cannot be denied.[21] In the case of Mary Bray, she left the convent after only a few months, in October 1701. She did not enjoy life there and she had begun lodging at Mrs Everard's, a widow whose late husband, Nicholas, had been one of Kehoe's associates. About his niece, Kehoe remarked 'I pray God direct her for the best for her future happiness', not entirely convinced that this was her best decision.[22] In contrast, and ironically around the same time, Helena's brother Nicholas and his wife begrudgingly accepted their daughter's move to become a nun, despite having striven to marry her into the merchant dynasty of the Walshes in a bid to strengthen business relations. In 1699, Nicholas complained that his daughter had refused to marry 'a good deserving honest man', chosen by him.[23] The young girl showed great aversion towards the union and the family blamed her young age, stating that her 'happiness was preferred to her future richness'. Usually, she was such an obedient daughter and Porter was utterly surprised by her behaviour. But the marital deal was not completed and the young girl concluded her life in a convent.

Within the Catholic mercantile community, more traditional female roles were certainly not denied and it is not the intent of this work to emphasise female independence. Catholic women were nuns, patrons, traders, but predominantly simply mothers or wives taking care of the family. However, this work shows that, when given the chance, women also worked in trade and acted in their own right, being possibly more reliable in trade and successful in forming relationships in business. By opening up about their health in the correspondence, they were arguably able to forge

---

[21]   A. Knox, 'The Convent as Cultural Conduit: Irish Patronage in Early Modern Spain', *Rocky Mountain Medieval and Renaissance Association*, accessed on www.northumbria.ac.uk.

[22]   AY 54 f. 4, Business Correspondence. Letter from Nicholas Kehoe in Puerto Santa Maria, on 7 November 1701.

[23]   AY 120, Personal Correspondence. Personal letters to John Aylward from Joseph Comerford and Nicholas Porter. Two letters about the breaking of Porter's daughter's engagement to Walsh, July–Oct. 1696.

stronger bonds with their commercial partners. Indeed, Mr Bake was very interested in Mrs Wyse's health, congratulating her on her recovery while discussing a trade deal. Mrs Aylward likewise often discussed her personal health and situation, disclosing her pain over the death of her husband to her partners. Furthermore, while worrying about work and the wellbeing of their associates, Catholic women continued to take care of their families, and among the letters of Mrs Aylward is personal correspondence from her own and her sister's children about the household.[24] For women, the business, the household, and the family were all nurtured side by side, something that is not evident among their male counterparts. With her sister, Helena Aylward discussed bereavement and mourning; with her daughters, marriage; and with her son, she expressed concern over his health after a bout of measles, *rougeole*.[25] In 1709, he was on the mend, lucky to be alive while some of his acquaintances had not been so lucky, which possibly explains why his mother wrote him out a recipe advising him to boil a mixture of white wine, pigeon's egg, and four lemons, leave it to set during the night and to drink it in the morning.[26] Whether this concoction actually helped is not clear, but either way Michael Trublet survived. This fascinating document suggests Helena Aylward abided by social conventions that in the early modern centuries saw women taking care of the family by administering home-made medical remedies. Preparing drugs to treat minor ailments was a housewife's duty and implied a mix of scientific and folkloristic knowledge as passed down the matrilineal line from one generation to the next. To prepare their concoctions, women usually used household items, using everything from plants and herbs, such as rhubarb and fennel, to eggs and milk, from white wine to exotic ingredients. They used kitchen utensils and recipes were prepared in an attempt to cure skin problems and various diseases, including gout and scurvy. Medicine was practised within the family and sometimes locally, with family remedies used alongside professional ones. Indeed, for illness, a physician was not always consulted unless to enquire about the deadliness of a disease if these homemade remedies were unsuccessful. Michael Trublet did not mention a professional in his letters, and did not ask his mother either. Nevertheless, Helena acted out of motherly love, sharing a knowledge possibly acquired from her own mother. Indeed, it was very common for middle-class women

---

[24]   AY 126, Business Correspondence. Letters addressed to her after her husband's death. Includes a few accounts and receipts (some for household expenses) May 1705–June 1711.

[25]   AY 128, Personal Correspondence. Letters from Helena Aylward to various relatives on the death of her husband, June and August 1705.

[26]   AY 123, Personal Correspondence. Recipe of Helena Aylward.

to invent recipes and to collect and compile medical books. This served as a form of charity and extended beyond the family into the community. For Helena it served as useful knowledge to pass on to her daughter, Mary, who married into the Howards – a family from which one of the first female medicinal books had been published in 1655.[27] It is undeniable therefore that Catholic women remained very aware of their social roles and the expectations upon them. They cared for their families and their community, both religious and mercantile, and strove to conclude strategic marital deals for their daughters in hope of strengthening relationships among co-religionists. Helena Aylward either married her daughters into the English gentry or sent them to convents.[28] Moreover, together with Mrs Wyse, the Brookings, and Mrs Comerford, she married them within the Catholic mercantile community so as to establish connections in areas where the family wanted to trade, consequently enforcing lasting religious and commercial bonds. Their work did not deny them their duty as women. They were aware of their responsibilities towards man and God, but nevertheless they seized the opportunities that this new economy offered.

Catholic Traders

Historical literature on women and the mercantile community proves how women worked in trade, and although not necessarily as merchants, in trade-related activities. They were involved in commerce and finance, showing knowledge of accounting, interest rates, and financial trends. Studies have shown that many women belonging to religious minorities such as Quakers, Presbyterians, and Jews engaged in the Atlantic economy, taking over the businesses when widowed so they could continue to operate along the same networks.[29] Catholic women shared the same rationale. They worked and they were able to sustain the family firm, showing business acumen in negotiating new deals, partnerships, and strategies, and

[27] Leigh Whaley, 'Motherly Medicine: Domestic Healers and Apothecaries' in *Women and the Practice of Medical Cares in Early Modern Europe, 1400–1800* (Basingstoke: Palgrave Macmillan, 2011), 155. Elaine Leong, 'Collecting Knowledge for the Family: Recipes, Gender and Practical Knowledge in the Early Modern English Household', *Centaurus*, 55 (2013): 81–103.

[28] T 30, Helena last Will and Testament 1713–1714; Julian Walton, *The Irish Genealogist*, 5 (1974). Helena's only son Michael Trublet died unmarried in 1755 in Paris.

[29] F. Tolles, *Meeting House and Counting House.* Haggerty, *The British-Atlantic Trading Community*, 79, 222; Sharpe, 'Gender in the Economy', 291; Froide, 'The Religious Lives of Single Women in the Anglo-Atlantic World', 60–78.

Helena Aylward shows how Catholic women were well acquainted with the dynamics of trade even before widowhood. Women at this time were usually believed to be risk averse, with their gender and emotion considered an impairment to business decisions, which as a result were left to the men. Women had problems in accessing capital and only widowhood seemed to have opened these new opportunities or given them any legal status. Helena Aylward became a widow for the second time in 1705, but in the 1680s had dealt with business transactions following the death of her first husband, and when the second, John, was absent. Being born into a family of merchants and married into another two provided the knowledge and training needed to understand commerce. She worked alongside her spouses and showed her abilities when suddenly bereaved. She closed those deals left open and went about remitting payments and collecting debts; she continued by taking charge of the household, caring for her children, and arranging marriages for her daughters while also thinking of new investments in weapons, artillery, and in the sea companies.

Helena worked with many families and her story is far from unique. Within the mercantile community, female merchants worked proactively in Atlantic–Mediterranean trade, both alongside their husbands as well as in widowhood. Among the most prominent families were the Wyses and the Brookings, who formed part of the vibrant mercantile community in Exeter. Mary Brooking married into the Wyse family and in the late 1680s, as we have seen, took over the family business when her late husband John Wyse passed away. Alice Brooking, possibly her sister, worked in Exeter, supervising the Anglo-Spanish deals, working with her family and ensuring she was kept informed of decisions when the male partners were absent.[30] The Brooking-Wyses worked extensively with London and Cadiz. The family firms had been established in the 1660s by Henry Wyse and continued to supply manufactured goods, mainly fabrics, to Spain and the American fleets. They imported Mediterranean fruit and Spanish wine and had started working in the Anglo-Spanish trade at least from the early 1670s. Mary Wyse took over the business in the late 1680s and carried it on into the eighteenth century. As a merchant involved in the Anglo-Spanish market, Mary invested in commodities including 'good sherrys' from Spain, especially during the Nine Years War when it filled a need in England while French wines were prohibited. Mary showed business acumen and the ability to diversify when needed as well as fuelling the exchanges between English ports and the Spanish empire. Mary and Alice's accounts

---

[30]   AY 111, Business Accounts. Account books of John Aylward at Malaga, 1674–1686. With notes to 1703.

record transactions between London, Exeter, and Cadiz where they worked with Catholic contacts as well as Protestants from London. Their rationale in commerce was like that of their former husbands and fathers; they never professed religious beliefs or commented on political events that could give away their allegiance. Their network was formed by Catholics as well as non-Catholics, they associated with the merchant house of Power & Hill which operated in London and Cadiz, and worked frequently with other associated merchants, including the Aylwards, Ryan, the Watkins, the Evans, and Benjamin Bake. Contacts in London helped to coordinate exchanges of fabrics that would be moved between Exeter and the capital and helped to smuggle goods in times of warfare. The Spanish partners were based in Malaga and Alicante from where they imported fruit and wine. Whether they were Catholic or not, their partnerships testify to the inter-faith cooperation among merchants moving within the British Isles. Catholics were not sectarian and would look outside their community if needed, and Protestant merchants in turn showed pragmatic acceptance. Both needed trustworthy partners in order to maximise profits and survive in international commerce and the Protestant and Catholic merchants worked together for decades. This association was not any the less when women took charge; indeed perhaps the books from that point actually became more accurate.

Indeed, Mrs Wyse for one carefully recorded credit and debts.[31] In 1688, she closed a transaction of £3,043 of 'raysin solis' and wine that had been opened in 1685. She needed to control three years' worth of exchanges and make sure that no one had been charged 'too little or too much'.[32] Meanwhile, she wanted assurances from John Aylward that he would order a friend in Exeter or in London to 'save and defend' her from the 'crooked' Mr Silvanus Evans, regarding a payment. Mr Evans was involved in a lawsuit with the Aylwards and he had quite a reputation in the community. Mrs Wyse was aware of her late husband's associates and had learn who to trust and who could be a liability. She also knew how to maximise profits and mitigate potential losses by investing in different deals. In fact, she was also part of the financial network of the Arthurs, mentioning them in her correspondence. The Arthurs were possibly one of the most powerful financial dynasties and their Catholicism never impaired their business. Throughout the decades, they lent money to various European monarchs and supervised many financial operations of the Aylwards and other associates. The widows continued working with them as their collaboration opened

---

[31] AY 103, f. 5, Peter Power's Accounts, bills for merchandise to Dec. 1689.
[32] AY 101, Business Accounts. Bills, accounts, receipts for merchandise to Dec. 1687.

opportunities to speculate in the sea companies, as Mrs Aylward did. In fact, Helena Aylward, like many widows in the mercantile communities, found herself with cash to invest, which offered the opportunity to look at the maritime companies and the military sector.[33] Helena subscribed to the South Sea Company and invested in the arms trade, as women could invest also in the East India Company's stocks.[34] If Mary Wyse did invest, she probably would have been as meticulous in trade, recording any single expense or money owed by the partners.

One member of the Wyse family's mercantile network operating in Atlantic and Mediterranean trade was Walter Ryan, a London merchant specialising in trading fabrics with Spain. Although working with the Wyses and the Aylwards, Ryan worked also with the Creaghs, Catholic merchants based in the Dutch ports of Rotterdam and Amsterdam, who had contacts across England, Italy, France, and the West Indies.[35] The Creaghs had various interests, from commerce to privateering, and possibly their strength lay in their ability to tap into various markets so as to secure the flow of trade even when exchanges in the Channel were disrupted by hostilities. From Rotterdam and also Ostend, they had contacts in Dunkirk which helped them monitor movements in those waters. Among their contacts was the prominent Lynch family, a mercantile dynasty which had worked in Atlantic–Mediterranean trade for over a century. The Lynch women do not seem to have been too involved in mercantile activities and, in fact, Dominick Lynch's wife was mentioned only once in the correspondence as he had married this widow 'who [had] offered'.[36]

Instead, the female Creaghs had a much more dynamic role, dealing with fabrics and manufactured goods for the Indies. In the early 1690s, they invested in transactions that could at once ship thimbles, 1,200 needles, 399 padlocks and boxes of musk. The Creaghs had been involved in Atlantic and Mediterranean trade for decades. They were of Irish origin

---

[33]   P. Walsh, *The South Sea Bubble and Ireland: Money, Banking and Investment, 1690–1721* (Woodbridge: Boydell Press, 2014), 27: Only in the 1780s, the Catholic Church would introduce new legislation on finance; Laurence, *Women and their Money*.

[34]   Margaret Hunt, 'Women and the Fiscal-Imperial State in Late Seventeenth and Early Eighteenth Centuries' in *A New Imperial History: Culture, Identity, and Modernity in Britain and the Empire, 1660–1840*, ed. Kathleen Wilson (Cambridge: Cambridge University Press, 2004), 29–47; Sharpe, 'Gender in the Economy', 301; Amy Froide, 'Learning to Invest: Women's Education in Arithmetic and Accounting in Early Modern England', *Early Modern Women: An Interdisciplinary Journal*, 10, 1 (2015): 3–26.

[35]   AY 28, Business Correspondence. Letters to John Aylward from David and Widow Creagh at Amsterdam, Jan. 1696–Dec. 1703.

[36]   AY 20, f. 28, Business Correspondence. Letter from Robert Butler in Cadiz.

and were based mainly in Amsterdam from where they maintained a vast correspondence and saw their business survive for decades. During the Nine Years War, they succeeded in trade through deals and contraband and by adopting accurate business strategies. They always attempted to sell in a timely manner and according to the movements of the American fleet; besides needles and thimbles, they exported the Dutch fabrics which were in high demand in Spain and in its colonial markets. However, the quality was not as good as English garments so this proved not to be their best-selling product, leaving them once debating what to do with a stained batch. One of the options was to take out the stains or perhaps to dye the fabrics which if not then completely clear could instead be sent to the Indies as the colonies did not demand the highest quality.

Business misjudgements aside, the Creaghs regularly closed successful deals, even in times of war as their vast network and family connections allowed them to deploy various tactics in order to continue in business. They worked with Catholics as well as others, with their deals not stopping even when Edward Creagh died in 1697 at the height of the hostilities. As was often customary in trade families, his widow took over the family business with her son David, but unfortunately, she is the only woman in the correspondence who never signed with her full name and the mail is always addressed to both her and her son. Among the Catholic merchants in the correspondence, Mrs Creagh took the least independent path, working with a guardian and not taking decisions on her own. Nevertheless, she contributed to leading the business into the eighteenth century when Europe was once again ravaged by yet another conflict. The War of the Spanish Succession presented a fresh challenge for merchants working in the Channel and in continental Europe; Britain was at war with France and Spain and the other European countries were indirectly involved in a conflict that seriously damaged economic exchanges. In 1701, when rumours of the hostilities began, Mrs Creagh became extremely concerned about the galleons and the *flota* coming back from South America as war would have meant an enemy fleet off the shore of Spain, looming to seize the precious cargoes. The family had heard of the alliance between England, Holland, and Brandenburg, and were certain that a new conflict would soon erupt, although they could never have predicted the extent of it. The scene was dire and their advice to the Aylwards was to 'be speedy' in their answer.[37]

---

[37] AY 28, f. 64, Business Correspondence. Letters to John Aylward from David and Widow Creagh at Amsterdam, Jan. 1696–Dec. 1703. The first partner of John Aylward was Edward Creagh; after his death in 1697, the partnership was maintained by David Creagh and Edward's widow.

During the last months of 1702, the Creaghs became concerned over Port St Mary in the bay of Cadiz, where they had their interests. The Spanish fleet had sailed to fight the Anglo-Dutch and the area had seen great upheaval, resulting in 2,000 casualties, 'among them many merchants'.[38] The Creaghs feared for the lives of their partners and the future of their businesses. They had heard that some families had been rescued by their privateers, but deemed trading almost impossible. In June 1702, the family was informed by a partner that one of the vessels shared with the Aylwards had been confiscated as it was among five French vessels seized when war had been declared. Luckily, there were no losses and thanks to the family connections, they were able to recover the cargo.

At this time, only through smuggling and privateering was it possible to run the family business, and the Creaghs were renowned for such activity. Their network in the Channel ensured that the colonial goods would ultimately reach English ports, usually after passing via Amsterdam. In Spain, they worked with Paul Den in Cartagena, with Woulfe & Trublet in El Puerto, and with Robert Skerret in Malaga. In France, they became acquainted with the Arthurs and their financial circle, contacts which would assure the supply of the merchandise and monitor American fleets. In return, the family received French and English fabrics, scarlet and white bays and large and narrow *kentins*. Such trade and partnerships were how they survived despite the disruptions. In Malaga, the market was at times 'dull', as Robert Skerret complained in 1702; however, American fleets continued loading and the Creaghs wanted to work.[39] Indeed, they continued corresponding with Helena Aylward even after the death of her husband in 1704. Although there is no direct correspondence between the two women, the family was mentioned in Mrs Aylward's accounts, suggesting how female-run business assured the survival of the enterprise and contributed to the continuity of the exchanges.

Another example of the efficiency of female enterprise is provided by Barbara Comerford. The Comerfords were cousins of the Aylward family, a Catholic merchant dynasty which had been in trade for decades, although their work was not outstanding. Patrick said they lived 'indifferent [and] quiet'; they were not necessarily successful in the dynamics of trade and the Aylwards had to bail them out more than once for having invested in the wrong deals or for being imprisoned. The Comerfords were intermarried

---

[38]   Ibid.

[39]   AY 81, f. 1, Business Correspondence. Letters to John Aylward from Robert Skerret at Cadiz and Malaga, Jan. 1700–Feb. 1702. In his correspondence Skerret mainly briefed Aylward about the galleons, their arrival and their departure, vital for doing business in Cadiz.

with the Catholic Goughs and the Whites, with networks extending to Spain, France, and the Flemish territories. Part of the family was in Ireland (mainly Waterford) and part in Ostend. They invested primarily in leather and herrings, and coordinated exchanges between Irish, Iberian, and Dutch ports. The female members of the family often took on traditional roles, yet some did not become involved in the family activities and instead were provided for by their husbands and brothers, a situation that caused even more distress to the male members of the family when worrying about their deals. Others lost touch with sisters who had been married off to other merchant families and now moved between Ireland and Ostend. Patrick Comerford commented that he was not exactly close to his sisters, not knowing where they were, and just hoped one would not leave his niece 'rambling'.[40] Other female members of the family seemed more proactive and reliable. There are no records of dire financial straits once the family activity was taken over by mother and head of the family Barbara Comerford after she was widowed. Barbara worked with the Aylwards in the late 1690s, and possibly worked alongside the family even before the death of her husband. She liaised with merchants in France, Ireland, and Spain[41] and was associated with Geraldin & Murphy in Nantes which helped her coordinate the exchanges between French and English ports. Meanwhile, she also invested in privateering in the Channel, introducing Spanish goods to England through Hamburg. She worked with the Aylwards and contributed to British trade at times of disruptions. Once she took charge of the family business, John Aylward received no more letters from the Comerfords begging to pay for their debts or bail them out of prison.

Even through preparing concoctions and running charities, Catholic women defy the stereotypes of simply being wives and daughters taking care of the family or waiting to marry. Instead, we can see that they fit within recent historiography on mercantile communities and widows in the economy. These were women with knowledge of the commercial transactions and who were more than able to master trading skills. As nuns, they worked and supported their community, and as merchants they were meticulous. They followed the same rationale in commerce as their husbands did before them, working with Catholic partners as well as not, and involving themselves in Atlantic–Mediterranean markets which enabled

---

[40] AY 7, f. 1, Business Correspondence. Miscellaneous letters to John Aylward, Jan.–Dec. 1692.

[41] AY 43, f. 3, Business Correspondence. Letters from and relating to Nicholas Geraldin, regarding a journey made to La Rochelle on his behalf by John Aylward, 1697.

them to sustain British trade on the continent even at times of war. They were able to coordinate exchanges between England and the Iberian ports as well as the Netherlands, France, and the West Indies. The strategies deployed were the same as those learnt and tested by their fathers and husbands before them. Their male relatives certainly introduced the figure of merchants in the Catholic historiography, but these women show that Catholics, both male and female, worked in its commerce; tapping into networks that had operated for centuries and showing the inclusivity of the community. Catholics did not operate only within their own religious circles and although not disregarding family ties or religious affiliation, men, and women worked with anyone deemed trustworthy in order to carry out the required deals. Catholic connections were useful when the British Isles came to be at war with France and Spain, but ultimately the aim was to introduce merchandise into England. The opportunity to access Catholic markets proved their strength but the will to move beyond the community assured the opportunity to survive in such a volatile environment. Catholic women were certainly no strangers to these dynamics. They defied social conventions of the time and the restraints on women's involvement in business. Undeniably, they did not access their businesses independently but were involved in making deals, fixing prices, and deciding on which commodities to trade once given the opportunity to do so. They worked alongside their men and took over when needed, showing a great competence, proactivity, and business acumen. Even having adult sons did not mean that they simply became domestic guardians once widowed. Mrs Creagh worked alongside her son David, and Mrs Aylward worked with her son Michael as a partner. We see that Catholic women's contribution was invaluable and crucial in navigating the business from one generation to the next and to ensuring its survival. Undeniably, these women helped sustain British commercial expansion in a vital economic time.

Conclusion

The initial aim of this work was to survey the Catholic community's economic involvement in the British economy in the long eighteenth century. When this project started in 2011, Gabriel Glickman had just re-opened the debate on Catholic integration, further challenging the widely held perception of a marginalised community. As this research progressed, the focus shifted to the mercantile community where a much wider picture started to show. Further inspired by the works of Trivellato, Haggerty, and Zahedieh, this work aimed to contribute to a much broader debate on religion, trade, and national identities, allowing for a deeper understanding of British Catholics in the early commercial age. One of the initial goals of the project was to dispel the myth of Catholic marginalisation and of the lack of entrepreneurial skills among the Catholic community, in turn refuting Max Weber's theory of how Catholicism clashed with capitalism. Although much debated, Weberian stereotypes long outlived his narrative, and there came a need to further discuss his interpretation. However, as this research progressed, the material also offered an opportunity to understand how the Catholic community was offered inclusion by the new commercial economy which eventually secured their widespread social integration. Catholic merchants challenged the prevailing models of segregation and decline, and like Hancock's Citizens of the World, they were successful in winning commercial success and social acceptance. Furthermore, Colley's work invited a reflection on the place of Catholics in the nation. Perhaps, like Weber's, even Colley's work could now be deemed outdated; undoubtedly, though, her work still invites historians to consider the nature of British national consciousness. The case of the Aylwards suggests that the contribution of Catholics to the emerging fiscal-military state ultimately earned them a place in the empire – and in the nation.

This book offers a link between two narratives: one around Catholicism in the British Isles, and the other centred on merchant communities in Atlantic–Mediterranean trade. It enriches the most recent findings on the involvement of Catholics in the economy and as entrepreneurs. Recent historiography has moved away from the theory of Catholicism in the British Isles as being a marginalised faith. Glickman has introduced the Catholic gentry as a group that reinvented itself. He discussed inclusion and political allegiance within a Protestant society and along with Colley has rethought the position of Catholics within the nation to suggest a more nuanced role where religion and political allegiance are not as clear-cut as previously thought. Along the same lines, this work on the Aylwards has looked at the Catholic middling sort, men and women involved in transatlantic and Mediterranean trades. The work of Trivellato, Zahedieh, Hancock, and Haggerty have offered a thorough analysis of the trading communities in the early commercial world and the Aylwards fit perfectly into this image of British Catholic merchants. Like Haggerty's traders, they acted merely for money, choosing associates based on trust, and like Trivellato's strangers moved beyond their community as blood ties and common religion could not guarantee commercial success. The Atlantic and Mediterranean trades required wider networks and Catholics simply adapted. Like Hancock's citizens they worked in the most profitable trades of the time; relying on reputable counting-houses and, after accumulating wealth, bought country retreats before eventually merging into the aristocracy. The rationale of Catholics as merchants does not show exceptionality; they abided by the same principles which moved all the mercantile communities at this time, crossing boundaries to work with the best men and always seeking the best deals. Yet they went against what was common in religious circles whereby working within the community was to be expected. They certainly acted along with family and co-religionists, but knew they needed wider networks in order to profit in trade, making it impossible to expect to know all of the agents involved. Religion was not openly discussed and was not a crucial factor in choosing partners, although the community was not disregarded as it could secure deals at times of warfare. These merchants show the willingness to trust in strangers for business and as a result, how they were able to carve out a place for Catholicism in the early days of British economy.

The traditional view of Catholicism in the British Isles is not being denied in this work. The community suffered penal restrictions right up until the late eighteenth century and it is perhaps through such restrictions that their involvement in business came about – either from being excluded from public office or as a way to adapt to a changing economy in which landowning was no longer profitable. However, within the business world, religion was certainly not an impediment on their journey to economic inclusion. From the British Isles, Catholics had the advantage of access to continental markets and, thereby, a competitive edge. Protestant traders needed them to access the south European ports which were vital in Britain's balance of trade. The new fiscal-military state needed funds and offered a wealth of commercial and financial opportunities; the religion of moneylenders was not relevant and religious policies were not of primary importance in the political agenda of the newly born British government. Catholics benefited from this shift. Along the lines of Trivellato's work, this book suggests pragmatic acceptance, though not implying cosmopolitanism. Catholic merchants did not deny any religious dimension, but due to the nature of their work there was simply no need to disclose personal beliefs or political allegiance. Their business culture and opportunities to work alongside Protestant partners for decades supported the building of the empire and ultimately led to a sense of national belonging.

This work analyses the impact of Catholic merchants in business from the 1670s through to 1714. In this time they were active players in the emerging imperial economy and were fostering the interests of their nation. They denied neither their community nor religious affiliation and the community was ultimately crucial in securing and sustaining a foothold in various markets. Their ties and religion proved advantageous in securing trading opportunities, yet was not crucial in choosing associates or in establishing market deals. At times of international warfare, community contacts offered Catholics in the British Isles opportunities to defy war policy and to prosper in an illegal trade. Ultimately however, the Catholics secured the survival of European exchanges, while also benefiting Protestant interests. Either through London, Exeter, Londonderry, or Waterford, provisions from Spain, France, and Italy were being constantly imported to meet demand.

Catholic merchants were entrepreneurs and reinvented themselves as a dynamic community. Their business acumen and economic activity highlight how Catholics contributed to the economy of Britain. They operated in long-standing commercial networks which had been established since the late middle ages and would continue to operate until the nineteenth century. Their advantage was their ability to move freely in Atlantic and Mediterranean ports – an ability that would prove to be crucial during twenty years of European warfare lasting from 1689 to 1714. Working in France and Spain did not only mean access to the continental provisions demanded in Britain, but also the possibility to establish inter-imperial networks; between the Spanish colonial possessions and the British and French West Indies. Indeed, it was so important that accessing the Spanish empire through Cadiz was a constant focus of the English government. Catholic merchants in those ports ensured this link; however, they also ensured access to the Americas through the French imperial markets when

Spanish trade was disrupted by warfare. The 'Romanist's Pass' offered Protestant merchants a stable foothold in colonial markets.

The activity of the Aylwards and their associates in Atlantic–Mediterranean trade prove that a new historical narrative is possible; one in which the Catholic community, both male and female, blended with trade and enterprise. Officially, until the late eighteenth century, Catholicism in Britain implied civil and political liabilities, but not economic impairment. The community was consistently persecuted and defined by bond of amity and marriage, yet this work shows that Catholics in the British Isles were not in the margins of society. They fit perfectly within the literature on commerce as their rationale focused solely on a desire to profit. They joined the most lucrative markets and chose partners based ultimately on bond and reputation, irrespective of their religion. Religious networks, blood ties, trustworthy partners, and outstanding skills all helped secure the role of Catholic merchants in international trade. British Catholicism and Atlantic–Mediterranean trade are part of the same narrative. Although barred from the British government, Catholics financed it; they simply adapted to the changing society, engaging in commerce which assured inclusion and great wealth. In European markets they moved between imperial networks, pursuing riches and proving that the ability to meet the needs of the Atlantic economy would secure integration in society, and eventually in civil and political rehabilitation. It proved the importance of continental commerce in strengthening the early British economy, before the British Isles began to negotiate its national identity at the end of the seventeenth century. The English acted according to economic needs; the Scots were possibly 'bought' for English gold after the failed attempt to emulate English commercial expansion in Darien, and the Anglo-Irish demanded inclusion but had nothing to offer in return, so ultimately their demands were refused. It was time for Catholics to rethink their allegiances and identities. Their support for the Catholic cause of Jacobitism or international Catholic powers was not as complete and unreserved as previously thought. Perhaps, as merchants, they wanted only to sustain their own activities and mainly concerned themselves with worrying about commercial disruptions. Nevertheless, they fundamentally contributed to the emerging British economy – an invaluable role which was acknowledged by the Protestants who, in exchange for business advantage through the 'Romanists' Pass', at last began to grant the Catholic community full civil freedom through the Relief Acts in 1778, and ultimately the Catholic Emancipation Act of 1829. I believe that the Aylwards as seen through the archives at Arundel have provided me with answers to many of the questions raised in 2011.

The Aylwards and their Partners 1672–1705

The Aylwards and their partners in Cadiz and Malaga, 1672–1687

Partners	Cities	Commodities	Years	Associations
Ambrose & Upton	Cadiz	Fruit, Fabrics, Wheat, Wine	1684	Harper, Cross & Palmer; Enys & Aldrington; Costa & Sanguineti; Warren, Caunter & Howe
Atkins, Aaron	Amsterdam, Port Royal	Wine, Fabrics, Sugar, Indigo, Pimento, Cinnamon	1686–1688	Power & Hill
Breedy	Cadiz	Corn	1685	
Brooking, Alice	Exeter	Fabrics	1678	Wyse family; John Brooking; Power & Hill
Brooking, John	Exeter, Leghorn, Bristol	Corn	1684–1685	Parker; the Wyses; Power & Hill; Alice Brooking
Burkin, James	Seville		1684–1685	
Butler, Peter	Dunkirk	Wine, Fabrics, Fruit	1685	Power & Hill
Chinchilla, Clemente		Tobacco, Iron, Currants	1686	
Clarke	Exeter	Fabrics	1683	
Enys, Richard	Cadiz	Tobacco, Fabrics, Hamburg goods	1682–1686	Power & Hill; John Searle; Aldrington & Bowles; widow Lepin
Furlong, Patrick	Bilbao	Tobacco, Iron, Currants	1684	
Hall, Henry	Port Royal	Slaves	1686	Brailsford; Power & Hill

Partners	Cities	Commodities	Years	Associations
Harper & Cross	Genoa	Currants, Olive Oil, Tobacco	1685	Power & Hill; Ambrose & Upton; Palmer & Co.
Hide, Thomas	Weymouth	Fruit	1683	Hide, William
Hollway, James	Bristol	Tobacco	1682	
Humphrey & Bauden	Exeter	Fabrics, Fruit	1686	
Gram(m)ar, William	London	Corn, Fabrics, Fruit	1680s	Power & Hill
Jefford, Thomas	Exeter	Wine, Fruit	1684	Palmer & Co
Knowles, Peter	Belfast	Fish, Fabrics	1683	
Lincoln, Nicholas	Dublin	Butter, Fish, Fruit, Wheat, Wine	1685	
Ludman, Henry			1684	
Martin, Richard	Cadiz, Plymouth	Needles, Cinnamon, Musk, Thimbles, Fish	1686	Thomas Aylward; Edward Creagh; Martin & Gardiner
Matthews, John	Malaga		1673	Butler family
Osmand, Nicholas		Wheat	1686	
Parker, Chris	Livorno	Corn	1684–1685	John Brooking
Parr, Peter	Exeter	Fabrics, Fruit	1683	John Wyse; Power & Hill
Pengelly, Thomas	London	Fabrics, Fruit	1674	
Pitts, Samuel	Cadiz	Fruit, Fabrics, Wheat, Beeswax	1684–1686	Ambrose & Upton
Porter, James	Malaga, Cadiz	Wheat, Corn, Fabrics	1684	Julien Grant; Power & Hill; Paul Den
Putt, John	Port St Mary		1677	Thomas Wyse; George Wyse
Sardness		Corn	1685	
Sealy	Exeter	Fabrics, Fruit, Wine, Olive oil	1683	
Searle, John	Malaga	Linens, Currants, Silks	1684–1686	Butler and Porter family; William Gramar; John Sitwell

Partners	Cities	Commodities	Years	Associations
Sitwell, John	London	Wine	1685–1686	
Speed, Thomas	Bristol	Currants	1685	
Warren & Caunter	Alicante	Fish, Fruit, Wheat, Olive oil	1684–1685	John Howe; Charles Horde; Ambrose & Upton
Watkins, Walter		Fabrics, Calicoes, Olive oil	1686	Power & Hill
Watts, Samuel	Alicante	Salt	1684	
White, Henry	Madrid	Butter	1684	Paul Den; Nicholas Kehoe
Wilcox	Cadiz, Topsham	Fabrics, Fruit	1683	
Wilmot, Robert	London	Wheat, Corn, Wine, Oranges, Lemons	1684–1687	Thomas Blake; John
Worldringham, Peter	Bristol	Currants	1680s	
Wyse, John	Exeter, London	Newfoundland Fish, Olive oil, Wine, Currants, Corn	1684–1685	Evans, Doliffe & Raudbourne; Humphrey & Boden; Watkins; Searle; Sardner
Wyse, Mary	Exeter	Fruit, Currants, Wine, Olive oil	1685–1688	Power & Hill; Benjamin Bake
Wyse, Thomas	Bristol, Dittisham	Butter, Wine	1678– 1681– 1683– 1686	Power & Hill; Brooking family

The Aylwards and their partners in St Malo 1687–1698

Partners	Cities	Commodities	Years	Associations
Arthur, Daniel	Paris	Fabrics, silver	1689– 1692–1693– 1696	Daniel Arthur Jr; Gough, Browne, Pincetti families; Nicholas Porter; Paul Aylward; Joseph Comerford; Murphy & Cruice; Helena Aylward
Arthur, Francis	Paris	Fabrics	1692	

Partners	Cities	Commodities	Years	Associations
Atkins, Aaron	Amsterdam, Port Royal	Wine, Fabrics, Sugar, Indigo, Pimento, Cinnamon	1688	Power & Hill
Brailsford, Thomas	London	Fruit, Fabrics, Logwood, Sugar	1688–1689	Hall family; Merrit; Wilson
Browne, Andrew	Ostend, Bruges	Irish goods	1691–1692	Fitzgerald, French, Lynch, Blake families
Butler, Robert	Cadiz	Fabrics, Silk, Rice, Wine, Fruit, Russia Hides	1687–1689–1690–1692–1693	Harper & Cross; Power & Hill; Lynch, Creagh, Ryan Walter, Porter, Evans, Watkin families, Paul Den
Butler, Thomas	Lisbon	Lemons	1689	Power & Hill; Porter family
Candiotti, Francis		Fabrics	1692	
Comerford, William	Waterford	Salt	1692	Grant, Walsh, Carew, White, Butler, Matthew, Lynch, French, and the Porter families
Cucco, Costa, Sanguineti	Genoa	Lemons, Mexican goods	1696	Ambrose & Upton; Power & Hill; Pincetti; Chamberlain, Slocombe & Lee
Den, Paul	Malaga, Faro, Cartagena, Antequera, Marseilles, Livorno	Wine, Olive oil, Fabrics, Oranges, Buttons, Buckles, Fabrics	1688–1693	Robert Skerret; Doliffe & Radbourne; John Searle; Wyse, Porter, Butler, Creagh, Goold families; James Rice
Emilie, John	London	French fabrics	1689	
Enys, Richard	Cadiz	Tobacco, Fabrics, Housewares, Hamburg goods	1695	Power & Hill; John Searle; Aldrington & Bowles; widow Lepin
Fitzgerald, George	Nantes		1691	Power & Hill; Blake, Walsh, Carew, Goold, Lynch, Butler, Comerford, Browne families
Frere, John	Malaga	Wine, Fruit	1693	

Partners	Cities	Commodities	Years	Associations
Geraldin & Murphy	Nantes	Hamburg goods	1697	
Grant, Julien	Lisbon	Fabrics, Butter, Oranges, Hamburg goods	1687–1695	Martin & Gardiner; the Porters
Hall, Emilie	Cadiz		1690	
Hall, Francis	Port Royal	Fabrics, Sugar, Indigo, Pimento, Butter, Logwood	1688	Thomas Brailsford
Hall, Thomas	Cadiz, Port Royal		1690	Probin
Hall, William	Port Royal	Fabrics, Sugar, Indigo, Pimento, Butter, Logwood	1688	Thomas Brailsford
Harper & Cross	Genoa	Currants, Olive Oil, Tobacco	1687–1688	Ambrose & Upton; Butler; Palmer
Helder, Richard	London	Dyes	1689	
Herkett, John	Rotterdam	Honey	1697	Creagh family
Hollway, Nicholas	Malaga		1693	
Horde, Charles	London	Wine, Indigo, Various dyes	1691–1692	Warren & Caunter
Knight, Thomas	Port St Mary, Chiclana	Corn	1690	Thomas Brailsford
Langton, Michael	Brest, Bristol	Wool, Leather	1691	
Lynch, Francis	Cadiz	Fabrics	1691	
Martin, Richard	Cadiz, Plymouth	Needles, Cinnamon, Musk, Thimbles, Fish	1697	Thomas Aylward; Edward Creagh
Morley, Will	Malaga	Soap, Almonds, Wine, Fruit	1693	
Peers, Charles	London	Fabrics, Dyes	1690	Thomas Brailsford; Hall family
Pincetti, Carlo	Genoa	Roses, Fruit, Wheat	1689–1690	Cucco, Costa & Sanguineti
Porter, James	Malaga, Cadiz	Wheat, Corn, Fabrics	1691	Julien Grant

Partners	Cities	Commodities	Years	Associations
Porter, John	Rouen	Russia hides, Fruit	1687–1692	Helena Aylward; Matthew Porter; Julien Grant
Power & Agnes	Bordeaux	Butter	1692	
Sherlocke, James	Waterford	Wine, Pepper, Tobacco, Fruit, Fabrics, Rice	1690	
Wyse, Mary	Exeter	Fruit, Currants, Wine, Olive oil	1688	Brooking family; Power & Hill; Benjamin Bake

The Aylwards and their partners in London, 1698–1705

Partners	Cities	Commodities	Years	Associations
Arthur, Daniel	Paris	Fabrics, Silver	1701–1703–1710	Daniel Arthur Jr; Gough family; Nicholas Porter; Pincetti family; Paul Aylward; Browne; Joseph Comerford; Murphy & Cruice; Helena Aylward; Richard Cantillon; Woulfe & Trublet
Archer, Edward	Middelburg		1702	Creagh family
Aylward, Helena	London	Fuzils, Carbins, Olive oil, Fabrics, Fruit	1680–1690–1700s	Lynch family; Edward Gough; Creagh family; Woulfe & Trublet; Arthur Daniel; Richard Cantillon
Aylward, Paul	Cadiz	Fabrics, fruit	1698–1700	Richard Enys
Barrett, Robert		fabrics	1701	
Browne, Andrew	Ostend, Bruges	Irish goods	1701	Joseph Comerford; Fitzgerald, French, Lynch, Blake families
Byrd, John		Sugar, Mattresses	1699	
Chamberlain, Slocomb, Lee	Messina	Silk, Wool	1698–1700	Vincenzo Marletta; Francesco Cardia; Carlo V

Partners	Cities	Commodities	Years	Associations
Comerford, Barbara	Ostend, Waterford	Fish, Fabrics	1697	Gough, White families; Geraldin & Murphy
Creagh, Daniel	Amsterdam	Fabrics	1700	Browne, Fitzgerald, French, Lynch, Blake families
Creagh, David and Creagh's widow	Amsterdam	Fabrics	1702	Browne, Fitzgerald, French, Lynch, Blake, Walter Ryan, Paul Den, Robert Skerret; Woulfe & Trublet
Creagh, Edward	Amsterdam	Cinnamon, Musk, Nutmeg, Thimbles, Needles, Fabrics	1710	Ryan Walter; Helena Aylward; Fitzgerald, French, Lynch, Blake families; Power & Hill
Den, Paul	Malaga, Faro, Cartagena, Antequera, Marseilles, Livorno	Wine, Olive oil, Fabrics, Fruit, Buttons, Buckles.	1698–1701– 1702	Robert Skerret; Doliffe & Radbourne; John Searle; Wyse, Butler, Porter families; Power & Hill; Woulfe & Trublet
Doliffe & Radbourne	Cadiz, Malaga	Corn, Salt	1700	Power & Hill; Radcliffe
England, Benjamin	Yarmouth	Herrings, Oil	1699	Doliffe & Radbourne
Enys, Richard	Cadiz	Tobacco, Fabrics, Hamburg goods	1700	Power & Hill; John Searle; Aldrington & Bowles; widow Lepin
Grant, Julien	Lisbon	Fabrics, Butter, Oranges, Hamburg goods	1699–1700	Martin & Gardiner; Porter family
Hacket, Andrew	Cadiz		1701	Thomas White; Robert Butler
Herkett, John	Rotterdam	Honey	1697	Creagh family
Hill, Richard	London, Cadiz	Cochineal, Fabrics, Oil	1672–1707– 1700	Walter Ryan
Horty, John	St Malo	Fabrics	1702	
Kehoe, Nicholas	Port St Mary	Fabrics	1701–1702	Nicholas Aylward; Woulfe & Trublet; Dominick White; Joseph Comerford

Partners	Cities	Commodities	Years	Associations
Lapthorne, John, George	Plymouth		1701	
Mahon, Franc	Rouen	Wine	1699	Woulfe & Trublet; Helena Aylward; Thomas Lynch; Browne
Martin & Gardiner	Cadiz	Fabrics	1700	Woulfe & Trublet
Shee, Robert	London		1709	
Walsh & Bennett	Bordeaux	Wines	1703	Francis White
White, James	Port St Mary	Wax, Salmon, Fabrics, Musk	1699–1690	Nicholas Porter; Francis White
White, John	Gallway		1700	Dominick White; Nicholas Geraldin; Comerford family
Woulfe, Patrick & Trublet Jacques de la Herse	Port St Mary	Grain, Fabrics, Lemons, Ginger, Wine, Rabbit wool, Beef	1698–1699–1706	Daniel Arthur; Martin & Gardiner; Paul Den

Bibliography

Primary Sources

Arundel Castle Archives: The Aylward Papers (1672–1717)

John Aylward

Business Correspondence

AY 1, Miscellaneous letters to John Aylward, 1672–1676.

AY 2, Miscellaneous letters to John Aylward, 1683.

AY 3, Miscellaneous letters to John Aylward, Jan.–Oct. 1684.

AY 4, Miscellaneous letters to John Aylward, Jan.–Dec. 1685.

AY 5, Miscellaneous letters to John Aylward, Jan.–Dec. 1686.

AY 6, Miscellaneous letters to John Aylward, Jan. 1687–Dec. 1691.

AY 7, Miscellaneous letters to John Aylward, Jan.–Dec. 1692.

AY 8, Miscellaneous letters to John Aylward, Jan.–May 1693.

AY 9, Miscellaneous letters to John Aylward, Mar. 1694–Nov. 1699.

AY 10, Miscellaneous letters to John Aylward, Jan. 1700–Dec. 1703.

AY 11, Letters to John and Helena Aylward from Daniel Arthur and Daniel Arthur Jr, in Paris, Oct. 1691–Nov. 1696.

AY 13, Letters to John Aylward from Aaron Atkins at Amsterdam and Port Royal, Apr. 1684–Jul. 1688.

AY 15, Three letters to John Aylward from Paul Aylward at Cadiz, one with a note from Richard Hore, Apr. 1699–Mar. 1700.

AY 16, Letters to John Aylward from Benjamin Bake, one also from Thomas Hill at Exeter, Aug. 1688–Aug. 1689.

AY 18, Letters to John Aylward from Thomas Brailsford and Richard Holder at London, Oct.1688–Sept. 1689.

AY 19, Joseph Comerford was the brother-in-law of the Brownes.

AY 20, Letters to John Aylward from Robert Butler at Malaga and Cadiz, May 1687–Dec. 1692.

AY 21, Letters to John Aylward from [Samuel] Caunter and [John] Howe at Alicante [first 5 letters signed, Warren, Caunter and Howe]. Feb. 1684–Dec. 1686.

AY 22, Letters to John Aylward from Chamberlin, Slocombe, and Lee at Messina, Oct. 1698–Dec. 1700.

AY 23, Letters to John Aylward from Messrs Champneys and Pitts at Seville, July 1684–Apr. 1686.

AY 28, Letters to John Aylward from David and Widow Creagh at Amsterdam, Jan. 1696–Dec. 1703.

AY 30, Letters to John Aylward from Paul Den at Malaga, one from Cadiz and one from St Malo, June 1685–Nov. 1703.

AY 35, Letters to John Aylward from Benjamin England at Yarmouth, Sept.–Dec.1699.

AY 36, Letters to John Aylward from Enys & Aldington and Aldington & Bowles, at Cadiz, one account for baize, 1695–Jan. 1702.

AY 37, Letters to John Aylward from Richard Enys and Eustace Power and one from Power, Hill, Enys & Company, one account for freight charges, all from Cadiz. Aug. 1682– Jul. 1687.

AY 43, f. 3, Letters from and relating to Nicholas Geraldin, regarding a journey made to La Rochelle on his behalf by John Aylward, 1697.

AY 49, Letters to John Aylward: two from Edward Hill at Livorno (1683), five from Thomas Hill at Exeter, one from old Mr Edward Hill at Priory (a personal letter), Dec. 1683, July 1685–Nov. 1688.

AY 51, Business letters to John Aylward from Charles Horde at London, Nov. 1691–July 1693. Most of the letters are counter-endorsed from Amsterdam by Philibert Brothers.

AY 54, Letters to John Aylward from Nicholas Kehoe at Puerto de Santa Maria, Mar. 1701–Mar. 1702.

AY 72, Letters to John Aylward from Peter Power and Richard Hill at London, May 1687– Aug. 1689.

AY 81, Letters to John Aylward from Robert Skerret at Cadiz and Malaga, Jan. 1700– Feb. 1702.

AY 83, Letters to John Aylward from Willoughby Swift at Lisbon, Mar. 1697–Sept. 1698.

AY 87, Letters to John Aylward from Francis White at St Malo, July 1698– Jan 1701.

AY 93, Letters to John Aylward from Woulfe and Trublet at Puerto de Santa Maria, Jan. 1698–Dec. 1700.

AY 94, Letters to John Aylward from Woulfe and Trublet, written mainly from Puerto de Santa Maria but a few from Cadiz and Jeres. From July 1702 signed mainly by Symon Michel and from May 1703 by Peter Willson.

AY 95, Letters to John Aylward and after his death to Helena Aylward from Woulfe and Trublet at Puerto de Santa Maria, May 1704– Oct. 1706.

Business Accounts

AY 96, Bills and accounts for merchandise to Dec. 1682.

AY 100, Bills and receipts for merchandise to Dec. 1686.

AY 101, Bills, accounts, and receipts for merchandise to Dec. 1687.

AY 102, Bills and accounts for merchandise to 1688.

AY 103, Accounts and bills for merchandise to Dec. 1689.

AY 104, Accounts and bills for merchandise to Dec. 1690. The partners involved were Cruice, Murphy, and Thomas Hease.

AY 109, Bills and accounts for merchandise to Dec. 1697.

AY 111, Account books of John Aylward at Malaga, 1674–1686. With notes to 1703.

AY 112, Rough account book of John Aylward relating to cargoes sent to and from Cadiz (entries very confused), c. Apr. 1689–Jan. 1693.

Business and Legal Papers

AY 117, Miscellaneous papers, agreements, a bond, and inventories of goods dispatched. One bundle of letters produced in a dispute involving Messrs Arthur and Forty, George Dusmaresq, David Cossart; letters neither addressed to nor sent by John Aylward. Aug. 1676–May 1705.

AY 118, Letter to John Aylward from Diouguel and Fossecave at Morlaix; note of papers relating to them and sent to Antoine Masson at Orleans by John Aylward. Letters to John Aylward from Francois Diouguel at Puerto de Santa Maria. Dec. 1697–Sept. 1701.

Personal Correspondence

AY 119, Letters to John Aylward on personal matters, mainly from relatives, July 1683–Mar. 1693. One to Helena Aylward relating to her niece, boarding at a convent at Rennes; correspondents include Richard Aylward, Isma White, Ann and Thomas Butler, and John Porter.

AY 120, Personal letters to John Aylward from Joseph Comerford and Nicholas Porter. Two about the breaking of Porter's daughter's engagement to Walsh, July–Oct. 1696.

Personal Accounts

AY 121, Accounts of John and Helena Aylward. (1) Accounts of John on behalf of Helena and her two brothers Nicholas and James in the matter of the effects and property of their father Matthew Porter, with an account for the latter's funeral expenses, 1697/8. (2) Accounts of Helena Aylward for money spent on behalf of her daughters, Marie and Jeannette, 1706–9.

AY 122, Accounts of Henry Lambe, (?)steward of John Aylward, and later of his wife, Helena, and of her executors [Sir] Francis More and Henry Charles Howard, Dec. 1704–May 1715.

Miscellanea

AY 123. Three medical recipes.

Helena Aylward

Business Correspondence

AY 124, Letters and accounts addressed to her before her marriage to John Aylward, May 1682– Sept. 1687.

AY 125, Letters to her from Edward Gough in Cadiz and Waterford, John Porter in Rouen, and Dominic Lynch in Cadiz, Jan. 1685– Jan. 1686.

AY 126, Letters addressed to her after her husband's death. Includes a few accounts and receipts (some for household expenses), May 1705–June 1711.

Business and Legal Papers

AY 127, Papers relating to the estate in Brittany she inherited from her first husband, Nov. 1682– May 1711.

Personal Correspondence

AY 128, Copy letters from Helena Aylward to various relatives on the death of her husband, June and Aug. 1705.

AY 129, Letters to Helena Aylward from Michel Trublet (her son) and one from her daughter, Madame Trublet de Permont, June 1709 and May and Dec. 1713.

Accounts

AY 130, General accounts of Helena Aylward. (1) Business accounts, June 1704–Dec. 1713. (2) As administratrix of John Aylward, May 1705– Dec. 1709. (3) Household accounts, June 1704– Dec. 1713.

Executors' Accounts

AY 131, Executors' accounts, receipts made out to the executors of John and Helena Aylward for debts owed by them at their deaths, May 1710– Mar. 1717.

AY 133, Receipts made out to the executors of John and Helena Aylward for debts owed by them at their deaths, May 1710–Mar. 1717.

AY 135–T 30, Helena's last Will and Testament, 1713–1714.

Devon Heritage Centre (South West Heritage Trust)

4210 Z/Z 108 a–e, Letter and shipping advice notes for John Aylward, merchant, 1683.

London Metropolitan Archives

MS 10137, Day Book of Charles Peers.

London, The National Archives

CO 110/152, Brailsford Papers, 1688–1692.

Oxford, Bodleian Library

MS, Eng. Lett c.192, Correspondence of John Aylward, Merchant and Banker.

Westminster Diocesan Archive

WDA, Register B 1536, Challoner's Ledger.
WDA, Register A 41:
A 41-20, Funds Belonging to the District.
A 41-57, Report about English Catholics.
A 41-113, Proposal for Asylum for Young Maids, 1770.
A 41-136, English Mission Report.
A 41-143, The Brent Fund.
A 41-152, Instructions and Directions for My Executor. May 8th 1776.
A 41-232, Respecting the Indictments of Priests and Others Under The Penal Laws.
WDA, Register A42:
A 42-1, Memorandum of Different Sums in my Name in the Stocks, 1751–5.
A 42-3, Bishop Petre's Fund.

Secondary Sources

Books and Articles

Ambrose, G. 'English Traders at Aleppo (1658–1758)', *The Economic History Review*, 3, 2 (1931): 246–267.

Amussen, Susan A., and Poska, Allyson M. 'Shifting the Frame: Trans-imperial Approaches to Gender in the Atlantic World', *Early Modern Women: An Interdisciplinary Journal*, 9 (2014): 3–24.

Aram, B., and Yun-Casalilla, B. (eds). *Global Goods and the Spanish Empire, 1492–1824: Circulation, Resistance and Diversity*. Basingstoke: Palgrave Macmillan, 2014.

Aslanian, S. D. *From the Indian Ocean to the Mediterranean: The Global Trade Networks of Armenian Merchants from New Julfa*. London: California University Press, 2011.

Aveling J. C. H. *The Handle and the Axe: The Catholic Recusants in England from Reformation to Emancipation*. London: Blond and Briggs, 1976.

Bailey, Craig. *Irish London: Middle-Class Migration in the Global Eighteenth Century*. Liverpool: Liverpool University Press, 2013.

-- ' The Nesbitts of London and their Networks' in *Irish and Scottish Mercantile Networks in Europe and Overseas in the Seventeenth and Eighteenth Centuries*, edited by David Dickson et al. Gent: Academia Press, 2006.

Barker, Hannah. *The Business of Women: Female Enterprise and Urban Development in Northern England, 1760–1830*. Oxford: Oxford University Press, 2006.

Barker, Hannah, and Chalus, Elaine. *Gender in Eighteenth-Century England: Roles, Representations and Responsibilities*. London: Routledge, 1997.

Barker, T. C. 'Smuggling in the Eighteenth Century: The Evidence of the Scottish Tobacco Trade', *The Virginia Magazine of History and Biography*, 62 (1954): 387–99.

Barry, Jonathan, and Brooks, Christopher. *The Middling Sort of People: Culture, Society and Politics in England, 1550–1800*. London: Macmillan, 1994.

Baskin, Jonathan B., and Miranti, Paul J. Jr. *A History of Corporate Finance*. Cambridge: Cambridge University Press, 1997.

Benjamin, Thomas. *The Atlantic World, Europeans, Africans, Indians and Their Shared History, 1400–1900*. Cambridge: Cambridge University Press, 2009.

Berg, Maxine. 'In Pursuit of Luxury: Global History and British Consumer Goods in the Eighteenth Century', *Past and Present*, 182 (2004): 85–142.

–– (ed.), with F. Gottmann, H. Hodacs, and C. Nierstrasz. *Goods from the East: Trading Eurasia*. Basingstoke: Palgrave Macmillan, 2015.

–– *Luxury and Pleasure in Eighteenth Century Britain*. Oxford: Oxford University Press, 2005.

Bergin, John. 'Irish Catholics and their Networks in Eighteenth-Century London', *Eighteenth-Century Life*, 39, 1 (2015): 66–102.

Bergin, Joseph. *The Seventeenth Century: Europe 1598–1715*. Oxford: Oxford University Press, 2001.

Black, Jeremy. *European International Relations, 1648–1815*. New York: Palgrave, 2002.

–– *European Warfare, 1660–1815*. London: Yale University Press, 1994.

Block, Kristen, and Shaw, Jenny. 'Subjects without an Empire: The Irish in the Early Modern Caribbean', *Past and Present*, 210 (2011): 33–60.

Bosher, J. F. 'Huguenot Merchants and the Protestant International in the Seventeenth Century', *The William and Mary Quarterly*, 52 (1995): 77–102.

Bossy, J. *The English Catholic Community, 1570–1850*. London: Darton, Longman & Todd, 1975.

Boulton, Jeremy. 'London Widowhood Revisited: The Decline of Female Remarriage in the Seventeenth and Early Eighteenth Century', *Continuity and Change*, 5, 3 (1990): 323–55.

Bowden, Caroline. 'The English Convents in Exile and Questions of National Identity, 1600–1688' in *British and Irish Emigrants and Exiles in Europe, 1603–1688*, edited by D. Worthington (Leiden: Brill, 2010), 297–314.

Bradshaw, B., and Morrill, J. (eds). *The British Problem c. 1534–1707: State Formation in the Atlantic Archipelago*. London: Palgrave Macmillan, 1996.

Bradshaw, B., and Roberts, P. (eds). *British Consciousness and Identity: The Making of Britain, 1533–1707*. Cambridge: Cambridge University Press, 1998.

Brady, C., and Gillespie, R. (eds). *Natives and Newcomers: The Making of Irish Colonial Society, 1534–1641*. Dublin: Irish Academic Press, 1986.

Braudel, Fernand. *The Wheels of Commerce: Civilization and Capitalism, 15th–18th Century*, vol. II. London: Collins, 1982.

Brewer, J. *The Sinews of Power: War, Money and the English State, 1688–1783*. London: Unwin Hyman, 1989, 185.

Brietz-Monta, S. 'Anne Dacre Howard, Countess of Arundel and Catholic Patronage' in *English Women: Religion and Textual Production 1500–1625*, edited by M. White, 59–82. Burlington: Ashgate, 2011.

Brilli, Catia. 'Genoese Migration to Cadiz: A Persisting Alliance' in Brilli, Catia, *Genoese Trade and Migration in the Spanish Atlantic*, 21–55. Cambridge: Cambridge University Press, 2016.

Bromley, J. S. *Corsairs and Navies,1660–1760*. London: Hambledon Press, 1987.

Brunelle, Gayle. 'The Price of Assimilation: Spanish and Portuguese Women in French Cities, 1500–1650' in *Women in Port, Gendering Communities, Economies, and Social Networks in Atlantic Port Cities, 1500–1850*, edited by Douglas Catterall and Jodi Campbell, 155–182. Leiden: Brill, 2012.

Canny, N., 'Identity Formation in Ireland: The Emergence of the Anglo-Irish' in *Colonial Identity in the Atlantic World, 1500–1800*, ed. N. Canny and A. Pagden. Princeton: Princeton University Press, 1987.

Canny, N., and Morgan, P. *The Oxford Handbook of The Atlantic World c.1450–c.1850*. Oxford: Oxford University Press, 2011.

Caplan, N. 'The Sussex Catholics, c. 1660–1800' in *Sussex Archaeological Collections*, vol.116. Lewes: S. A. C., 1978.

Chapman, Stanley. *Merchant and Enterprise in Britain from the Industrial Revolution to World War I*. New York: Cambridge University Press, 1992.

Cipolla, C. M. *Allegro ma non troppo*. Bologna: Il Mulino, 1988.

Claydon, Tony, and McBride, Ian. *Protestantism and National Identity: Britain and Ireland, c. 1650–1850*. Cambridge: Cambridge University Press, 1998.

Coe, S. D., and Coe, M. D. *The True History of Chocolate* (London: Thames and Hudson, 1996), 165–175.

Colley, Linda. *Britons: Forging the Nation, 1707–1837*. New Haven: Yale University Press, 1992.

Corish, P. J. *The Catholic Community in the Seventeenth and Eighteenth Centuries.* Dublin: Helicon, 1981.

Croft, Pauline. 'Englishmen and the Spanish Inquisition, 1558–1625', *The English Historical Review*, 87, 343 (1972): 249–268.

—— 'Trading with the Enemy, 1585–1604', *The Historical Journal*, 32, 2 (1989): 281–302.

Cullen, L. M. *An Economic History of Ireland since 1660.* London: B. T. Batsford, 1972.

—— 'Galway Merchants in the Outside World, 1650– 1800' in *Galway: Town and Crown, 1484–1984*, ed. D. O'Cearbhaill. Dublin: Gill and Macmillan, 1984.

—— 'Galway Merchants in the Outside World, c.1650–1800' in *Economy, Trade and Irish Merchants at Home and Abroad*, edited by L. M. Cullen, 165–192. Dublin: Four Courts Press, 2012.

—— 'The Smuggling Trade in Ireland in the Eighteenth Century', *Proceedings of the Royal Irish Academy. Section C: Archaeology, Celtic Studies, History, Linguistics, Literatu*re, 67 (1968/1969): 149–175.

—— 'The Two Fitzgeralds of London, 1718–1759' in *Irish and Scottish Mercantile Networks in Europe and Overseas in the Seventeenth and Eighteenth Centuries*, edited by David Dickson et al. Gent: Academia Press, 2006, 251–270.

D'Angelo, M. *Mercanti Inglesi a Livorno, 1573–1737.* Messina: Istituto di Studi Storici Gaetano Salvemini, 2004.

Davis, Ralph. 'English Foreign Trade, 1660–1700', *The Economic History Review*, 7 (1954): 150–166.

Deane Jones, I. *The English Revolution: An Introduction to English History, 1603–1714.* London: Heinemann, 1966.

Dickson, D. 'Catholics and Trade in Eighteenth Century Ireland: An Old Debate Revisited' in *Endurance and Emergence: Catholics in Ireland in the Eighteenth Century*, edited by T. P. Power and Kevin Whelan. Dublin: Irish Academic Press, 1990.

Dickson, P. G. M. *The Financial Revolution in England: A Study in the Development of Public Credit, 1688–1756.* London: Macmillan, 1967.

Doe, H. 'Waiting for her Ship to Come in? The Female Investor in Nineteenth⊠century Sailing Vessels', *Economic History Review*, 63, 1 (2010): 85–106.

Duffy, Eamon. 'Richard Challoner 1691–1781: A Memoir' in *Challoner and his Church: A Catholic Bishop in Georgian England*, edited by Eamon Duffy, 1–26. London: Darton, Longman and Todd, 1981.

Ellis, S. G., and Barber, S. (eds). *Conquest and Union: Fashioning a British State, 1485–1725.* London: Routledge, London, 2013.

Emmett, C. R. *Papist Devils: Catholics in British America, 1574–1783.* Washington DC: The Catholic University of America Press, 2014.

Erickson, Amy L. 'Married Women's Occupations in Eighteenth-Century London', *Continuity and Change*, 23, 2 (2008): 267–307.

Fattacciu, I. 'The Resilience and Boomerang Effect of Chocolate: A Product's Globalisation and Commodification' in *Global Goods and the Spanish Empire, 1492–1824: Circulation, Resistance and Diversity*, edited by B. Aram and B. Yun-Casalilla, 255–273. Basingstoke: Palgrave Macmillan, 2014.

Findlay, Ronald, and O'Rourke, Kevin. 'World Trade, 1650–1780: The Age of Mercantilism' in *Power and Plenty: Trade, War, and the World Economy in the Second Millennium*, edited by Ronald Findlay and Kevin O' Rourke, 227–310. Princeton: Princeton University Press, 2007.

Fisher, F. J. 'London's Export Trade in the Early Seventeenth Century', *The Economic History Review*, 3 (1950): 151–161.

Fisher, H. E. S. *The Portugal Trade: A Study of Anglo-Portuguese Commerce 1700– 1770.* London: Methuen & Co., 1971.

Francis, A. D. 'John Methuen and the Anglo-Portuguese Treaties of 1703', *The Historical Journal*, 3 (1960): 103–124.

Froide, Amy M. 'Learning to Invest: Women's Education in Arithmetic and Accounting in Early Modern England', *Early Modern Women: An Interdisciplinary Journal*, 10, 1 (2015): 3–26.

—— 'The Religious Lives of Single Women in the Anglo-Atlantic World: Quaker Missionaries, Protestant Nuns, and Covert Catholics' in *Women, Religion and the Atlantic World (1600–1800)*, edited by Daniella Kostroun and Lisa Vollendorf, 60–78. Toronto: University of Toronto Press, 2009.

—— *Silent Partners: Women as Public Investors during Britain's Financial Revolution.* Oxford: Oxford University Press, 2017.

Furber, H. *Rival Empires of Trade in the Orient, 1600–1800: Europe and the World in the Age of Expansion*, vol. II. London: Oxford University Press, 1976.

Fusaro, Maria. *Political Economies of Empire in the Early Modern Mediterranean: The Decline of Venice and the Rise of England, 1450–1700*. Cambridge: Cambridge University Press, 2015.

Gardina Pestana, Carla. *The English Atlantic in the Age of Revolution 1640–1661*. London: Harvard University Press, 2004.

Gauci, Perry. *Emporium of the World: The Merchants of London, 1660–1800*. London: Bloomsbury, 2007.

— — *The Politics of Trade: The Overseas Merchant in State and Society, 1660–1720*. Oxford: Oxford University Press, 2003.

Glickman, Gabriel. 'Catholic Interests and the Politics of English Overseas Expansion 1660–1689', *Journal of British Studies*, 55 (2016): 680–708.

— — *The English Catholic Community, 1688–1745: Politics, Culture and Ideology*. Woodbridge: Boydell Press, 2009.

Goffman, D. *Izmir and the Levantine World, 1550–1650*. Seattle: University of Washington Press, 1990.

Gooch, Leo. 'Priests and Patrons in the Eighteenth Century', *Recusant History Journal*, 20 (1990): 207–211.

Goodrich, J. 'Ensigne-Bearers of St Claire: Elizabeth Evelinge's Early Translations and the Restoration of English Franciscanism' in *English Women Religion and Textual Production* 1500–1625, edited by M. White, 83–101. Burlington: Ashgate, 2011.

Grafe, Regina. *Distant Tyranny: Markets, Power and Backwardness in Spain, 1650–1800*. Princeton: Princeton University Press, 2012.

Grassby, Richard. *Kinship and Capitalism: Marriage, Family, and Business in the English- Speaking World, 1580–1740*. Cambridge: Cambridge University Press, 2001.

Greif, Avner. 'Coercion and Exchange: How did Markets Evolve?' (Stanford University, 2008) in Institutions, Innovation and Industrialisation: *Essays in Economic History and Development*, edited by A. Greif, L. Kiesling, and J. V. C. Nye. Princeton: Princeton University Press, 2015

Haggerty, Sheryllynne. *The British Atlantic Trading Community, 1760–1810: Men, Women and the Distribution of Goods*. Leiden: Brill, 2006.

— — *'Merely for money'? Business Culture in the British Atlantic, 1750–1815*. Liverpool: Liverpool University Press, 2012.

Hancock, David. 'Atlantic Trade and Commodities, 1402–1815' in *The Oxford Handbook of The Atlantic World c.1450–c.1850*, edited by Nicholas Canny and Philip Morgan, 324–340. Oxford: Oxford University Press, 2011.

— — *Citizens of the World: London Merchants and the Integration of the British Atlantic Community, 1735–1785*. Cambridge: Cambridge University Press, 1995.

— — *Oceans of Wine: Madeira and the Emergence of American Trade and Taste*. New Haven: Yale University Press, 2009.

Hanley, Thomas O' Brien. *The American Revolution and Religion: Maryland 1770–1800*. Washington: Catholic University of America Press, 1971.

Haring, C. H. *The Spanish Empire in America*. New York: Harcourt, Brace & World, 1952.

Haydon, C. *Anti-Catholicism in Eighteenth Century England, c. 1714–80: A Political and Social Study*. Manchester: Manchester University Press, 1993.

— — 'Eighteenth-Century English Anti-Catholicism: Contexts, Continuity, and Diminution' in *Protestant–Catholic Conflict from the Reformation to the Twenty-first Century*, ed. John Wolffe. Basingstoke: Palgrave Macmillan, 2013, 46–70.

Hayton, D. W. *The Anglo-Irish Experience, 1680–1730: Religion, Identity and Patriotism*. Woodbridge: Boydell Press, 2012.

Hayton, D. W. 'The Williamite Revolution in Ireland, 1688–91' in *The Anglo-Dutch Moment: Essays on the Glorious Revolution and its World Impact*, ed. J. I. Israel. New York: Cambridge University Press, 1991.

Herzog, Tamar. *Defining Nations: Immigrants and Citizens in Early Modern Spain and Spanish America*. New Haven: Yale University Press, 2003.

Hillman, H., and Gathmann, C. 'Overseas Trade and the Decline of Privateering', *The Journal of Economic History*, 71, 3 (2011).

Hoppit, J. 'The Landed Interest and the National Interest, 1660–1800' in *Parliaments, Nations and Identities in Britain and Ireland, 1660–1850*, edited by J. Hoppit, 83–102. Manchester: Manchester University Press, 2003.

Hughes, Philip. *The Reformation in England*. New York: Macmillan, 1951.

Hunt, Margaret R. *Women in Eighteenth-Century Europe*. London: Routledge, 2014.

–– 'Women and the Fiscal-Imperial State in the Late Seventeenth and Early Eighteenth Centuries' in *A New Imperial History: Culture, Identity, and Modernity in Britain and the Empire, 1660–1840*, edited by Kathleen Wilson, 29–47. Cambridge: Cambridge University Press, 2004.

Johnson, C. *Developments in the Roman Catholic Church in Scotland, 1789–1829*. Edinburgh: John Donald, 1983.

Kaplan, B. J., Moore, B., Van Nierop, H., and Pollmann, J. (eds). *Catholic Communities in Protestant States: Britain and the Netherlands, c. 1570–1720*. Manchester: Manchester University Press, 2009.

Kinoulty, Mary K. *A Social Study of Roman Catholicism in West Sussex in the Eighteenth Century*. Chichester: West Sussex Record Office, 1982.

Kinsella, Eoin. 'In Pursuit of a Positive Construction: Irish Catholics and the Williamite Articles of Surrender, 1690–1701', *Eighteenth-Century Ireland*, 24 (2009): 11–35.

Kishlansky, M. A Monarchy Transformed: Britain 1603–1714. London: Penguin, 1996.

Knights, Mark. '"Meer religion" and the "church-state" of Restoration England: The Impact and Ideology of James II's Declaration of Indulgence' in *A Nation Transformed: England after the Restoration*, edited by A. Houston and S. Pincus, 41–70. Cambridge: Cambridge University Press, 2001.

–– *Representation and Misrepresentation in Later Stuart Britain: Partisanship and Political Culture*. Oxford: Oxford University Press, 2006.

Koenigsberger, H. 'English Merchants in Naples and Sicily in the Seventeenth Century', *The English Historical Review*, 62, 244 (1947): 304–326.

Lamikiz, Xabier. *Trade and Trust in the Eighteenth Century Atlantic World: Spanish Merchants and their Overseas Networks*. Woodbridge: Boydell Press, 2010.

Langford, Paul. *A Polite and Commercial People: England 1727–1783*. Oxford: Clarendon Press, 1989.

Lario de Oñate, María del Carmen. 'The Irish Traders of Eighteenth Century Cadiz' in *Irish and Scottish Mercantile Networks in Europe and Overseas in the Seventeenth and Eighteenth Centuries*, edited by David Dickson, Jan Parmentier, and Jane Ohlmeyer, 211–230. Gent: Academia Press, 2006.

Laurence, Anne. 'Lady Betty Hastings (1682–1739): Godly Patron', *Women's History Review*, 19, 2 (2010): 201–213.

Laurence, Anne, Maltby, Josephine, and Rutterford, Janette (eds). *Women and their Money 1700–1950: Essays on Women and Finance*. London: Routledge, 2009.

Lay, Jenna. 'An English Nun's Authority: Early Modern Spiritual Controversy and the Manuscripts of Barbara Constable' in *Gender, Catholicism and Spirituality: Women and the Roman Catholic Church in Britain and Europe, 1200–1900*, edited by L. Lux-Sterritt and Carmen M. Mangion, 99–114. New York: Palgrave, 2011.

Leong, Elaine. 'Collecting Knowledge for the Family: Recipes, Gender and Practical Knowledge in the Early Modern English Household', *Centaurus*, 55 (2013): 81–103.

Lock, Alexander. *Catholicism, Identity and Politics in the Age of Enlightenment: The Life and Career of Sir Thomas Gascoigne, 1745–1810*. Woodbridge: Boydell & Brewer, 2017.

Magee, Brian. *The English Recusants: A Study of the Post-Reformation Catholic Survival and the Operation of the Recusancy Laws*. London: Burns, Oates and Washbourne, 1938.

Maltby, William S. *The Rise and Fall of the Spanish Empire*. London: Macmillan, 2009.

Marichal, C. 'The Spanish-American Silver Peso: Export Commodity and Global Money of the Ancien Regime, 1550–1800' in *From Silver to Cocaine: Latin American Commodity Chains and the Building of the World Economy, 1500–2000*, edited by S. Topik, C. Marichal, and Z. Frank, 25–52. London: Duke University Press, 2006.

Marshall, Peter, and Scott, Geoffrey. *Catholic Gentry in English Society: The Throckmortons of Coughton from Reformation to Emancipation*. Burlington: Ashgate, 2009.

Marzagalli, S.'Trade Across Religious and Confessional Boundaries in Early Modern France' in *Religion and Trade: Cross-Cultural Exchanges in World History, 1000–1900*, ed. F. Trivellato, L. Halevi, and C. Antunes. Oxford: Oxford University Press, 2014.

Mathew, David. *Catholicism in England, 1535–1935*. London: The Catholic Book Club, 1936.

Mathias, Peter. 'Risk, Credit and Kinship in Early Modern Enterprise' in *The Early Modern Atlantic Economy*, edited by John J. McCusker and Kenneth Morgan, 15–36. Cambridge: Cambridge University Press, 2000.

McCabe, I. B. 'Small Town Merchants, Global Ventures: The Maritime Trade of the New Julfa Armenians in the Seventeenth and Eighteenth Centuries' in *Maritime History as Global History*, edited by M. Fusaro and A. Polónia. Newfoundland: International Maritime Economic History Association, 2010.

McCreery, D. 'Indigo Commodity Chains in the Spanish and British Empires, 1560–1860' in *From Silver to Cocaine: Latin American Commodity Chains and the Building of the World Economy, 1500–2000*, edited by S. Topik, C. Marichal, and Z. Frank, 53–75. London: Duke University Press, 2006.

McFarlane, A. *The British in the Americas, 1480–1815*. London: Longman, 1992.

McLachlan, Jean O. *Trade and Peace with Old Spain, 1667–1750: A Study of the Influence of Commerce on Anglo-Spanish Diplomacy in the First Half of the Eighteenth Century*. Cambridge: Cambridge University Press, 1940.

McLoughlin, Thomas. *Contesting Ireland: Irish Voices Against England in the Eighteenth Century*. Dublin: Four Court Press, 1999.

Mendelson, Sara, and Crawford, Patricia. *Women in Early Modern England, 1550–1720*. Oxford: Clarendon Press, 1998.

Meyer, A. O. *England and the Catholic Church under Queen Elizabeth*. London: Kegan, Trench, Trubner & Co., 1916.

Meyer W. R. 'English Privateering in the War of 1688 to 1697', *The Mariner's Mirror* 67 (1981): 259–272.

–– 'English Privateering in the War of the Spanish Succession, 1702–1713.' *The Mariner's Mirror*, 69 (1983): 435–446.

Miller, J. *Popery and Politics in England, 1660–1688*. Cambridge: Cambridge University Press, 1973.

Minchinton, W. E. *The Growth of the English Overseas Trade in the Seventeenth and Eighteenth Centuries*. London: Methuen, 1969.

Monod, Paul. 'Dangerous Merchandise: Smuggling, Jacobitism, and Commercial Culture in Southeast England, 1690–1760', *The Journal of British Studies*, 30 (1991): 150–182.

–– *Jacobitism and the English People, 1688–1788*. Cambridge: Cambridge University Press, 1989.

Monod, P., Pittock, M., and Szechi, D. (eds). *Loyalty and Identity: Jacobites at Home and Abroad*. Basingstoke: Palgrave Macmillan, 2010.

Morgan, Kenneth. *Bristol and the Atlantic Trade in the Eighteenth Century*. Cambridge: Cambridge University Press, 1993 and 2004.

Morieux, Renaud. *The Channel: England, France and the Construction of a Maritime Border in the Eighteenth Century*. Cambridge: Cambridge University Press, 2016.

Moring, B., and Wall, R. *Widows in European Economy and Society, 1600–1920*. Woodbridge: Boydell Press, 2017.

Morrill, J. *Oliver Cromwell and the English Revolution*. London: Longman, 1990.

Muldrew, Craig. 'Credit and the Courts: Debt Litigation in a Seventeenth Century Urban Community', *Economic History Review*, 46 (1993): 23–38.

Murphy, Anne. 'Financial Markets: The Limits of Economic Regulation in Early Modern England' in *Mercantilism Reimagined: Political Economy in Early Modern Britain and its Empire*, edited by Philip J. Stern and Carl Wennerlind, 264–279. Oxford: Oxford University Press, 2014.

Murphy, Antoin E. *Richard Cantillon: Entrepreneur and Economist*. Oxford: Clarendon Press, 1986.

Nadri, G. A. 'The Indigo Trade: Local and Global Demand' in Nadri, G. A., *The Political Economy of Indigo in India, 1580–1930: A Global Perspective*, 85–123. Leiden: Brill, 2016.

Nash, R. C. 'The English and Scottish Tobacco Trades in the Seventeenth and Eighteenth Centuries: Legal and Illegal Trade', *The Economic History Review*, 35 (1982): 354–372.

–– 'Irish Atlantic Trade in the Seventeenth and Eighteenth Centuries', *The William and Mary Quarterly Journal* 42 (1985): 329–356.

Norman, Edward. *Roman Catholicism in England: From the Elizabethan Settlement to the Second Vatican Council*. Oxford: Oxford University Press, 1985.

Norton M., 'Tasting Empire: Chocolate and the European Internalisation of Mesoamerican Aesthetics', *The American Historical Review*, 211, 3 (2006).

O'Cearbhaill, Diarmuid. *Galway: Town and Crown, 1484–1984*. Dublin: Gill and Macmillan, 1984.

O'Ciosain, Eamon. 'Hidden by 1688 and After: Irish Catholic Migration to France 1590–1685' in *British and Irish Emigrants and Exiles in Europe, 1603–1688*, edited by D. Worthington, 125–138. Leiden: Brill, 2010.

O'Flanagan, Patrick. *Port Cities of Atlantic Iberia, c.1500–1900*. Burlington: Ashgate, 2008, 85.

O'Scea, Ciaran. 'Special Privileges for the Irish in the Kingdom of Castile (1601–1680): Modern Myth or Contemporary Reality?' in *British and Irish Emigrants and Exiles in Europe, 1603–1688*, edited by D. Worthington, 107–124. Leiden: Brill, 2010.

Ohlmeyer, J. 'Driving a Wedge within Gaeldom: Ireland & Scotland in the Seventeenth Century', *History Ireland* (1999).

Oresko, R. 'The Glorious Revolution of 1688–89 and the House of Savoy' in *The Anglo-Dutch Moment: Essays on the Glorious Revolution and its World Impact*, edited by J. I. Israel, 365–388. Cambridge: Cambridge University Press, 1991.

Pagano de Divitiis, G. *Mercanti Inglesi Nell'Italia del Seicento: Navi, Traffic, Egemonie*. Venice: Marsilio Editori, 1990.

Panzac, D. 'Plague and Seafaring in the Ottoman Mediterranean in the Eighteenth Century' in *Trade and Cultural Exchange in the Early Modern Mediterranean: Braudel's Maritime Legacy*, edited by Maria Fusaro, Colin Heywood, and Mohamed-Salah Omri. London: Tauris, 2010, 45–68.

Parmentier, Jan. 'The Irish Connection: The Irish Merchant Community in Ostend and Bruges during the Late Seventeenth and Eighteenth Centuries', *Eighteenth Century Ireland* 20 (2005): 31–54.

—— 'The Sweets of Commerce: The Hennessys of Ostend and their Network in the Eighteenth Century' in *Irish and Scottish Mercantile Networks in Europe and Overseas in the Seventeenth and Eighteenth Centuries*, edited by David Dickson, Jan Parmentier, and Jane Ohlmeyer Jane, 67–92. Gent: Academia Press, 2006.

—— 'A Touch of Ireland: Migrants and Migration in and to Ostend, Bruges and Dunkirk in the Seventeenth and Eighteenth Centuries', *The International Journal of Maritime History*, 27, 4 (2015): 662–679.

Parrish, David. *Jacobitism and Anti-Jacobitism in the British Atlantic World, 1688–1727*. Woodbridge: Boydell & Brewer, 2017.

Paul, Helen J. *The South Sea Bubble: An Economic History of its Origins and Consequences*. New York: Routledge, 2011.

Phillips Rahn, C. 'The Growth and Composition of Trade in the Iberian Empires, 1450–1750' in *The Rise of Merchant Empires: Long Distance Trade in the Early Modern World, 1350–1750*, ed. J. D. Tracy. Cambridge: Cambridge University Press, 1990, 34–101.

Pincus, Steve. *1688: The First Modern Revolution*. London: Yale University Press, 2009.

—— 'Rethinking Mercantilism: Political Economy, the British Empire, and the Atlantic World in the Seventeenth and Eighteenth Centuries', *The William and Mary Quarterly*, 69 (2012): 3–34.

Pizzoni, Giada. 'Mrs Helena Aylward: A British Catholic Mother, Spouse and Businesswoman in the Commercial Age (1705–1714)', *British Catholic History*, 33, 4 (2017): 603–621.

—— '"A Pass is not Denied to any Romanist": Strategies of the Catholic Merchant Community in the Atlantic World', *Cultural and Social History Journal*, 11, 3 (2014): 349–365.

Poggi, Gianfranco. *Calvinism and the Capitalist Spirit: Max Weber's Protestant Ethic*. London: Macmillan Press, 1983.

Power, T. P., and Whelan, Kevin. *Endurance and Emergence: Catholics in Ireland in the Eighteenth Century*. Dublin: Irish Academic Press, 1990.

Price, J. M. 'What Did Merchants Do? Reflections on British Overseas Trade, 1660–1790', *The Journal of Economic History* 49 (1989): 267–284.

Questier, Michael. *Catholicism and Community in Early Modern England: Politics, Aristocratic Patronage and Religion, c. 1550–1640*. Cambridge: Cambridge University Press, 2006.

Quinn, F. *The French Overseas Empire*. Westport, CT: Praeger, 2002.

Rabuzzi, D. 'Women as Merchants in Eighteenth-Century Northern Germany: The Case of Stralsund, 1750–1830', *Central European History*, 28, 4 (1995): 435–456.

Recio Morales, Oscar. 'Identity and Loyalty: Irish Traders in Seventeenth Century Iberia' in *Irish and Scottish Mercantile Networks in Europe and Overseas in the Seventeenth and Eighteenth Centuries*, edited by David Dickson, Jan Parmentier, and Jane Ohlmeyer, 197–210. Gent: Academia Press, 2006.

Roseveare H. *Market and Merchants of the Late Seventeenth Century: The Marescoe-David Letters, 1668–1680*. Oxford: Oxford University Press, 1987.

Scammell, G. V. *The First Imperial Age: European Overseas Expansion, c.1400–1715*. London: Routledge, 1992.

Schofield, Nicholas, and Skinner, Gerard. *The English Vicars Apostolic, 1688–1850*. Oxford: Family Publications, 2009.

Schuller, Karin. 'Irish–Iberian Trade from the Mid-Sixteenth to the Mid-Seventeenth Centuries' in *Irish and Scottish Mercantile Networks in Europe and Overseas in the Seventeenth and Eighteenth Centuries*, edited by David Dickson, Jan Parmentier, and Jane Ohlmeyer, 175–196. Gent: Academia Press, 2006.

Sharpe, Pamela. 'Gender in the Economy: Female Merchants and Family Businesses in the British Isles, 1600–1850', *Social History/Histoire Sociale* 34 (2001): 283–306.

Shephard, Alexandra. 'Minding their own Business: Married Women and Credit in Early Eighteenth-Century London', *Transactions of the RHS*, 25 (2015): 53–74.

Smith, R. S. 'Indigo Production and Trade in Colonial Guatemala', *The Hispanic American Historical Review*, 39, 2 (1959): 181–211.

Smyth, J. 'The Communities of Ireland and the British State, 1660–1707' in *The British Problem c. 1534–1707: State Formation in the Atlantic Archipelago*, edited by B. Bradshaw and J. Morrill. London: Palgrave Macmillan, 1996.

–– 'Like Amphibious Animals: Irish Protestants, Ancient Britons 1691–1707', *Historical Journal* (1993).

–– *The Making of the United Kingdom, 1660–1800: State, Religion and Identity in Britain and Ireland*. London: Longman, 2001.

Snyder, Holly. '"Under the Shadow of Your Wings": Religiosity in the Mental World of an Eighteenth Century Jewish Merchant', *Early American Studies: An Interdisciplinary Journal* 8 (2010): 581–622.

Sommerville, P. 'Papalist Political Thought and the Controversy over the Jacobean Oath of Allegiance' in *Catholics and the Protestant Nation, Religious Politics and Identity in Early Modern England*, edited by Ethan H. Shagan. Manchester: Manchester University Press, 2005.

Symcox, G. 'Britain and Victor Amadeus II: Or, the Use and Abuse of Allies in England's Rise to Greatness, 1660–1763' in *England's Rise to Greatness, 1660–1763*, edited by Stephen B. Baxter, 151–184. Berkeley: University of California Press, 1983.

Starkey, David J. *British Privateering Enterprise in the Eighteenth Century*. Exeter: University of Exeter Press, 1990.

Steensgaard, N. *The Asian Trade Revolution of the Seventeenth Century: The East India Companies and the Decline of the Caravan Trade*. Chicago: University of Chicago Press, 1973.

Stephens, W. B. *Seventeenth Century Exeter: A Study of Industrial and Commercial Development, 1625–1688*. Exeter: University of Exeter Press, 1958.

Thomson, J. *Mercenaries, Pirates and Sovereigns: State Building and Extra Territorial Violence in Early Modern Europe* (Princeton: Princeton University Press, 1994).

Todd, Barbara J. 'The Remarrying Widow: A Stereotype Reconsidered' in *Women in English Society, 1500–1800*, edited by Mary Prior, 54–85. London and New York: Routledge, 1985.

Tolles, Frederick B. *Meeting House and Counting House: The Quaker Merchants of Colonial Philadelphia, 1682–1763*. New York: Norton & Co., 1963.

Tracy, J. D. (ed.) *The Rise of Merchant Empires: Long-Distance Trade in the Early Modern World, 1350–1750*. Cambridge: Cambridge University Press, 1990.

Trivellato, Francesca. *The Familiarity of Strangers: The Sephardic Diaspora, Livorno and Cross-Cultural Trade in the Early Modern Period*. London: Yale University Press, 2009.

Truxes, Thomas. *Defying Empire: Trading with the Enemy in Colonial New York*. New Haven: Yale University Press, 2008.

–– *Irish–American Trade, 1660–1783*. Cambridge: Cambridge University Press, 1988.

Van Den Heuvel, Danielle, and Van Nederveen Meerkerk, Elise. 'Partners in Business? Spousal Cooperation in Trades in Early Modern England and the Dutch Republic', *Continuity & Change* 23, 2 (2008).

Vanneste, Tijl. *Global Trade and Commercial Networks: Eighteenth Century Diamond Merchants*. London: Pickering & Chatto, 2011.

Walker, Christine. 'Pursuing her Profits: Women in Jamaica, Atlantic Slavery and a Globalising Market, 1700–60', *Gender and History*, 26, 3 (2014): 478–501.

Walker, Claire. '"When God Shall Restore them to their Kingdoms": Nuns, Exiled Stuarts and English Catholic Identity, 1688–1745' in *Religion and Women in Britain, c. 1660–1760*, edited by S. Apetrei and H. Smith, 79–98. Burlington: Ashgate, 2014.

Walsh, Patrick. *The South Sea Bubble and Ireland: Money, Banking and Investment, 1690–1721*. Woodbridge: Boydell Press, 2014.

Walton, Julian. *The Irish Genealogist*, 5 (1974): 216–222.

Walvin, James. *Britain's Slaves Empire*. Gloucester: Tempus, 2008.

Ward, Bernard. *The Dawn of the Catholic Revival in England 1781–1803*. London: Longmans, Green and Co., 1909.

Watkin, E. I. *Roman Catholicism in England from the Reformation to 1950*. London: Oxford University Press, 1957.

Weber, Max. *The Protestant Ethic and the Spirit of Capitalism*. London: Routledge, 1992.

Weir, Alison. *Henry VIII: King and Court*. London: Vintage Books, 2002.

Whaley, Leigh. *Women and the Practice of Medical Cares in Early Modern Europe, 1400–1800*. Basingstoke: Palgrave Macmillan, 2011.

Whatmore, L. E. 'The Birthplace and Parentage of Bishop Challoner: An Enquiry', *Recusant History* 4 (1973): 254–260.

Wrigley, E. A. 'British Population during the Long Eighteenth Century, 1680–1840' in *The Cambridge Economic History of Modern Britain: Industrialisation 1700–1860*, vol. I, edited by R. Floud and P. Johnson. Cambridge: Cambridge University Press, 2008, 57–95.

Zahedieh, Nuala. *The Capital and the Colonies: London and the Atlantic Economy, 1660–1700*. Cambridge: Cambridge University Press, 2010.

—— 'Making Mercantilism Work: London Merchants and Atlantic Trade in the Seventeenth Century', *Transactions of the Royal Historical Society*, 6th series (1999): 143–160.

—— 'The Merchants of Port Royal, Jamaica, and the Spanish Contraband Trade, 1655–1692', *The William and Mary Quarterly* 43 (1986): 570–593.

—— 'Overseas Expansion and Trade in the Seventeenth Century' in *The Oxford History of the British Empire: The Origins of Empire*, edited by Nicholas Canny, Alaine Low, and W. Roger Louis, vol. I, 398–421. Oxford: Oxford University Press, 2011.

Web Based Sources

A Brief and True Report of the New Found Land of Virginia by Thomas Hariot (1585), Documenting the American South, University of North Carolina, 2003, accessed via the University of Warwick website: www.warwick.ac.uk.

Knox, A. 'The Convent as Cultural Conduit: Irish Patronage in Early Modern Spain', Rocky Mountain Medieval and Renaissance Association, accessed via Northumbria University website: www.northumbria.ac.uk.

Index